THE OVERPRODUCTION TRAP IN U.S. AGRICULTURE

THE OVERPRODUCTION TRAP IN U.S. AGRICULTURE

A Study of Resource Allocation
from World War I to the Late 1960's

Edited by Glenn L. Johnson, Project Director,
and C. Leroy Quance

Published for Resources for the Future, Inc.
by The Johns Hopkins University Press, Baltimore and London

RESOURCES FOR THE FUTURE, INC.
1755 Massachusetts Avenue, N.W., Washington, D.C. 20036

Resources for the Future is a nonprofit corporation for research and education in the development, conservation, and use of natural resources and the improvement of the quality of the environment. It was established in 1952 with the cooperation of the Ford Foundation. Part of the work of Resources for the Future is carried out by its resident staff; part is supported by grants to universities and other nonprofit organizations. Unless otherwise stated, interpretations and conclusions in RFF publications are those of the authors; the organization takes responsibility for the selection of significant subjects for study, the competence of the researchers, and their freedom of inquiry.

This book is one of RFF's studies in land use and management, which are directed by Marion Clawson. The manuscript was edited by Kathleen Sproul. The illustrations were drawn by Frank J. Ford and Clare Ford. The index was prepared by Helen Eisenhart.

RFF editors: Henry Jarrett, Vera W. Dodds, Nora E. Roots, Tadd Fisher.

The Johns Hopkins University Press, Baltimore, Maryland 21218
The Johns Hopkins University Press Ltd., London

Library of Congress Catalog Card Number 77-186509
ISBN 0-8018-1387-5

Library of Congress Cataloging in Publication data will
be found on the last printed page of this book.

Foreword

At Resources for the Future, we have always been concerned with agriculture, for a number of reasons: it employs many men and women, and, although employment in farming has declined greatly, employment in the activities that service farming has risen; it is a large sector of the whole economy and includes an important component of our foreign trade; an adequate supply of food and fiber at reasonable prices is important to the national well-being; and, above all, agriculture (including grazing) utilizes a great deal of land—far more than any other use of land in the United States. Moreover, agriculture has been the subject of large-scale federal programs for a full generation—programs grown increasingly expensive and increasingly dubious in the context of the present-day society and economy.

At the same time, we at RFF are acutely aware that the federal government has a Department of Agriculture and that each state has a Land Grant College, all conducting important and highly competent research on agricultural problems. If we were to duplicate their work, or to supplement it only modestly, this would be a wasteful dissipation of our research capability and opportunity. It is our conviction that research supported by the private foundations has both a unique opportunity and a unique responsibility to tackle difficult (and often ill-defined) problems which, for one reason or another, cannot well be dealt with by the public agencies.

For American agriculture, our research efforts at RFF have fallen mostly in two categories. In the first place, we have studied agriculture in contrast to other activities; in *Land for the Future*, the demand for land by agriculture was contrasted with the demand for land for other activities, such as urban occupancy and recreation; in *Resources in America's Future*, agriculture as a source of raw materials was compared with other sources, such as minerals and fuels. Secondly, we have sought to look at agriculture as a whole or at some major aspect of agricultural programs, in an overall policy sense. Thus, in two books, *Governing*

Soil Conservation: Thirty Years of the New Decentralization and *Soil Conservation in Perspective*, we looked at one broad range of programs affecting the land resource. In *Policy Directions for U.S. Agriculture: Long-Range Choices in Farming and Rural Living*, we took a comprehensive look at the whole of agriculture, including the way farm and rural people live, and tried to outline some policy directions for the future.

It was in connection with the last-named study that we approached Glenn L. Johnson at Michigan State University, to suggest that he undertake some appraisal of past federal agricultural programs. Although there has been an enormous amount of writing about those programs, and although some studies have attempted to show the effect of the federal programs on the prices of agricultural commodities, we felt that there existed an altogether inadequate understanding of the overall effect of the long-continued federal programs for agriculture, particularly their effect upon the allocation of manpower, capital, and land to the production of agricultural commodities. With characteristic thoroughness, Johnson undertook a number of studies, utilizing graduate students to make detailed analyses of particular problems. This method of attack necessarily took some time, and has produced several detailed specialized studies, unpublished. In this volume, the major conclusions of those studies have been brought together, and synthesized, through a theoretical framework which Johnson has developed over the years.

The prime focus of this book is on resource allocation—how much labor, capital, and land have been directed to the production of agricultural commodities, on what basis the resource allocations were made, and by whom, and what the effect has been on agricultural incomes, on payments to factors of production, and on agricultural output. Some persistent tendencies to overinvestment of capital (accompanied at times by some underinvestment), a persistent tendency to overallocation of manpower to agriculture, and a consequent persistent tendency to a level of output not planned for when the resource allocation was initially made, are described in quantitative terms. The results of this resource allocation are measured in terms of resulting output and of factor remuneration. It is thus a study in resource use and efficiency; it does not directly face the problems of rural and farm welfare, although it does provide much information and some new analytical concepts that we think should be most thought-provoking to the welfare economist, to the sociologist, and to the agricultural policymaker.

We are happy to offer this book as a contribution to a better understanding of American agriculture and as a foundation upon which agricultural policy might be built—or rebuilt.

Marion Clawson
Resources for the Future, Inc.

Preface

This book represents the efforts of eight agricultural economists to describe the impact of selected U.S. agricultural programs from 1917 to the late 1960's on output and resource utilization of U.S. agriculture. These programs have been and are admired by many countries in the world, but they are encumbered with a number of problems. The descriptive and analytical results—both non-normative and normative—of our study are intended to be helpful to students who are seeking to understand the U.S. agricultural policies and to policy makers who are faced with evaluating present U.S. and foreign agricultural policies and formulating future ones.

Because the direct impact of public policies is on resource use and is revealed over time, resources and time are important dimensions of the study. Building around the descriptive and theoretical model of the agricultural sector that I present in Part I, Francis Van Gigch, Leroy Quance, Venkareddy Chennareddy, Bob Jones, Arne Larsen, and George Rossmiller study, first, the overall pattern of production, product utilization, income and resource use, and then capital, labor, and land resources across the policy evaluation and time dimensions in Part II. Price expectations are a necessary ingredient to study the ex ante resource earnings expectations on which farmers base production decisions. Thus, Milburn Lerohl's major study on product price expectations precedes Part II's resource-oriented chapters. The input-oriented studies are partial studies of individual resource markets in which product market considerations are injected via expected and actual product prices. These are dynamic studies in that imperfections in knowledge (ex ante as opposed to ex post resource earnings) are recognized and analyses are conducted over time and varying government policies. Francis Van Gigch provides an initial integration of the input-oriented studies that are the basis for Chapter 10 in Part III, and I provide evaluative conclusions and recommendations in Chapter 11 to complete the book.

Because many of the research components contributing to this study originated as Ph.D. dissertations with differing completion dates, there is some variation in the ending dates for important estimates and none are completely current. But time is the important dimension over which resource adjustments are studied, and the period 1917 to the mid-1960's is of sufficient length to provide lessons of the past useful in predicting an unknown future. And, where possible, more current secondary data is provided depicting the farm sector in the late 1960's. We contend that data for the late 1960's and early 1970's will confirm the historical analysis presented herein.

The study is interdisciplinary, with economics, statistics, mathematics, and history contributing importantly to Parts I and II. And in Part I (via the chapter on basis for evaluation) and in Part III (via evaluative conclusions and recommendations), the book draws on philosophic value theory in a significant recognition of the non-Pareto nature of many private as well as public resource use decisions in agriculture.

Due to the breadth and interdisciplinary nature of the book, we owe considerable gratitude to several fellow social scientists. Agricultural economists offering considerable assistance are Professors Dale E. Hathaway, Lester V. Manderscheid, James D. Shaffer, and Vernon Sorenson of Michigan State University, and Dr. David H. Boyne, Chairman, Economics Department, Ohio State University. Assistance of a historical nature was provided by Dr. Gladys L. Baker, Head, Historical Research Section, Agricultural History Branch, Economic Research Service, U.S. Department of Agriculture, Washington, D.C. The unique use of philosophical value theory benefited from the perceptive comments of Dr. Lewis K. Zerby, Professor of Philosophy, Michigan State University. Recognition is also due Dr. Larry L. Boger, Dean of Agriculture and Natural Resources, Michigan State University, for administrative assistance, and Dr. Marion Clawson, director of Resources for the Future's program in land use and management, for professional assistance.

The contribution by Dr. Quance represents research completed during his graduate study at Michigan State University and does not represent official views or estimates of the U.S. Department of Agriculture unless so specified.

Glenn L. Johnson

Contributors

VENKAREDDY CHENNAREDDY, Department of Economics, Wisconsin State University, River Falls, Wisconsin

GLENN L. JOHNSON, Department of Agricultural Economics, Michigan State University, East Lansing, Michigan

BOB F. JONES, Department of Agricultural Economics, Purdue University, West Lafayette, Indiana

ARNE LARSEN, Det Okonomiske Sekretariat, Slotsholmsgade 12, BK-1116, Copenhagen, Denmark

MILBURN L. LEROHL, Agricultural Economics Research Council of Canada, Ottawa, Ontario, Canada

C. LEROY QUANCE, Natural Resource Economics Division, Economic Research Service, U.S. Department of Agriculture, Washington, D.C.

GEORGE E. ROSSMILLER, Department of Agricultural Economics, Michigan State University, East Lansing, Michigan

FRANCIS VAN GIGCH, International Bank for Reconstruction and Development, Washington, D.C.

Contents

List of Tables

Table

List of Figures

THE OVERPRODUCTION TRAP IN
U.S. AGRICULTURE

The Problem of Problems in a Dynamic Agriculture

Most people agree that the United States has a "farm problem." But there is much disagreement in defining, explaining causes and impacts, and in prescribing public policies for alleviating the chronic adjustment needs in agriculture. The areas of disagreement depend on understanding the area of agreement—i.e., what *is* the "farm problem"? The most difficult part of our inquiry is its initiation. Before a problem can be solved, it must be correctly defined and a mode of communications established. The four chapters of Part I, in discussing important characteristics of the U.S. agricultural economy, summarizing a theoretical model that will serve as an analytical framework, and then discussing a basis for evaluation, provide the initiation of our inquiry.

CHAPTER 1

Introduction

GLENN L. JOHNSON

Since 1917 (and possibly some time before), United States agriculture has been characterized by a capacity to expand production every twenty to twenty-five years by as much as it produced in 1875. Further, this impressive rate of growth has been accompanied by an almost chronic tendency to expand production (both before and since the introduction of price and production controls) to the point at which product prices fail to cover investments and expenditures in producing farm products. Results have been (1) relatively abundant supplies of low-priced food for consumers and (2) either low returns and capital losses for producers or taxes to shift the burden of losses from individual farmers to the public at large.

More fundamentally, there has been a substantial loss to the American economy from the commitment of resources to produce relatively less-needed farm products instead of needed (1) infrastructures such as roads and schools; (2) means of relieving domestic poverty; (3) military means to fulfill our international commitments; and (4) means to assist underdeveloped countries to attain viable self-sustaining economies. The need to improve allocative efficiency in the United States agricultural economy is not alleviated by the facts that some of the capital losses to farmers were offset by inflationary gains and that the overall growth of the American economy much more than offset the adverse consequences of overcommitted resources in agriculture.

Clearly, the resource allocating mechanism of the United States agricultural economy requires careful study. A basic question is: how do we manage this important sector to minimize losses (to investors, consumers, and/or taxpayers) without sacrificing ability to grow and to supply products to consumers at reasonable prices? This book attempts to join a somewhat original theoretical approach to the problem with new and on-going empirical work for the 1917-69 period. We hope that this will create a clearer understanding of how the United States agricultural economy operates, and provide a basis for making recommendations to improve its operations.

The general thesis of the book is that United States agriculture has an empirically observed tendency to use such large amounts of labor and capital and to value land so highly that, in general, marginal earnings of all three resources fail to cover investments in, and expenditures on, the resources. The explanation for this behavior which appears, superficially, perverse is found in ordinary classical economic theory provided it is recognized (1) that entrepreneurs are imperfectly informed about continuously recurring changes in technology, institutions, and people and (2) that there are costs for transferring resources from sector to sector, region to region, farm to farm, and enterprise to enterprise.

Among the theoretical implications of such reasoning is the conclusion that the ex post consequences of decisions by individual entrepreneurs often impose economic losses on other entrepreneurs. Such losses would not exist in either (1) an economy operated by perfectly informed entrepreneurs or (2) an economy characterized by zero costs of transferring assets from one use to another. The theoretical existence of these imperfections precludes the application of evaluative criteria which implicitly assume the absence of such losses. Yet it is precisely these criteria that are often used by some economists, politicians, and policy students in evaluating the operation of economic sectors and total economies—and rejected by others. Our book tries to get at this "root of the farm problem" and, as such, provide a theoretical and empirical basis for understanding the problems of appraising and improving the operations of a mixed control (private and public) sector of our national economy.

We stress that, while allocative efficiency has a great deal to do with welfare, the book is not a study of welfare or of poverty, per se; instead, it is a study of the efficiency with which the United States allocates its agricultural resources. In Chapter 2, we describe the main structural characteristics of the agricultural economy; in Chapter 3, the theoretical consequences of taking these structural characteristics into account are ascertained. Chapter 4 provides a basis for evaluation. Following is a historical analysis extending over several chapters. Product price expectations, a necessary ingredient for studying resource allocation, are studied in Chapter 5. Chapter 6 examines the overall pattern of production, consumption, exports, and carryovers, 1917 to date, while Chapters 7 to 11 look at capital, labor, and land utilization, 1917 to date. Chapter 10 summarizes the preceding chapters, and Chapter 11 evaluates and yields suggestions for improving the operation of the U.S. agricultural economy.

CHAPTER 2

Characteristics of
U.S. Agricultural Economy

GLENN L. JOHNSON

Our objective in this chapter is to determine those characteristics of the national agricultural economy that have underlying significance for gaining theoretical understanding of how farm resources are allocated. Economic abstractions based on realistic assumptions with respect to such characteristics should imply, predict, or indicate the operating characteristics. Therefore, it is left mainly to later chapters to examine the correspondence or lack of correspondence *between* (1) the theoretical consequences of the structural characteristics summarized here, and (2) the operating characteristics. The presence or absence of this correspondence determines the advisability of using the theoretical formulation and empirical analysis presented in this study as a basis for designing changes in U.S. agricultural policies and programs. However, some attention must also be given to operating characteristics at this point to assure a relevant theoretical formulation in the sense that appropriate dependent variables are studied.

In the following pages attention is given characteristics of (1) U.S. agricultural factor markets, (2) product markets, and (3) the managerial units for agricultural firms. Much structural significance is revealed when: (1) factor markets are examined in a broad sense, including attention to technological and institutional change; (2) product markets are examined, including attention to increases in demand due to population growth, changes in per capita income, and changes in income distribution; (3) the managerial units producing farm products are described; and (4) the aggregate behavior of U.S. agricultural output is described.

5

AGRICULTURAL FACTOR MARKETS

The classical categorization of factors—land, labor, and capital—is useful, particularly if capital is divided into land-saving, labor-saving, neutral (with respect to land and labor), and a mix produced as a result of labor-saving, land-saving, and other technological developments.

The most important single characteristic of *land* for theoretical purposes is probably the space it occupies on the face of the earth. Its other productive characteristics are relatively easy to replace or reproduce, as demonstrated by fertilizer factories, irrigation systems, and drainage facilities. But space, in which the energy of the sun can be collected is to date a characteristic not readily reproducible by man. While land becomes increasingly passive as a factor of production [Schultz, May 1951, pp. 204 ff.], the impact of the space it occupies remains important in the operation of factor markets.[1]

One square mile is required for four 160-acre farms. Of necessity, some of the farms within an area of a thousand 160-acre farms must be almost 20 miles away from a single central supply point for factors of production in the nonfarm sector. For farm-produced factors, such as feeder animals and feed, supplying and demanding farms even within a single group of a thousand farms average several miles apart and transportation costs are of substantial importance.

Given regional specialization in farm-produced inputs and sector specialization in producing tractors, machinery, trucks, etc., by the nonfarm economy, transportation costs for durable inputs are clearly of major importance. These costs grow out of the space-occupying characteristics of land. In turn, transportation costs create substantial differentials between acquisition costs and disposal values of storable production factors, both durable factors which are used repeatedly—such as tractors—and nondurable factors which are used but once—such as feed or gasoline. In addition to transportation costs, there are other costs of transferring resources from one use to another including commissions, brokerage fees, taxes, loss of knowledge, changes in interest rates, etc. Thus, it is necessary for economic analysis to account for differentials between acquisition costs and salvage values growing out of transportation costs made necessary by the space-occupying characteristic of land.

As land itself is not transported, the differential between land acquisition costs and salvage values is less affected than are the acquisition cost and salvage value differentials for factors associated with land. However, large differentials develop for prices of comparable lands in varying locations. Von Thunen's theory on the location of agricultural production does not adequately handle the role of opportunity cost necessarily introduced by positive differentials between acquisition costs and salvage values. In theoretical analyses of static equilibria

---

[1] Bracketed names and/or dates (and sometimes page numbers) refer to the Bibliography following the final chapter.

based on the assumptions that farmers are perfectly informed, this makes little difference; however, an analysis which recognizes the mistakes likely to be made by imperfectly informed farmers must take into account the price at which farmers can salvage their mistakes if salvage prices are lower than acquisition costs.

As noted earlier, physical capital associated with land is either durable or nondurable. Viewed technologically, physical capital is further classed as land-saving, labor-saving, relatively neutral, or mixed—with respect to its impact on land and labor use.

Durable, land-saving capital includes irrigation facilities, land leveling, terraces, and drainage facilities. These are often heavy, expensive structures, sometimes created in place. As such, their salvage values may be less than zero, i.e., it costs money to destroy or eliminate some of them entirely, though, of course, they may have some value when the land is sold to another farmer. Because such facilities are expensive to acquire and often have negative salvage value, their value in use depends, like that of land, on the price of the products they produce and can vary from negative to as high as their original or present acquisition cost.

Nondurable, land-saving capital includes irrigation water, highly soluble fertilizers, and pesticides—items that tend to have values in use quite near acquisition costs. Though often storable, these items are generally acquired as they are used, mainly within a current production period, and farmers make fewer mistakes of overcommitment than they do for durables such as drainage facilities which may produce services for several decades.

Thus, for a substantial proportion of land-saving capital used in agriculture, acquisition costs exceed salvage values. Whether or not this proportion is increasing is an empirical question not easily answered. The use of durable land substitutes is expanding rapidly and is in many instances driving marginal lands out of cultivation. Use of nondurable, land-saving capital (mainly fertilizer, improved seed, and feed-saving technology) and product-conserving technology is also expanding rapidly. Though these nondurables have low salvage values once acquired, they tend to be used quickly with their earning power covering acquisition costs.

Durable labor-saving capital ranges from fences and buildings through tractors, trucks, horses, and combines, to hoes, pitchforks, and electric sheep-shearing equipment. At one extreme are heavy and expensive items that are produced in place. At the other extreme are light, inexpensive, and easily transported items. Some items, such as milking machines and hay bailers, are specialized even within agriculture. Others, such as plows, are specialized to agriculture, but flexible between the agricultural and nonagricultural sectors. Generally, it is clear that transportation costs for durable, labor-saving capital, plus its tendency to be specialized, combine with the space-occupying characteristics of agriculture to create substantial differentials between acquisition costs and salvage values for a high proportion of the labor-saving, durable capital used in agriculture. As labor-saving technology advances, the proportion of labor-saving durables increases in the factor mix used.

Nondurable labor-saving capital used in U.S. agriculture includes gasoline, electricity, herbicides, and pesticides. These one-use items, like the nondurable land-saving capital items discussed above, are generally acquired as farmers are convinced that their earnings will cover acquisition costs. Thus, the substantial differential which the space-occupying characteristics of land introduces between acquisition costs and salvage values for these items is of less practical significance than for durable labor-saving capital.

The importance of labor-saving capital is steadily increasing in the factor mix for United States agriculture. Since 1917 there has been an almost complete replacement of horse feed by petroleum products, both of which substitute for human labor. On the durable capital side, a corresponding replacement of horses with tractors and trucks occurred. Thus, it is difficult to judge whether the difference between acquisition costs and salvage values for labor-saving capital has grown relatively more important or less important. However, it is clear that the difference is important.

Durable capital that is relatively neutral with respect to land and labor use is also important. This category includes items produced both on and off farms. Examples of the former include breeding stock, orchards, and improved pastures; examples of the latter (not previously mentioned) are dryers, pelleting machines, processing equipment, etc. While superior capital items of this type may reduce both labor and land requirements per unit of output, they are primarily items that perform services not readily provided by either land or labor.

Farm-produced, neutral capital is sometimes produced in place. In other instances, it is moved from a producing farm to a using farm. In either case, transportation costs introduced by the space-occupying characteristics of agriculture introduce such differentials between acquisition and salvage values over the lifetime of these durables that high acquisition costs may be associated with negative salvage values, as in the case of orchards.

Nondurable agricultural capital that is relatively neutral with respect to land and labor utilization includes such farm-produced factors of production as livestock feed, seed, and feeders. Some nonfarm produced factors of production, such as drugs, are relatively neutral or mixed, but are also relatively unimportant compared with the nondurable land and labor substitutes produced by the nonfarm economy.

The relatively neutral, farm-produced nondurables are extremely important in our agricultural economy. Since they are often moved from producing to utilizing farms, transportation costs introduce substantial differentials between acquisition costs and salvage values. On farms which both produce and then utilize these factors of production, the productive value can range from acquisition cost to salvage value. Acquisition cost is the expense of producing or buying the input from another farmer and then moving it to the utilizing farm. The cost of buying involves, of course, the cost of transferring title from seller to buyer—including commissions, fees, taxes, dealers' profits, and interest charges. The salvage value is what the using farmer can obtain for the input in its next best alternative use if he decides to withdraw the input from its present employment.

AGRICULTURAL PRODUCT MARKETS

Markets for United States agricultural products have several structural characteristics important in formulating theoretical structures for use in understanding how resources are allocated. Historically, U.S. farmers have attempted with and without governmental assistance to gain control over the marketing of their products. However, success in attaining such control without the assistance of government has been sporadic and unsustained. With state and federal legislation, marketing orders have been established for specialized commodities and/or local areas and regions. Then, too, federal production and marketing controls have been used with varying success to control production and marketing and to raise prices. Nonetheless, the individual farmers behave mainly as competitive buyers and sellers rather than as monopsonists and monopolists.

On the buying, processing, and distribution side of U.S. agricultural product markets, less competition exists. There have been historical concerns with monopolistic practices in transportation and meat packing, and in tobacco, grain, and cotton exporting. The National Commission on Food Marketing found no strong tendency toward monopolization by the four largest firms, but did find some increased tendency toward monopolistic competition among a fairly substantial number of firms operating in a specific geographic or commodity area, such as food retailing and meat packing. Much of the concentration and increase in firm size which is taking place appears to be a result of: (1) technological advances in materials handling, transporting, processing, and retailing; (2) advancing wage rates; and (3) changes in consumer tastes and preferences accompanying higher per capita incomes, increased urbanization, and increased monetization of the U.S. economy. The space-occupying nature of the farm firm means that agricultural product markets are characterized by substantial transportation costs, and hence large geographic price differentials.

Finally, U.S. agriculture produces for both foreign and domestic consumers. Domestically, the ultimate consumers are characterized as having increasing per capita incomes with low-income demand elasticities for starchy unprocessed food, higher-income demand elasticities for processed and/or tasty, high-protein foods and/or low caloric fruit and vegetables, and very-high-income demand elasticities for products incorporating services which save consumer labor. Historically, consumer incomes have been unstable due to the business cycle, but this form of instability has been less pronounced since World War II. Characteristically, the foreign consumers of U.S. products provide a large but unstable market. This results from wars that disrupt foreign production, the increasing role of other governments in international markets for agricultural products, and the role of the U.S. government export programs.

THE U.S. FARM-FIRM AND ITS ENVIRONMENT

For purposes of understanding the operation of the U.S. agricultural economy, the characteristics of the farm-firm of most interest have to do with its size and decision-making capacity. In this section we discuss eight of the most significant characteristics in this regard.

First, the most outstanding characteristic of the American farm is that it has remained essentially a family operation. While its size has grown steadily when measured in terms of output, acreage, and capital utilized, it has not grown substantially in labor used.

Second, the farm-firm is atomistically competitive. Very few producing farms are large enough either to buy enough of any input or to sell enough of any product to see themselves as capable of influencing product or factor prices except with the assistance of associations, cooperatives, and/or governmental regulations.

Third, the farm-firm has apparently been unable to obtain perfect knowledge of the extremely changeable environment in which it operates. On the institutional side there have been great changes in taxation, production controls, credit availability, food and drug regulation, minimum wages, social security, farm organizations, local schools, roads, markets, etc. Further, consumers of farm products are an unstable lot (as noted in the section above). Consumer incomes have both grown and fluctuated widely over the ups and downs of prosperity and depressions. As the incomes of domestic consumers increased, relative demands for common starches, fats, and oils fell, while demands for high-quality meats, cheeses, fruits, etc. increased [Schultz, 1945]. Generally, in periods of depression, prices that consumers must pay fall rapidly relative to prices in prosperity. At all times the demand for food is relatively inelastic and any substantial increase in output per capita has quickly depressed prices [Cochrane, May 1947]. Internationally, consumers of United States farm products are also an uncertain market that fluctuates widely with wars, international prosperities and depressions, and nationalistic changes in import and exchange control policies and programs. Imperfect knowledge of these changes on the demand or consumption side has been an important cause of investment errors on the part of farm entrepreneurs.

On the production side, the environment of U.S. agriculture is at least as unstable as on the demand side. Almost since the beginning, American agriculture has been labor extensive and has sought and obtained major changes in labor-using (saving) technology. The changes come at least as rapidly as corresponding changes for the nonfarm economy. More recently, the pressure has been on land-saving technology, and thus changes have come rapidly for fertilizers, crop improvements, irrigation, etc. Most of the U.S. agricultural production takes place in a continental climate. Stallings' weather index [February 1960] indicates that weather alone was capable of shifting the index of gross farm production from 69 to 120 percent of normal for selected years between 1930 and 1957. For individual products the range is wider, and for individual farms the range is still wider. As the agricultural production process is biological rather than mechanical or chemical, there is the added uncertainty of disease and insect infestation. However, this uncertainty is coming under greater control with improved disease- and pest-control technology. Nevertheless, atomistically organized family-farm entrepreneurs operating in a rapidly changing environment are imperfectly informed about rapidly changing technology, demand, weather, diseases, pests, and institutions with which they must deal.

Fourth, American farm prices have typically not been high enough to cover simultaneously the acquisition costs for labor and the different kinds of capital plus the value assigned to land by the market; thus, substantial capital losses have been incurred. These losses are, however, offset in part by secular inflation and, since 1933, by government payments. Table 1 shows the extent of capital gains and losses in current dollars, by asset category, annually from 1911 to 1959. Table 2 shows capital gains and losses in constant dollars, by asset category, annually from 1940 to 1960, and indicates that secular inflation in land values has not covered the capital losses incurred. But substantial capital losses are offset by government payments that have ranged up to $3 billion per year; the expectation of these payments has maintained agricultural capital values. It is also interesting to note that William Kost [1967] found that random investments in the stock market would have yielded a 17.9 percent rate of return from income and price gains, whereas farm real estate earned but 9.3 percent from 1950 to 1963.

Capital losses, of course, originate in factor earnings that do not cover acquisition costs. Information on the earnings of labor, capital, and land is available from a variety of sources. However, in this chapter only superficial attention is devoted to this subject, since later chapters take it up in detail. Here we are only

TABLE 1. Changes in Current Value of Assets in Agriculture Due to Price Changes, by Sectors and in Total, 1911-1959

(millions of dollars)

| Year | Net change in asset position of | | | | Total change in asset position of agriculture |
	Real estate	Livestock	Machinery	Crops	
1911	932	-155.3	6.5	323.1	1,106.8
1912	822	590.9	7.7	-509.7	910.8
1913	815	347.5	4.3	431.3	1,598.1
1914	-345	-145.0	-4.9	-315.2	-810.0
1915	2,357	-155.2	101.8	67.8	2,371.4
1916	2,922	573.5	65.7	898.2	4,259.4
1917	4,046	1,291.2	590.1	1,742.2	7,669.5
1918	4,153	477.6	841.1	284.0	5,755.6
1919	11,341	-280.4	-228.3	89.0	10,921.3
1920	-5,369	-1,896.5	-368.9	-2,878.9	-10,513.3
1921	-7,029	-1,290.9	-1,150.6	-906.3	-10,376.8
1922	-929	270.7	-279.1	650.1	-287.4
1923	-2,031	-182.3	670.8	232.8	-1,309.7
1924	-546	188.3	-48.0	554.8	149.1
1925	-182	535.7	145.7	-591.3	-91.8
1926	-1,874	220.2	3.1	-348.0	-1,998.7
1927	-849	489.4	-101.9	222.9	238.5
1928	-217	548.9	136.8	-52.2	416.5
1929	-719	-158.1	75.9	74.7	-726.5
1930	-4,765	-1,707.1	-418.8	-553.0	-7,443.9
1931	-7,118	-1,425.5	-175.8	-1,029.5	-9,748.8
1932	-6,899	-665.7	-314.9	-571.2	-8,450.7
1933	999	123.4	70.7	785.0	1,978.0
1934	644	600.6	388.2	816.4	2,449.2
1935	597	1,723.4	159.8	-1,056.6	1,423.7
1936	884	-31.9	157.2	866.0	1,875.2
1937	-78	50.0	185.1	-1,358.5	1,201.4
1938	-1,120	-31.6	-139.3	-335.3	-1,626.2
1939	-483	-188.1	-394.6	362.2	-703.5
1940	697	135.5	273.6	-15.6	1,090.6
1941	2,597	1,461.5	626.1	785.6	5,470.2
1942	3,494	2,079.9	343.8	593.4	6,511.1
1943	6,014	-362.0	-462.7	1,371.6	6,560.9
1944	5,009	-101.6	741.9	-30.4	5,618.9
1945	6,354	1,018.4	-2,079.5	43.9	5,336.7
1946	7,234	2,644.2	954.2	896.9	11,729.2
1947	4,996	1,946.0	2,579.8	2,820.8	12,342.5
1948	2,738	1,393.5	1,038.4	-3,514.9	1,654.9
1949	-1,597	-1,991.5	-22.7	-546.9	-4,158.1
1950	11,316	4,227.0	-534.3	1,181.0	16,189.8
1951	9,197	1,383.0	1,297.3	1,320.2	13,197.4
1952	641	-5,131.8	-1,337.1	200.3	-5,627.6
1953	-1,948	-2,696.9	105.3	-1,289.5	-5,829.1
1954	4,092	-660.0	-415.6	-636.3	2,380.2

Table 1. Continued.

(millions of dollars)

| Year | Net change in asset position of | | | | Total change in asset position of agriculture |
	Real estate	Livestock	Machinery	Crops	
1955	3,872	−732.2	690.8	−1,220.0	2,235.5
1956	6,817	633.3	801.2	546.5	8,543.4
1957	6,799	3,160.6	39.3	1,014.7	11,013.6
1958	8,818	4,304.4	1,473.0	15.9	14,611.3
1959	4,009	−2,598.8	579.0	−1,582.3	407.0

Source: Computations by Glenn Johnson, modified by Dale Hathaway and extended by Willard Sparks.

setting forth a general picture of what tends to happen in U.S. agriculture so that we may then suggest a theoretical apparatus capable of corresponding with reality.

When returns to the operator and family labor are computed residually by subtracting modest interest charges, the hourly rate of return varies for selected, typical, family-operated commercial farms (Table 3) from an average low of − $0.56 per hour to a high of $3.47 for 1956–59.

In the past twenty years, around fifty functional analyses of farm business records were carried out by agricultural economists, principally in Iowa, Kentucky, Michigan, North Carolina, and Montana. Though these analyses have yielded nonresidual estimates of marginal earnings and were more rigorous than farm records and typical farm studies, conclusions derived from them in general agree with those from analyses based on farm accounts and the typical farm data presented in Table 4. Indications are that the earning power of labor on commercial farms was lower but less variable from year to year than the farm account studies indicate. The lower level of labor earnings shown by functional analyses was probably "real," since the residual method is arbitrary in this respect. This difference in variability is expected in that the residual method of computation followed in the typical farm records analyses gives family and operator labor the benefit of all the fortunate things which happen to a farm business in a favorable year as well as imposes upon it the consequences of all the unfortunate events of unfavorable years.

These different sources also furnish some evidence concerning capital earnings. If the typical farm and farm records residual analyses are modified with a charge being made for family and operator's labor instead of for capital, the residual returns are for capital. Generally speaking such computations show low to modest returns on capital so long as the labor charge is a modest one running below the industrial wage rate. If, however, the charge for family and operator's labor is made at industrial wage rates, residual returns to capital are low or negative. Both functional and residual studies show, by and large, that marginal

TABLE 2. Changes in Purchasing Power of Farm Operator-Owned Price-Sensitive Assets, and Monetary Assets and Liabilities, Measured in Constant Dollars for Calendar Years 1940–1959

(billions of 1910–14 dollars)

Year	All farm real estate (1)	Percentage owned by farm operators (2)	Operator-owned farm real estate (3)	Machinery and motor vehicles (4)	Livestock (5)	Crop inventories (6)	Total for price-sensitive assets (7)	Monetary assets and liabilities (8)	Total real wealth gain (+); loss (−) (9)
1940	0.26	73.0%	0.19	0.14	0.05	-0.02	0.37	0.01	0.38
1941	0.33	72.9	0.24	-0.07	0.90	0.44	1.52	0.21	1.73
1942	-1.08	72.9	-0.79	0.38	0.68	0.13	0.40	0.05	0.45
1943	1.21	72.8	0.88	0.21	-0.77	0.82	1.14	-0.14	1.00
1944	1.45	72.8	1.05	0.39	-0.46	-0.23	0.76	-0.28	0.48
1940–44	2.17	–	1.58	1.06	0.40	1.15	4.18	-0.15	4.03
1945	2.81	72.7	2.04	-0.84	0.37	-0.02	1.56	-0.36	1.20
1946	0.02	72.2	0.02	-0.56	0.87	0.05	0.38	-0.39	-0.01
1947	-3.07	71.7	-2.20	-0.03	-0.07	0.66	-1.65	-0.41	-2.06
1948	-0.92	71.2	-0.66	0.16	0.24	-1.22	-1.47	0.01	-1.46
1949	0.12	70.7	0.08	0.22	-0.43	-0.20	-0.32	0.13	-0.19

1945–49	-1.04	–	-0.72	-1.06	0.99	-0.72	-1.51	-1.02	-2.53
1950	4.02	70.2	2.82	0.09	1.52	0.29	4.72	-0.21	4.51
1951	0.26	70.1	0.18	-0.06	0.05	0.18	0.35	-0.10	0.25
1952	-0.56	70.0	-0.39	0.01	-1.94	-0.18	-2.51	0.01	-2.50
1953	-0.73	69.8	-0.51	0.07	-1.02	-0.21	-1.67	0.00	-1.67
1954	1.20	69.7	0.83	0.02	-0.20	-0.06	0.59	-0.01	0.58
1950–54	4.18	–	2.93	0.12	-1.59	0.01	1.48	-0.31	1.17
1955	1.24	69.6	0.87	0.11	-0.19	-0.39	0.40	0.00	0.40
1956	1.72	69.5	1.20	0.29	0.17	0.04	1.70	-0.02	1.68
1957	1.07	69.4	0.74	-0.05	1.04	-0.57	1.16	-0.02	1.14
1958	2.24	69.2	1.55	0.14	1.08	0.04	2.81	0.00	2.81
1959	1.00	69.1	0.69	0.14	-0.91	-0.02	-0.10	0.00	-0.10
1955–59	7.27	–	5.04	0.63	1.19	-0.90	5.97	-0.04	5.93
1940–59	12.58	–	8.84	0.75	1.00	-0.47	10.12	-1.52	8.60
1940–59ᵃ	36.47	–	25.63	2.17	2.90	-1.36	29.35	-4.41	24.94

Source: Boyne [1964, Table 11, pp. 39–40].
ᵃExpressed in dollars of 1960 purchasing power as approximated by the Farm Family Living Index.

TABLE 3. Returns per Hour of Family and Operator's Labor on Selected, Typical, Commercial, Family-Operated Farms, 1946-50, 1956-59, and 1966

	Dollar returns per hour of family and operator's labor			
			1966	
Type of farm	1946-50	1956-59	At current interest	At 4.1% interest
Dairy farms:				
Central northeast	$0.69	$0.74	$0.98	$1.21
Eastern Wisconsin	.66	.25	–	–
Grade A	–	–	1.29	1.58
Grade B	–	–	.54	.75
Western Wisconsin	.53	.52	–	–
Grade B	–	–	1.15	1.30
Dairy-hog farms, S. Minn.	–	–	1.24	1.49
Broiler farms, Maine	–	–	.49	.78
Corn Belt farms:				
Hog-dairy	1.08	1.02	2.64	3.01
Hog-beef fattening	2.29	1.55	1.76	2.43
Cash grain	1.97	.84	2.29	3.67
Cotton farms:				
Southern Piedmont	.36	.33	–.04	.31
Texas, High Plains				
(irrigated)	3.34	3.47	3.77	4.67
Tobacco farms:				
Tobacco-livestock				
Kentucky	.80	.66	–	–
Inner Bluegrass	–	–	1.07	1.77
Tobacco-beef				
Pennyroyal	–	–	.22	.75
Wheat farms:				
Spring wheat–small grain–				
livestock, Northern Plains	1.89	1.09	2.73	3.14
Winter wheat, Southern Plains	2.90	1.74	1.35	2.02
Cattle ranches:				
Northern Plains	.86	.29	.59	.99
Southwest	.38	–.56	–1.67	–.47

Source: USDA, ERS.

TABLE 4. Marginal Earnings of Labor, Selected Types of Farms in Selected Locations, at Indicated Dates

Description of study and date	Marginal earnings of labor per month
Trigg County, upland, Kentucky, 1951[1]	$ 52
Trigg County, bottomland, Kentucky, 1951[1]	97
Graves County, bottomland, Kentucky, 1951[1]	43
Ingham County, dairy, Michigan, 1952[2]	25

Table 4. Continued.

Description of study and date	Marginal earnings of labor per month
North Lower Peninsula, Michigan, 1952[3]	12
Burnside Township, Lapeer Co., Michigan, 1953[4]	113
Almount Township, Lapeer Co., Michigan, 1953[4]	84
N.W. Illinois, hog enterprise, 1950[5]	8
N.W. Illinois, dairy enterprise, 1950[5]	126
N.W. Illinois, crop enterprise, 1950[5]	132
Ogemaw-Arenac Co., Michigan, beef, 1953[3]	182
Ogemaw-Arenac Co., Michigan, process milk, 1953[3]	137
Ogemaw-Arenac Co., Michigan, fluid milk, 1953[3]	114
Marshall Co., Kentucky, upland, 1950[6]	32
Grayson Co., Kentucky, upland, 1951[7]	61
McCracken Co., Kentucky, upland, 1951[6]	32
Calloway Co., Kentucky, upland, 1951[1]	8
Calloway Co., Kentucky, bottomland, 1951[1]	38
Calloway Co., Kentucky, bottomland, large farms, 1951[1]	53
McCracken Co., Kentucky, upland, large farms, 1951[8]	53
Central Indiana, hog-feeder cattle, 1953[9]	218
Central Indiana, hog-dairy cattle, 1953[9]	277
S. Central Michigan, soil B, dairy, 1953[2]	37

[1] Glenn L. Johnson, *Sources of Income on Trigg, Calloway, and Graves County Bottomland Farms, 1951*, Progress Report No. 13, Kentucky Agricultural Experiment Station (Lexington: University of Kentucky with Tennessee Valley Authority Cooperating, May 1953).

[2] Robert Vance Wagley, "Marginal Productivities of Investments and Expenditures, Selected Ingham County Farms, 1952," M.S. thesis, Michigan State College, East Lansing, 1953.

[3] Gerald I. Trant, "A Technique of Adjusting Marginal Value Productivity Estimates for Changing Prices," M.S. thesis, Michigan State College, East Lansing, 1954.

[4] Carl Eicher, "The Use of Cobb-Douglas Analysis in Evaluating the Michigan Township Extension Program," M.S. thesis, Michigan State University, East Lansing, 1956.

[5] Christoph Beringer, "A Method of Estimating Marginal Value Productivities of Input and Investment Categories on Multiple Enterprise Farms," Ph.D. thesis, Michigan State University, East Lansing, 1955.

[6] Glenn L. Johnson, *Sources of Incomes on Upland Marshall County Farms*, Progress Report 1, Kentucky Agricultural Experiment Station, University of Kentucky, Lexington, 1952.

[7] Thomas G. Toon, "Marginal Value Productivities of Inputs, Investments, and Expenditures on Upland Grayson County Farms during 1951," M.S. thesis, University of Kentucky, Lexington, 1953.

[8] Glenn L. Johnson, *Sources of Income on Upland McCracken County Farms, 1951*, Progress Report No. 2, R & MA 60, Kentucky Agricultural Experiment Station (Lexington: University of Kentucky with Tennessee Valley Authority Cooperating, September 16, 1952).

[9] Clark Edwards, "Estimation of Farm Resource Productivities from Central Indiana Accounting Records," M.S. thesis, Purdue University, Lafayette, Indiana, 1956.

earnings of capital at values placed on it by farmers in agriculture have been fairly satisfactory under the conditions prevailing in recent years. However, much of the capital has been revalued by farmers to take account of the capital losses which they suffered.

It is rather common for machinery investments in farming to be returning an estimated earning of 10 to 15 or 20 percent at the margin, which is a reasonable return in view of taxes and the life spans for most major items of machinery. Typically, returns for investments in land are just about sufficient to sustain the current prices being paid by farmers for land, if the interest rate is figured at 5 or 6 percent, which is low on the current market. Returns on investments in livestock and improved pasture appear high at first appraisal, running in the neighborhood of 25 to 40 percent; however, this return is not high when the high depreciation rates involved in investments in breeding and milk stock are considered. The typical dairy cow, for instance, stays in a herd between three and four years. The average cow in a herd has been in that herd for half of these three or four years. Thus, the depreciation charge for an ordinary cow is very high even after allowance for her cull value. In the case of capital, functional analyses indicate that current earnings are more stable than residual analyses indicate. The greater stability is expected from the difference in method.

More detail for 1966 is provided in Table 5 for the United States and for Michigan. Despite the favorable price situation that existed in this year, both the

TABLE 5. Percent of Sample of Michigan Farms with Parity Returns or Better, 1966

| Type of farm | Size of farms (gross sales) | | | |
	Over $40,000	$20,000–39,999	$10,000–19,999	$5,000–9,999
Dairy	52%	34%	3%	0%
Cash grain	44	38	33	0
Livestock	36	20	0	0
General	50	31	16	20

Source: Hathaway and Duvick [1967].

Note: Michigan data are computed from Telfarm records. Parity returns are defined "to be the value of a rental return on equity capital, plus a wage for the farm operator and unpaid family labor equivalent to what the labor could earn (would have earned had he left the farm as a boy) in any other occupation."

federal census and Michigan State University Telfarm[2] data show that overall returns were not at parity levels, where parity is defined as returns favorable enough to cover, simultaneously, reasonable annual charges on the price of land,

[2] Computerized farm account system operated by the Michigan State University Agricultural Extension Service.

the cost of providing the different kinds of capital involved, and operator and family labor at rates varying from $1.91 per hour for unpaid family labor on small farms to $2.62 per hour for operators on large farms. Table 6 shows the distribution of farms by income level. The Michigan Telfarm system oversamples large farms and undersamples the small ones. The year 1967 was much worse for Michigan farmers than 1966. The 1967 index of prices received fell 1 percent, while the index of prices paid rose over 1 percent in the face of expanded investments and usage of nondurable factors of production. These changes dropped total net income of farm operators from $16.2 billion in 1966 to $14.9 billion in 1967. Clearly, then, technical advances, the international food gap, farm reorganizations, and changes in scale had not changed the general situation prevailing in American agriculture for many years. Now, as in the past, gross returns for the vast majority of farmers are not high enough to cover land values, acquisition costs for capital, the cost of hired labor, and reasonable charges for operators and family labor.

TABLE 6. Proportion of Michigan Commercial Farms by Economic Class

| | Economic class and income interval | | | | | | |
| | I | II | III | IV | V | VI | All |
Item	$40,000– or more	$20,000– 39,999	$10,000– 19,999	$5,000– 9,999	$2,500– 4,999	$50– 2,499	commercial farms
1964 Census of Agriculture	4%	12%	22%	25%	27%	10%	100%
1965 Michigan Telfarm system	31	48	18	2	1	0	100
1966 Michigan Telfarm system	36	48	13	2	1	0	100

Fifth, another characteristic of agriculture is that its labor has been and still is born into the farm-family firm. Further, there is an excess of natural net accretions to the number of rural youth ready to enter the labor force over the net increase (decrease) in agricultural employment. Agriculture is thus a net supplier of manpower to the rest of the nation [Chennareddy and G. L. Johnson, August 1968].

Sixth, for the typical U.S. agricultural firm the farm is generally (though far from entirely so) a profit and utility maximizing organization. This is clear from (1) the way in which the output of individual products quickly responds to changes in relative prices [Cochrane, May 1947]; and (2) studies of the behavior of individual farm managers [Johnson et al., 1961, Chaps. 4, 5, and 7]. There is evidence that midwestern farmers know a substantial amount about the theory of the firm [Ibid., p. 83 and elsewhere] and the principles of price determination. The farmers also appear to understand the technique of maximizing the expected utility of uncertain future events well enough for a significantly high proportion to answer randomly presented questions in a manner consistent with that technique [Halter, 1956]. This is not to state that all farmers are maximizers at all times under all conditions of risk and uncertainty. However, they do enough maximization so that theoretical maximizing models are useful in analyzing that part of their behavior having to do with response to price and resource allocation.

Seventh, the U.S. farm-firm entrepreneur is aware that he must adjust to change from the position in which he exists. This is recognized by the extension worker's axiom "start with the farmer where he is and with the problems he faces." Halter's study of 1,075 midwestern farmers in the mid-1950's revealed extensive use by farmers of analytical managerial systems that start out from fixed conditions over which the farmer has no control. Farmers with fixed land resources employed a land-use approach, others with fixed labor but variable land resources employed a labor-utilization approach [Halter, 1956, pp. 62, 63, and 77-81]. Still others employed other fixed resource approaches.

Eighth, most farm firms are technologically and, in a sense, economically obsolete. To show a foreign visitor a really up-to-date farm in almost any part of the United States, I would probably need to drive past many (perhaps 200) farms before proudly showing off the "special case." The bypassed farms are characterized by investments in less-advanced technologies, which the farmer now wishes he had not made and from which he is now suffering capital losses. The losses are not recoverable and cannot advantageously be liquidated.

THE NATURE OF AGGREGATIVE RESPONSES OF
U.S. AGRICULTURE

U.S. agriculture displays a greater capacity to expand than to contract production in the aggregate. This characteristic is most pronounced when national indexes are examined but it is also prominent for individual commodities [G. L. Johnson et al., 1958]. Recent estimates [Tweeten and Quance, 1969] indicate that the aggregate supply elasticity for U.S. farm output is 0.15 in the short run and 1.50 in the long run for increasing prices. However, the supply elasticity drops to 0.10 in the short run and 0.80 in the long run for decreasing farm prices.

SUMMARY

The following structural characteristics of American agriculture should be reflected in the assumptions underlying economic theories used to explain its operation:

1. The U.S. farmer operates, in substantial part, as a profit and/or utility maximizer or as a loss and/or disutility minimizer. Further, he knows quite a bit about the process of maximization.

2. The entrepreneur or farmer operates subject to risk and uncertainty in an environment characterized by large and continuous changes in technology, institutions, and human behavior.

3. Farmers make substantial errors in their attempts to maximize and minimize.

4. Transportation and other ownership transfer costs introduce substantial differentials between the acquisition costs and salvage values of identical or substantially similar factors of production. Salvage values are negative in some instances while acquisition costs may approach infinity. Rarely are acquisition costs and salvage values precisely the same.

5. In organizing and managing their businesses, American farmers follow various fixed resource approaches, the particular one used depending on which resource they find to be fixed.

The following operating characteristics of the United States agricultural economy are well enough established and known that economic theories used to explain the operation of the economy should not preclude their occurrence: (1) failure of product prices to cover acquisition costs in the long-run; (2) long-run simultaneous failure to equate the earnings of labor and capital in agriculture with their acquisition costs; (3) long-run reoccurring capital losses; and (4) non-Pareto optimum adjustments as a result of a freely operating price mechanism.

At this point a disclaimer is required. Many of the characteristics summarized in this chapter are not unique to agriculture. Indeed, even the combination of characteristics may not be unique though Hathaway [1963] and we think it is unique enough to require theoretical recognition. In any event the object in recognizing the characteristics of American agriculture is not to develop an argument in defense of special treatment for agriculture, but to develop theoretical formulations with more explanatory, diagnostic, and prescriptive power. To the extent that other industries have the characteristics described above, the theoretical formulations in the next chapter have explanatory, diagnostic, and prescriptive power for them as well.

CHAPTER 3

Theoretical Considerations

GLENN L. JOHNSON

Before developing our theoretical model that will be the basis of Part II, it is useful to examine two valuable modifications of neoclassical economic theory made respectively by T. W. Schultz and D. Gale Johnson. In addition, certain other lines of reasoning that concern American agriculture's tendency to expand, but not to contract, production are given attention in this chapter.

THE SCHULTZIAN SECULAR MODIFICATION

Schultz's modification, presented in his book *Agriculture in an Unstable Economy* [1945], applied to the long-run or secular analysis advanced by the classical and neoclassical economists and is essentially also a modification of John Stuart Mill's *Principles of Political Economy*, Book 4 [1849].

Schultz argued (1) that birth and mortality rates in farm population result in a supply of farm labor which, in view of labor-saving technological advances, exceeds agricultural demand for the supply, (2) that per capita real incomes rise rapidly in western societies such as the United States, and (3) that the income demand elasticities for most foods and fibers are so low that prices of farm products are depressed relative to prices of nonfarm products. He also noted that technological advance is labor saving and involves the substitution of capital for labor in agriculture at a rate at least as rapid as in industry. Some theoretical consequences of these observations are (1) a rate of growth in the supply of farm products with low elasticities of demand exceeding the rate of growth in demand for these same products with, (2) a consequent cost-price squeeze on the producers of the low-elasticity farm products with the prices averaging below long-run equilibrium levels, (3) an excess supply of labor devoted, at low returns, to the production of farm products, and (4) returns to capital above competitive levels because of the long-run need to transfer capital into agriculture to substitute for the labor transferred out.

D. GALE JOHNSON'S RISK AND UNCERTAINTY MODIFICATION

The D. Gale Johnson modification involved the addition of certain nonstatic concepts (borrowed mainly from Frank Knight [1941]) to the short-run competitive theory of the firm. In Johnson's book, *Forward Prices for Agriculture* [1947, Chap. 4], the risk and uncertainty analysis explains certain phenomena in agriculture that, in turn, imply the wisdom of farm policies and programs based on forward prices. This modification of neoclassical theory of the competitive firm is not "long run" as is the Schultzian modification. Instead of assuming that producers have perfect knowledge of future prices for both products and factors of production, Johnson used the much more realistic assumption that farmers are imperfectly informed about the future.

His model of producer behavior under these conditions includes attention to the various safeguards which producers take to protect themselves against the adverse effects of imperfect knowledge. These safeguards involve various forms of formal and informal insurance. An important type of informal insurance is the discounting of anticipated future returns to establish (1) safety margins to meet unfavorable contingencies and (2) reserves to take advantage of favorable events. Under the law of diminishing returns, such discounting results in restriction of output and average prices higher than the "certain" prices necessary to call forth sufficient output to equate supply with demand. The theoretical result is underproduction rather than overproduction of a specific commodity and average farm prices high enough to cover more than the actual acquisition costs.

D. Gale Johnson's model would cause us to expect that the introduction of price stability through price supports would increase the willingness of farmers to produce at any given average level of prices. At least three rather detailed studies—of dry edible beans, burley tobacco, and potatoes [respectively by Hathaway, May 1955; G. L. Johnson, February 1952; and Gray, Sorenson, and Cochrane, 1954]—indicate that this theory is valid. However, Johnson's modification of the comparative model economy does not account for such characteristics of the agricultural as (1) its tendency to overinvest in productive capacity, (2) the presence of a high proportion of obsolete production units, (3) lower, rather than higher, competitive average actual earnings of labor and capital in agriculture, (4) capital gains and losses received by farmers, and (5) agriculture's meager ability to contract production. The risk and uncertainty analysis simply does not explain why farmers make mistakes of overproduction which result in excess productive capacity, low product prices, inability to contract production when prices fall, low earnings, and capital losses.

The neoclassical analysis, as modified secularly by Schultz and in the short run by D. Gale Johnson's adoption of Knight's risk and uncertainty analysis, does not need to be replaced; instead, further modification of the analytical apparatus is needed so that it will more adequately account for low product prices, overproduction at prices less than sufficient to cover factor acquisition costs, capital losses, greater capacity to expand rather than to contract production, and technologically obsolete farms.

OTHER MODIFICATIONS AND EXTENSIONS

At least three different lines of reasoning have some importance as explanations of the tendency of American agriculture to expand but not contract production. The first and most important of these deals with technological advance. The second deals with improvements in the human agent. The third has to do with the role that various economic adjustments, mainly specialization, play in increasing productivity.

The most widespread of the above three "explanations" of overproduction involves technological advances. W. W. Cochrane [1958] is emphatic in stressing the technological advance role. Further, he argues that the irreversibility of technological advance also accounts for American agriculture's inability to contract production when need for expanded production disappears. The work of Cochrane and other agricultural economists on the technological variable is supplemented by sociologists studying the diffusion of new farm practices and the adoption of technological advance by farmers [Rogers, 1958]. The "technological advance" explanation is strengthened further by various projections of production based largely on technological considerations which have proven quite accurate. Included among these projections are those by Black and Bonnen [1956], as well as some U.S. Department of Agriculture projections [e. g., Daly, 1967, pp. 82-119].

However, several considerations make for uneasiness about using technological advance to explain all of the above-listed characteristics of American agriculture. These include: (1) some tendency to define technological advance so as to include all economic adjustments such as changes in the amount of nitrogen fertilizer used on corn in response to a decrease in the price of nitrogen relative to other fertilizer nutrients; (2) the very high proportion of obsolete units of production in American agriculture; and (3) the changes in production and resource flows into and out of agriculture relative to changes in product and factor prices as demonstrated by the research Hathaway presented at the hearings of the Joint Economic Committee in December 1958 [Hathaway, 1958, pp. 51-76] and by an article entitled, "Supply Functions: Some Facts and Notions," published in the proceedings of a conference sponsored by the North Central Farm Management Research Committee [Johnson et al., 1958, Chap. 5].

Schultz joined Cochrane, momentarily at least, in stressing technological advance, and, in addition, stressed improvements in the human agent as a parallel consideration. Schultz also noted that ratios between incremental output and incremental input for American agriculture are greater than one. Though serious problems exist in measuring both total output and total inputs, accurate observation of such ratios would not necessarily mean that improvement occurred in either nonhuman agents (called technological advance) or in the human agent (education and training). Without either technological advance or improved training of individuals, several types of adjustment can occur that can result in an increase in output with no increase in input. (Several of these types of adjustments are discussed in the next paragraph.)

Another explanation of irreversible overproduction receives some attention among agricultural economists. Fundamentally, it involves economic adjustments, especially those that concern specialization between the farm sector and the nonfarm sector, among regions of the United States, and among farms within regions [G. L. Johnson, November 1957]. Specialization can account for ratios between incremental output and incremental input greater than one. So can diversification or, in fact, any profit maximization or efficiency adjustment which, by definition, either expands production more than the use of resources or contracts production less than the use of resources. A full understanding of these adjustments requires a theory to explain when and under what circumstances production is expanded or contracted or allowed to remain unchanged.

In recent decades very significant specializations have occurred. For instance, agriculture abandoned the production of its own power units and fuel by turning from horses to the purchase of tractors and fuel. In addition, there were very substantial shifts in production among regions of the United States. Notable among them were the shifts with respect to grapefruit, poultry, potatoes, apples, and cotton. Significant specialization is also occurring farm by farm among the farms in a region. Such adjustments are often associated with technological advances, institutional developments, and the creation of transportation and marketing facilities, some of which are irreversible. Adjustments of this type are capable of explaining much of the capacity of American agriculture to expand production, some of its failure to contract production, and capital gains and losses associated with such adjustments. However, the economic adjustment hypotheses do not explain fully *either* the failure of American agriculture to contract production *or* the presence of a high proportion of obsolete production plants.

One commonly advanced explanation for the willingness of farmers to overcommit their lives and resources to agricultural production and to pay too much for land is based on the idea that farmers regard farming as a superior way of life. This "superior" industry argument holds that people are willing to work in agriculture for less than they would earn elsewhere, to take losses on their expenditures and investments, and to pay more for land than can be recovered. There are a number of difficulties with this argument. A contrary argument, also commonly held, is that agriculture is a socially inferior industry and that a person should have extra pay for the long hours, hard disagreeable labor, poor community services, etc., associated with it. The "inferior" industry argument is often advanced to explain why it is so hard to (1) keep young men and, especially, young women "down on the farm" and (2) recruit farm laborers from the nonfarm economy. Another disturbing consideration for the "superior" industry argument is the dissatisfaction expressed by farmers when they fail to cover acquisition costs. In discussing this matter, they sound quite unwilling to subsidize the rest of the economy for the privilege of working in a "superior" industry.

The neoclassical, competitive model employed by Schultz, D. Gale Johnson, and many other agricultural economic analysts is based on the assumption that producers can sell variable factors of production at the prices paid for them. The assumption is applied to durables (after appropriate adjustments for depreciation, obsolescence, and repairs), as well as to stocks of unused expendable inputs such as feed, silage, gasoline, and oil. Though the discussion in Chapter 2 demonstrated the contrary-to-fact nature of this assumption for U.S. agriculture, its serious theoretical and empirical consequences are not considered in most theoretical and empirical studies of agricultural supply responses and of policies and programs designed to support prices and control production. When it is possible for a producer to dispose of an input at the price he paid for it, mistakes of overinvestment and overproduction are corrected without loss. Consequently, production expansions in response to price changes are reversible by opposite price changes; no one is hurt, and some benefit. Both the expansions and contractions either increase welfare or leave it unchanged.

By contrast, in the real world, inputs are seldom salable at prices paid for them; instead (as indicated in Chapter 2) acquisition costs exceed salvage prices as a result of (1) distances between farms, between suppliers and farms, and between farms and markets, and (2) the institutional costs of changing titles, particularly for immovable durables, from one farmer to another. Unwise increases in production induced by erroneously anticipated higher product prices are not always completely correctable by lower actual product prices as, in many instances, durables and stocks of expendables cannot be liquidated without losing more than would be lost by maintaining production. A substantial gain in explanatory power is achieved when the neoclassical analysis is modified: (1) to recognize *explicitly* that acquisition costs may be less than, or equal to, infinity but greater than, or equal to, salvage values which, in turn, can be greater than, equal to, or less than zero; (2) to recognize imperfect knowledge (as D. Gale Johnson did) of the technology, education,. and other changes studied by Schultz, Cochrane, and others.

A FURTHER EXTENSION OF NEOCLASSICAL THEORY

In the remainder of the chapter, a brief verbal and geometric presentation of a neoclassical analysis based on a more realistic set of assumptions is presented. (More technically minded readers are referred to the Appendix for a more rigorous mathematical treatment.)[1]

Several important consequences for ordinary neoclassical theory emerge when we explicitly assume (1) differentials between acquisition costs and salvage values and (2) imperfect knowledge. Under such assumptions, some errors of underproduction can be completely corrected in the sense that the farm can be reorganized to the high-profit organization defined by acquisition costs for inputs and product prices. Other errors of underproduction, however, can be only partially corrected without incurring additional unnecessary losses and then only by producing more than would be produced at the original high-profit organization. When errors of overproduction are considered, the neoclassical apparatus indicates that no such errors can be completely corrected without incurring additional losses unless acquisition prices are equal to salvage values for all inputs involved. In some instances, errors of overproduction are partially corrected on a least-loss basis only by further expansions in production which reduce losses. In other instances, some errors of overproduction are partially corrected on a loss minimization basis by reducing production but not to the level of the original high-profit organization for acquisition costs. In other instances, there are no corrections of errors of overproduction advantageous from the standpoint of either maximizing profit or minimizing losses.

The analytical apparatus indicates further that the aggregative responses of producers to price increases is very different from their aggregative responses to price decreases. That these responses are different follows from the preceding statements about correcting errors of overproduction and underproduction. When a product price falls below prices anticipated at the time durable invest-

---

[1] Glenn L. Johnson and Lowell Hardin, *The Economics of Forage Evaluation*, Purdue Agricultural Experiment Station Bulletin No. 623, 1955; Clark Edwards, "Resource Fixity and Farm Organization," *JFE*, November 1959; Glenn L. Johnson, "Supply Functions— Some Facts and Notions," *Agricultural Adjustment Problems in a Growing Economy* (Iowa State University Press, 1958); Glenn L. Johnson, "The State of Agricultural Supply Analysis," *JFE*, May 1960, pp. 441–42; Glenn L. Johnson, "Implications of the IMS for Study of Responses to Price, *A Study of Managerial Processes of Midwestern Farmers*, edited by Johnson et al. (Iowa State University Press, 1961); and Warren Vincent, ed., *Economics and Management in Agriculture* (Prentice-Hall, 1962), pp. 113–44.

Recent examples of policy and farm business applications of this theory include Dale Hathaway, *Government in Agriculture* (Macmillan, 1963), and the Phase II model of the NC–54 study of feed grain and livestock production in the midwest. Other applications are by Theodor Heidhues, "A Recursive Programming Model of Farm Growth in Northern Germany," in *JFE*, August 1966, and Robert Young, *An Economic Study of the Eastern Beet Sugar Industry*, Michigan State University Agricultural Experiment Station, Bulletin No. 9, 1965.

ments are made, an error of overproduction occurs. The preceding statements indicate that some such errors are not correctable at all, that some are corrected by further expansions in production, and that still others are partially corrected by profit-maximizing and loss-minimizing entrepreneurs. Under these conditions, responses to price declines are far from the reverse of responses to price increases. The result is a supply function for increases in prices that differs from that for decreases in prices. Reversible supply functions and elasticities do not exist except in special cases where (1) acquisition costs equal salvage values and (2) there is perfect knowledge.

Further, with continuous imperfect knowledge of ongoing technical, institutional, and human change, the neoclassical model, under our price assumptions, indicates that low-factor earnings relative to acquisition costs and capital losses would be associated with all errors in organization other than those errors of underproduction which can be completely corrected. The presence of these capital losses means that there is no way of constructing a competitive model which will eliminate the possibility of adjustments benefiting one or more persons at the expense of damaging one or more other persons. This means that conventional neoclassical economists cannot evaluate economic adjustments with techniques included as part of what is commonly referred to as "modern welfare theory." Instead, other bases are required for evaluating consequences of overinvestment in productive capacity and of the losses which such investments impose upon persons making them. (The method used in this book is outlined in Chapter 4.)

Consider Figure 1. Let Y stand for the output (measured in dollars) of a given farm using labor (L), capital (V), and fixed resources (F). The fixed resources are assumed fixed in the sense that, under all conditions considered, the amount presently employed is worth more employed by this firm than anyone will pay for it but not enough to justify acquiring more. Because of the fixity of F, the law of diminishing returns applies to the use of labor (L) and capital (V).

Two problems must be faced squarely at this point. One has to do with stock/flow conversions, and the other deals with the meaning of acquisition costs and salvage values. Figure 1 can be interpreted as either a stock or a flow diagram. If it is a stock diagram, then the acquisition and salvage values for capital reflect the costs of acquiring and the sales value of the equipment being used. The difference between acquisition cost and salvage value is the difference between the cost of buying another unit of capital *identical* to that on hand and the net which would be realized if a unit on hand were sold. If the diagram is interpreted on a flow basis, the acquisition cost of capital is the cost of acquiring another identical unit of capital service (by buying and operating a unit of stock) while the salvage value is the net which would be received from disposing of a unit of service (by selling a unit of stock). If the stock interpretation is used, the marginal value product (MVP) of a unit of stock is the discounted present value

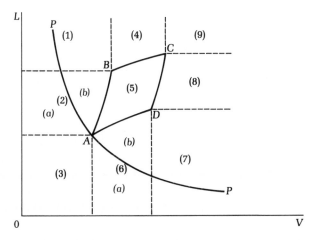

Figure 1. The modified neoclassical representation of a firm's factor-factor relationships.

of the future stream of MVP's produced by the stream of services it generates. If, on the other hand, the flow interpretation is used, then the MVP is merely the MVP of the unit of service generated in the time period under consideration.

For labor, the interpretations are more difficult, though essentially similar to those for capital. The first point is that we are dealing with the acquisition and disposal of units of labor identical to those on hand at a given point in time. Thus, if we are dealing with 45-year-old laborers possessed of given skills and characteristics, then that is what we are dealing with, whether they are being acquired or disposed of and whether we are treating them as stocks or flows. Stock acquisition cost is the cost of attracting a laborer into the business for more than one unit of time. Salvage value is the net value received by releasing that stock of labor services from the business. In the case of an owner-operator, stock acquisition cost is the cost of adding another similar employee to the business, perhaps for his lifetime. For the owner-operator, (the stock) salvage value is the present value of the MVP's of the future stream of labor (excluding capital earnings and land rents) services which he would generate if he left the farm. Interpreted on a flow basis, the acquisition cost of an owner-operator is the cost of acquiring a unit of service for one unit of time through the acquisition of another unit of owner-operator stock. Also on a flow basis, the salvage value of a unit of owner-operator labor is the net received for giving up a unit of owner-operator service in this time period by disposing of an owner-operator.

In Figure 1, L is on the vertical axis and V on the horizontal axis. As F is fixed, it is not shown as a variable. In this diagram, the line PP represents combinations of L and V which produce a given amount of Y. The line is chosen so that it contains the most profitable amounts (and combination) of L and V to use when profits are figured on the basis of the acquisition costs of L and V. That combination is designated A, the *high-profit* point.

In addition to line PP and the high-profit point A, we are interested in segments of four other lines. There is a line AB beyond which (to its right) the use of more capital would not yield a return (MVP) that would cover its acquisition cost. This line passes through A, the high-profit point defined by acquisition costs. We are interested only in the segment of this line above A and below its intersection with another line at B. The second line considered, BC, is a line above which the use of labor (L) is contracted because it can be sold for more than it is earning but on which the marginal earnings of labor are equal to its off-farm salvage value. The line BC intersects the line DC which is a similar line for capital. Quantities of V falling beyond CD earn less than enough to cover their salvage value and, hence, are advantageously sold. The bottom line AD is the line above which more L would earn less than the cost of acquiring it. If dotted vertical and horizontal lines are extended outward from the corners of the enclosed area $ABCD$, Figure 1 is divided into nine areas of particular interest to the analyst. Each of these is assigned a number. Areas 2 and 6 are subdivided into (a) and (b) depending on whether production is greater or less than at point A.

In Figure 2 areas 2, 4, 5, 6, and 8 do not exist, due to the *contrary-to-fact* assumption that labor and variable capital can be disposed of at salvage values equal to their acquisition costs. It is the presence of these areas in our modification of the neoclassical apparatus that gives our model power to explain the several major characteristics of the United States agricultural economy discussed in Chapter 2.

Without specifying, for now, why mistakes are made, it is instructive to inquire about the consequences of making the mistakes of organizing a farm in areas 2a, 2b, 4, 5, 6a, 6b, and 8 of Figure 1. None of these areas would exist if acquisition costs were equal to salvage values. No such mistakes would be made by perfectly informed managers. (Areas 1, 3, 7, and 9 are considered later.)

Area 5. When a farm is organized in area 5 (other than at point A): (1) overproduction occurs in the sense that more is being produced than will yield marginal returns high enough to cover acquisition costs; (2) the mistakes are not corrected until stocks of L and V are exhausted, because their earning powers make them worth more in production than anyone will pay for them; (3) capital losses occur with respect to the original acquisition costs of the committed stocks of L and V; (4) originally anticipated earnings of L and V are not obtained; and (5) it is not clear whether welfare is increased or decreased as a loss is imposed on the farmer which may or may not more than offset someone else's gain.

Area 2a. When a farm is mistakenly organized to fall in area 2a: (1) underproduction occurs, initially; (2) less than the maximum profits realizable at A

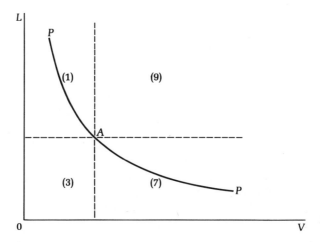

Figure 2. The unmodified neoclassical representation of a firm's factor-factor relationships.

are obtained; (3) the maximum profit (or minimum loss) which can be made involves expanding the use of V to the edge of 5 (L cannot be sold advantageously because it is, or can be made, worth more on the farm than anyone will pay for it); (4) the maximum profit which can be made is less than at point A; (5) when the maximum profits obtainable are obtained, *over*production occurs despite the initial mistake of *under*production; (6) capital losses occur with respect to labor (in the case of family and operator's labor this loss can sometimes be interpreted as the current value of the difference between the earning power of farm and industrial labor over a lifetime); (7) originally anticipated earnings on labor are not obtained; and (8) it is not clear whether general welfare is increased or decreased but the farmer incurs a loss.

Area 2b. When a farm is mistakenly organized to fall in area 2b, the consequences are the same as for 2a except that: (1) *over*production instead of *under*production occurs, initially; and (2) obtainable profits are maximized or losses are minimized by *expanding* production despite the initial mistake of *over*production.

Areas 6a and 6b. When a farm is mistakenly organized to fall in areas 6a and 6b, the consequences are essentially the same as for 2a and 2b. In these cases, however, the use of L is expanded while V is fixed, the capital loss occurs with respect to V instead of L and anticipated earnings on V are not obtained.

Area 4. When a farm is mistakenly organized to fall in area 4: (1) overproduction occurs; (2) mistakes are partially corrected by disposing of part of L and moving vertically to a point on the line BC, reducing production; and (3) after the mistake is partially corrected (it cannot be completely corrected to point A by a profit-maximizing or loss-minimizing entrepreneur), overproduction will still occur, capital losses are imposed for both L and V, the earning power of V will more than support its salvage value, the earning power of L will just support its salvage value, and anticipated earnings are not obtained for either L or V.

Area 8. When a farm is mistakenly organized to fall in area 8, conclusions for area 4 hold, except that it is capital (V), not labor (L), which is sold; hence, capital, not labor, will have earnings at the edge of area 5 which just support its salvage value while labor, not capital, will have earnings which more than support its salvage value but do not cover its acquisition costs.

We now compare the four areas common also to the analysis when acquisition costs are assumed equal to salvage values. Areas 1, 3, 7, and 9 of the modified neoclassical theory have counterpart areas in the unmodified analysis which assumes salvage values equal to acquisition costs. Figure 2 diagrams the usual neoclassical analysis and is to be compared to Figure 1. Areas 2, 4, 5, 6, and 8 of Figure 1 disappear and points A, B, C, and D of Figure 1 converge to the single point A in Figure 2.

Area 3. The interpretations of area 3 are the same for both figures. Errors of organization in this area are completely correctable. Earnings of both L and V exceed acquisition costs. Expansion of production to point A is possible and will increase profits without lowering returns to L and V below acquisition costs which are equal to salvage values. No capital losses are imposed in either case. Such profit-maximizing adjustments are judged to increase welfare, since the entrepreneur can make himself better off without making anyone worse off.

Area 9. In both Figure 1 and Figure 2, mistakes of organizing farms in area 9 are corrected by moving to the lower lefthand corner of that area. The differences arise because point C does not correspond to point A in Figure 1, whereas it does in Figure 2. Thus, with respect to area 9: (1) errors of overproduction are completely correctable in Figure 2 but not in Figure 1; (2) capital losses result from errors of overproduction with respect to both L and V in Figure 1 but not in 2; (3) inflation and deflation can create capital gains and losses in both analyses; (4) anticipated earnings just sufficient to cover acquisition costs will be realized in Figure 2 but not in 1; and (5) the change in welfare resulting from partially correcting the error of overproduction in Figure 1 is not Pareto-better, since the entrepreneur recovers only salvage and not acquisition cost on the L and V sold whereas the result of correcting the overproduction error on Figure 2 is a movement toward Pareto-optimality as acquisition costs equal salvage values.

Area 1. With respect to area 1, mistakes of overproduction and underproduction can be made on both figures. The differences between the two diagrams arise with respect to the possibilities and consequences of correcting these mistakes. In Figure 2, all area 1 mistakes of overproduction and underproduction can be completely corrected, whereas the best that can be done on Figure 1 is to move to point B which: (1) is a point of overproduction; (2) yields returns to L which just support its salvage value and hence results in capital losses on L;

(3) yields returns to V which support its acquisition costs; and (4) involves the imposition of losses as well as gains for different individuals which are not, therefore, Pareto-optimal.

Area 7. With respect to area 7, the conclusions for area 1 apply except that V, not L, is the disadvantaged input.

Differences between Figure 1 and Figure 2 are basic to understanding why the earlier modifications by Shultz and D. Gale Johnson were crucial but incomplete. It is imperfect knowledge (as stressed by D. Gale Johnson) of technological, human (as stressed by Cochrane and Schultz), and other changes that causes the entrepreneur to make the errors that place them in areas 1 through 9. However, areas 2, 4, 5, 6, and 8 do not exist unless we recognize that acquisitions costs may be greater than salvage values. This difference characterizes the markets for a high proportion of production resources used in agriculture. Further, it is imperfect knowledge, which produces errors of organizing in these areas, plus the differences between areas 1, 7, and 9 in the two diagrams that give us a theory capable of explaining (1) partially irreversible supply responses, (2) production of such large quantities of products that market clearing prices do not cover factor acquisition costs, and (3) the imposition on entrepreneurs of non-Pareto-better capital losses, which are the source of so much political dissension and analytical difficulty for evaluative policy analysts.

QUESTIONS OFTEN RAISED CONCERNING THE MODIFIED ANALYSIS

Several theoretical issues have been raised by colleagues concerning the analysis of Figure 1. Generally speaking, they arise because our modified theory seems to fly in the face of much that is taught and accepted. Typical discussions of the issues indicate that recognition of both imperfect knowledge and differentials between acquisition costs and salvage values does much to clarify vague, murky areas in common uses of the neoclassical apparatus.

Some of the issues raised deal with the opportunity cost principle, quasi-rents, cost of production, length of run, aggregate supply responses, factor-demand responses, discounting and long-run equilibria, and the conflicting "superior" and "inferior" industry ideas. Each of these issues is discussed below, in the hope that this will be helpful to readers having concerns along these lines.

The opportunity cost principle has long been an important aspect of the neoclassical analysis but has not been handled adequately.[2] Essentially, the opportunity cost principle is used when market prices are not applicable in solving

[2] See, for example, Richard H. Leftwich, *The Price System and Resource Allocation* (Rinehart and Company, 1955), pp. 132–33, which considers primarily off-farm opportunity costs but which ignores use of the opportunity cost principle in allocating fixed resources among competing uses within the firm. Paul Samuelson, *Economics*, 1st ed. (McGraw-Hill, 1948) does not give explicit attention to the principle. George Stigler, *The*

resource allocation problems. A resource fixed for a farm as a whole is fixed because its earning power is too low to justify purchase of more of it at the acquisition (market) price and too high to justify its liquidation at salvage (market) value (price), acquisition costs being higher than salvage values because of transportation and ownership transfer costs. Thus, rigorous application of the opportunity cost principle in both theory and practice depends on the explicit recognition of the differential between acquisition costs and salvage values. The inadequacy of the usual neoclassical presentations stems either from an assumption that acquisition costs are equal to salvage values or from a hidden unrecognized assumption that acquisition costs can exceed salvage values.

Modern linear programming literature, on the other hand, concentrates almost wholly on the opportunity cost principle. It addresses itself primarily to allocating fixed resources among alternative uses. Commonly, a slack activity provides for disposition at zero salvage value while the absence of acquisition activities introduces, in effect, an infinitely high acquisition cost. Recently, more appropriate linear programming analyses have replaced slack with salvage activities at realistic salvage values and introduced acquisition activities at realistic acquisition costs. These activities (plus appropriate credit and financial constraints and activities) produce analyses consistent with the theory presented in this chapter; they are capable of allocating resources according to opportunity cost, acquisition cost, and salvage values, and, most importantly, of determining endogenously which resources are fixed and variable. As such, the analyses are far superior to the usual, incomplete neoclassical analysis and to earlier linear programming analyses.

Quasi-rents, too, are vaguely handled in the unmodified neoclassical analysis. In connection with fixed assets, the analysis notes that the earning power of quasi-rents, like that of land, is determined by product prices. Some writers, when comparing earnings (marginal value products) with replacement (acquisition) costs, conclude that certain fixed assets yield negative quasi-rents. Other writers compare earnings with salvage values and conclude that quasi-rents are positive. However, explicit recognition that assets are fixed when their current and expected earnings are less than acquisition costs but greater than salvage values does much to clarify the quasi-rent concept; i.e., such recognition fixes a range within which quasi-rents are confined and makes it clear that they can be calculated in either of two ways, one of which yields quasi-rents greater than or less than zero while the other yields quasi-rents less than or equal to zero.

Average variable, average fixed, and marginal costs in relation to product price are also vaguely handled in the unmodified neoclassical analysis. One text

---

Theory of Price (Macmillan, 1946), does not note the principle in the index or table of contents. Kenneth Boulding, *Economic Analysis* (Harper and Brothers, 1948), has references on pp. 30, 33, and 46, and E. O. Heady, *Economics of Agricultural Production and Resource Use* (Prentice-Hall, 1952), pp. 680–81, 367–69, and 214.

after another indicates that that portion of the marginal cost function above the average variable cost function defines the range over which product prices can vary without prompting the firm to go out of business. With respect to a diagram such as Figure 3, it is generally concluded that a farm producing milk will stay in business as long as the price exceeds $2 per cwt. When this was explained to me as an undergraduate farm boy at the University of Illinois, I sensed intuitively that something was wrong, and I later discovered what it was. The diagram assumes zero salvage values for the fixed resources which invoke the law of diminishing returns to give the two curves their shape. But the conclusion is simply *not so*, if the fixed resources are such things as dairy cows, land, pasture, silos, milking machines, etc., which they must surely be. Long before the price of milk gets to $2, the MVP of a dairy cow, for instance, falls so low that she is worth more to the butcher than to the dairy farmer and she is sold. Similarly, there are alternative uses for the motor on the milking machine, and the rest can be sold as scrap. The pasture, barn, and silo, too, can be devoted to beef production before the price of milk falls to $2—at which point their earning power in milk production would be zero.

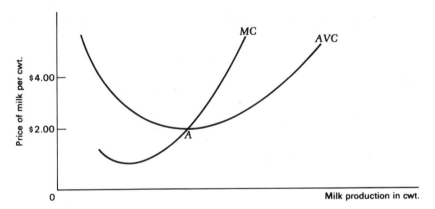

Figure 3. An example of a firm's cost curves under unmodified neoclassical theory.

A more appropriate diagram, Figure 4, is implied by recognizing that acquisition costs may be less than infinite and, in turn, may be greater than salvage values which, in turn, may be greater than zero, equal to zero, or less than zero [Vincent, 1962, p. 126]. Figure 4 has two average total cost lines, one based on acquisition costs and the other on salvage values for fixed assets. It indicates that if the price of milk falls below $2.50, the dairy farmer finds it advantageous to reorganize his farm by selling some part of his previously fixed assets. Conversely, if the price goes above $3.50, the diagram indicates that the dairy farmer finds it advantageous to reorganize his farm by buying more of certain previously fixed assets. As soon as either one of these actions is taken, the original

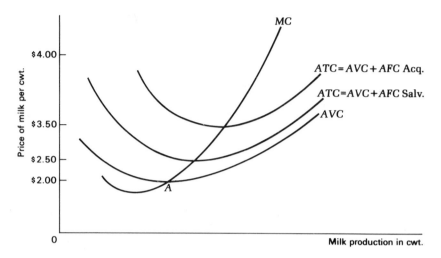

Figure 4.   An example of a firm's cost curves under modified neoclassical theory.

MC curve is irrelevant and a new MC curve based on a different set of fixed resources must be computed [Vincent, 1962, pp. 127 ff.] .

Length of run in the unmodified neoclassical analysis is often discussed in two contexts. In one context there is the distinction between the ultimate short run when all factors are fixed, the intermediate run in which only some factors are fixed, and the ultimate long run in which all factors are variable. When differentials between acquisition costs and salvage values are recognized, the classification of factors as fixed or variable becomes endogenous, or internal to the analysis. Consequently, exogenous short, intermediate, and ultimate long-run distinctions become restrictive, troublesome, and confusing. In the second context, the long run refers to situations in which resource MVP's are adjusted to equal their acquisition cost, while the short run refers to situations in which these adjustments have not been made. If changes take place repeatedly, and entrepreneurs are imperfectly informed about them, differences between acquisition costs and salvage values would prevent attainment of the long-run conditions defined in the second context.

Supply functions and supply responses are also inadequately handled in the usual neoclassical analysis [G. L. Johnson, May 1960, pp. 435–52] . Traditionally, partial equilibrium and industry supply responses are regarded as the horizontal summation for all firms producing the product of their MC curves above the intersection of the AVC curves. The validity of this procedure depends on (1) variable inputs having salvage values equal to acquisition costs and (2) fixed inputs having infinite acquisition costs and zero salvage values. When acquisition costs are less than infinity but greater than salvage values that are, in turn, greater than zero, only part of the MC curve is relevant. Further, portions of the other MC curves from other more profitable or other less unprofitable re-organizations of the farms become part of the industry supply function. Still further, output responses to increases in product prices may differ for a subsequent fall in prices from the opposite of the response to the price increase. Thus, industry supply responses are not generally reversible like those shown in the ordinary textbook—and which are still taught, alas, to many graduate students in agricultural economics. Instead, the rate of response at any level of output is a function of the direction and amount of the price change. In some instances, no output response would occur and in other instances substantial responses would occur dependent on the initial relationship among the MVP, acquisition cost, and salvage value of each of the factors of production [Vincent, 1962, pp. 131-44, 193 ff.].

Students interested in the demand for factors of production have also raised questions about the consequences for their work if both imperfect knowledge and differentials between acquisition costs and salvage values are recognized. The consequences are substantial. The quantities of factors demanded are functions of both the magnitude and direction of the change in the price of the factor. Still further, they are a function of the initial relationships, for each factor, among that factor's earning power, acquisition cost, and salvage value [Manderscheid, 1965].

It is generally observed that a high proportion of U.S. farms are obsolete relative to existing technologies. This is to be expected with imperfectly foreseen change and with technology embedded in durable capital so long as salvage values of the durable capital items are substantially less than acquisition cost appropriately adjusted for depreciation and usage. If salvage values were equal to acquisition costs less depreciation and usage charges, a farmer could sell his obsolete capital and reinvest in capital carrying the more modern technology. However, as matters typically stand, the farmer is constrained to continue to use the older capital items until such time as the discounted value of the expected MVP's falls to or below salvage values despite failure to recover the original investment. The low rates of return obtained by farmers on their capital investment and the presence of so much obsolete capital combine to support the conclusion that U.S. farms are more obsolete than they would be if farmers were more perfectly informed or if salvage values were equal to acquisition costs adjusted for depreciation and usage. In effect, farmers repeatedly overinvest in new technologies (relative to prices), still newer technologies yet to materialize, and stocks of fixed obsolete capital on hand. The result is that the present is always characterized by a stock of obsolete capital that is fixed but is not capable of covering its original acquisition costs.

A question about discounting has been raised by one or two colleagues. This is essentially a question as to whether the D. Gale Johnson analysis is adequate. With acquisition costs equal to salvage values and with sufficiently stable probability distributions for Frank Knight's risk situation [1941] to prevail, risk discounting would lead to ex post actual returns in excess of acquisition costs and underproduction in the sense that, if average prices actually received were guaranteed with certainty, production would be higher. With a differential between acquisition costs and salvage values and uncertainty (in the Knightian sense), as well as risk, we would expect entrepreneurs to fail to realize their risk discounts and to overproduce relative to their discounted earnings and acquisition costs.

Some people argue that, *in the aggregate, supply and demand responses* (for factors of production) are in accord with the reversible functions commonly presented in textbooks, and that in the long run, an equilibrium will be attained that equates marginal earnings with acquisition costs, with mistakes of overcommitment and undercommitment averaging out. Here the theoretical problem is that mistakes will not average out if similar circumstances cause large numbers of producers and factor buyers to make similar mistakes of overproduction as opposed to underproduction.

Another idea is that, in the long run, *entrepreneurs depreciate overcommitted resources and replace them without further errors* and thus attain long-run equilibria with marginal earnings equal to acquisition costs. The difficulty here is that change, imperfect knowledge, and transfer costs are long-run as well as short-run phenomena and that the long-run adjustment is never attained when changes take place continuously for imperfectly informed managers. In the chapters that follow, numerous instances are examined empirically in which widespread, commonly held misinformation caused extensive errors of overcommitment and overinvestment on the part of a large proportion of agricultural producers.

With respect to the arguments in this chapter and Chapter 2, it seems obvious (1) that the empirical truth of the assumption that errors are compensating is most questionable, (2) that we have had no long changeless period in which to attain long-run equilibrium, and (3) that resource transfer costs do not disappear in the long run.

Closely related to the discounting problem is another problem created by the conflicting argument that farmers regard agriculture as either a *superior* or an *inferior industry*. The addition of subjective premiums to costs and/or the subtraction of subjective discounts from returns would help explain why actual ex post earnings do not cover acquisition costs. However, with imperfect knowledge, acquisition costs in excess of salvage values, and continuous change, our modification of the neoclassical analysis would indicate that, ex post, entrepreneurs would fail to cover their discounts and/or premiums. If, on the other hand, agriculture is regarded as an inferior industry, the analysis presented herein is also capable of explaining ex post earnings below acquisition costs as a result of failure to attain subjectively discounted earnings and/or to cover subjective premiums added to costs. Further, whether agriculture is regarded as superior, inferior, or equal, the theoretical apparatus we present here is capable of explaining disappointed expectations as a result of overinvestment and, hence, the generally observed discontent of farmers.

INTRODUCING A LITTLE DYNAMICS

The full superiority of the modified theory over the unmodified theory is even more apparent when the analysis is made slightly more dynamic. This can be done by assuming, in accord with the characteristics of United States agriculture outlined in Chapter 2, that farmers are imperfectly informed about the nature and consequences of changes occurring in their economic, technical, political, and social environment.

Relaxation of the assumption of perfect knowledge so common in analyses of agricultural policies introduces into the theory the possibility that farmers make errors in organizing farms. The theoretical apparatus then permits the analyst to see the probable consequences of:

(1) failure of beginning farmers to foresee relative advances in nonfarm wage rates and levels of living;

(2) failure to foresee advances in technology and improvements in the human agent;

(3) failure to see the overall consequences (in terms of product and factor prices) of similar actions by large numbers of producers;

(4) failure to foresee inflations and deflations;

(5) failure to foresee shifts in demand resulting from war, changes in the foreign situation (particularly in demand), and changes in real per capita incomes;

(6) failure to foresee institutional changes, i.e., social security, income tax, etc.;

(7) failure to foresee the consequences of specialization among farms, regions, and sectors of the economy; and

(8) failure to distinguish between capital gains due to inflation and the earning power of resources devoted to production.

The consequences of continuing change and imperfect knowledge include overproduction at prices which do not cover acquisition costs, whereas the introduction of imperfect knowledge in the Knight/D. Gale Johnson risk and uncertainty analysis indicates underproduction at prices with average marginal value products in excess of acquisition costs.

Ability to see how different kinds of imperfect knowledge cause overexpanded production leads, in turn, to greater ability to predict the consequences of changes in policies and programs.

With changes occurring, errors of overproduction lead to overcommitments (fixing) of assets and to low earnings for both labor and capital in agriculture. Such fixities invoke the law of diminishing returns which limits the size of firm that can be developed.[3] Low earnings of both labor and capital make it difficult for larger-than-family farms to compete in the open market for capital and labor. The number of family farms tends to be perpetuated beyond the number required by "fixing" in agriculture excess labor produced by farm families in accord with Schultz's analysis. This tends to make the size of business which can be handled by one family's fixed labor the maximum attainable size. Thus, the application of neoclassical theory along with Schultz's modification explains the persistence of the family farm [G. L. Johnson, 1969, Chap. 11].

Larger-than-family businesses in nonfarm sectors and in certain farm sectors of the United States, as well as elsewhere, appear to result from:

(1) the stability of nonbiological production processes which are not affected by weather;

(2) greater control over aggregate production and hence greater ability to control and predict prices;

(3) greater aggregate control over the production and prices of inputs;

(4) farm labor supplies which are not free or which do not have the opportunity of leaving agriculture;

(5) institutional arrangements that permit complete disassociation of families which produce labor from businesses and/or the absence of a tendency to produce surplus labor; and

(6) local, particularly favorable, prices for farm products.

SUMMARY

The superiority of the theoretical modification presented here rests on two considerations: (1) its ability to explain important characteristics of the agricultural economy not explained by the more usual model and (2) its ability to suggest the realistic consequences of imperfect knowledge. It is also comforting to note that this modification (1) makes it possible to retain the advantages of the earlier Schultzian and Johnsonian (D. Gale) modifications and (2) provides a basis for advancing systematic explanatory hypotheses about the roles of such commonly considered variables as technological advance, improvements in the human agent, economic adjustment (including sector, regional, and farm-by-farm specialization), the impact of capital gains, the impact of price support operations, and the introduction of contract farming and vertical integration.

[3] Studies that reveal constant returns to scale in agriculture are based on comparisons between farms. Hence, such estimates reveal the consequences of varying inputs that are actually fixed for the individual farms.

CHAPTER 4

Basis for Evaluation

GLENN L. JOHNSON

The main objective of our study (as noted earlier) is to investigate the efficiency of both the private and public mechanisms for allocating resources in American agriculture. Therefore, the problems of poverty, welfare, and equality in the distribution of resource ownership are not the study's concerns, except as they arise in connection with mechanisms that control the use, as contrasted to ownership, of resources. However, since such problems do arise in connection with the on-going operations of the allocative mechanisms as well as with attempts to modify the operations of the mechanism, we must address ourselves to them in a limited way.

In operating resource-allocating mechanisms, losses and benefits are conferred on farm persons at the expense of taxpayers, consumers, and, in some instances, other farmers, while the market itself confers capital losses on imperfectly informed farmers and benefits on the consumers in the form of low-cost food produced by the overinvestment that created the capital losses. How do we evaluate such changes and the policies and programs used to alleviate them?

A basic problem for present-day evaluative economic analysts arises from the inability of economists to measure losses and gains imposed on different persons in such a way as to permit their summation into a measure of change in total welfare [Arrow, 1951]. Such a statement as "the greatest good for the greatest number" is vague and unclear. Yet as we shall see in succeeding chapters, recent U.S. agricultural policies and programs and the day-to-day operations of resource-allocating mechanisms both impose losses and confer gains on different people.

The classical writers who established the rationale behind our systems of economic analysis were not concerned with the problem of making interpersonally valid measurements of welfare, because they assumed that such measurements could be or had been made. This led some of them to the erroneous conclusions that an economy which reached competitive equilibrium would be the best of all possible economies. The idea is still widely held by some economists and also relatively well-educated laymen. However, few reputable economists argue that an economy is necessarily in an optimum organization just because the competitive adjustments of a free economy are made and a point of equilibrium reached. Most recognize that redistribution of rights, privileges, and benefits might (note that neither "would" nor "could" is used) establish a different equilibrium (also, a free, competitive equilibrium) superior to the old one. However, while recognizing this possibility, many economists feel unable to determine whether the new equilibrium is better or worse than the old.

The theoretical circumstance under discussion in the above paragraph is another application of the "theory of second best" presented and generalized by Lipsey and Lancaster [1955-56]. That theory indicates that when a new constraint prevents attainment of a previously possible Pareto-optimal situation the new Pareto-optimal alternative among the new or remaining open alternatives may be inferior to, superior to, or equal to the original Pareto optimum. The theory of second best has been used to deal with the consequences of introducing or removing taxes, monopolies, subsidies, import duties, and so on. The situation dealt with in this chapter results from the introduction of the particular constraints growing out of the mistakes of one or more managers. When such a mistake is made, non-Pareto-better losses are imposed by the constraining consequences of the mistake unless, of course, as pointed out above, the mistake is completely correctable. The reasoning presented in this chapter indicates that the loss-minimizing adjustments necessary when a fixed resource has to be priced according to the opportunity cost principle involves an application of the theory of second best. It is comforting to note, therefore, that the conclusions reached herein concerning the operation of a free market system under uncertainty and in the presence of acquisition costs greater than salvage prices leads to the same indeterminant evaluations reported in considering scientific tariffs [Harry G. Johnson, 1960] and in considering the consequences of imperfect markets [Fishlow and David, 1961].

Economists tend to avoid facing up to the problem. As they become more aware of their inability to make interpersonally comparable measurements of welfare, they restrict their evaluative analyses to situations in which it is unnecessary to make such measurements. Consequently, present-day systems of economic analysis are of limited usefulness in evaluating precisely the kinds of changes that have been made in policies and programs of U.S. agriculture and that occur in freely operating economies such as in the United States.

In addition to the above problem of attaining interpersonally valid utility measures, which was examined by Hicks [1941], there are three other problems that plague the evaluative analyst.

The second is the question of whether or not all values are expressible in terms of a common denominator, even for a single person. Economists tend to use "utils," or dollars and cents, or something called welfare as if these constituted common denominators [Parsons, 1949]. This question combines with the one on interpersonally valid welfare measures to make it extremely difficult to judge non-Pareto-better changes involving such disparate "goods" as income, freedom, pride of workmanship, and self-reliance, and such disparate "bads" as expenses, hunger, ego damage, and the feeling of dependence. Yet all of these goods and bads (and many others) are consequences of the changes that have taken place in U.S. agriculture before and since 1917, as a result of public programs and policies and of the ongoing operation of the economy.

The third problem is the frequent encountering of changes that are not so ordered that we can conceive of a maximum difference between the good and bad consequences of following the various alternatives, even if we grant the possibility of an interpersonally valid, universal, common denominator of values. With respect to institutional change, technological advances, and the education of people, nothing is apparently comparable to the laws of diminishing returns and utility to ensure the second order conditions necessary for a maximum difference between the "goods" and "bads" produced by public action and by the ongoing operation of the economy.

The fourth problem is the basis for choices under risk and uncertainty. In evaluating a policy or a program, do we conclude, for instance, that a certain program is better than another because the value of the expected future stream of net differences between the "good" and "bad" consequences of the program is higher than for the alternative? Or do we follow a minimax rule in making the choice? Perhaps, if an interpersonally valid universal common denominator of value is not present, we should vote. If so, would it be one vote per man or two senators per state? Or, perhaps it would be better to flip a coin or fight a civil war?

The four difficulties discussed above are so horrendous for the evaluative analyst that he despairs of objectivity in evaluating the way our agricultural economy has allocated its resources under public policies and programs of the 1917–70 period. Yet, somehow or other, agriculture policies and programs and the operations of the agricultural economy have been assessed and evaluated by political bodies, deliberative committees, and economists helping to make such evaluations. Thus, our study is required to go beyond competitive, perfect-knowledge, equilibrium economics, and the poor measuring ability of modern welfare economists. We need to use whatever knowledge we can find of the processes of human, technical, and institutional change, and, further, of the bases for choice. Only in this way can we try to evaluate what has gone on with respect to the allocation of resources in the U.S. agricultural economy from 1917 to 1970 and to suggest improvements.

EVALUATIVE METHOD

In the evaluative method used in this book a sharp distinction is drawn between "goods" and "bads" on one hand, and "rights" and "wrongs" on the other [C. I. Lewis, 1955]. Situation, conditions, things, attitudes, etc., are described as good or bad; in contrast, actions are designated as right or wrong. Right or wrong actions represent compromises among the goods and bads involved in a given situation in view of what is, will be and/or what is possible. An action which accomplishes more good than is sacrificed by not executing an alternative action is more right than the alternative, other things equal. An action which only avoids more bad than an alternative would, while neither attains any good, is probably more right than the alternative, other things equal. An action which accomplishes the same good but is accompanied by less bad than an alternative is more right than the alternative, other things equal. If the reverse were true in the above examples, the actions would be less right or more wrong than their alternatives.

The discussion in the above paragraph presumes that all difficulties discussed before with respect to universal interpersonally valid welfare measures, second-order conditions, and the choice of decision rule have been handled. Yet, in practice, they have not. However, before discussing how we will face up to these difficulties, we must look at the prior problem of whether it is possible to have objective knowledge of the normative as well as the nonnormative.

Evaluation of farm programs and policies and the operation of the economy requires nonnormative concepts of conditions, situations, and things. Nonnormative or positive concepts have nothing to do with the goodness or badness of conditions, situations, or things. Normative concepts are those having to do with "goodness" and "badness" of conditions, situations, and things. As outlined above, it is in the light of both nonnormative and normative concepts that actions taken with respect to agricultural policy and programs are evaluated as right or wrong.

Nonnormative concepts about how the economy operates, how it would operate if various changes were made, and how it would operate regardless of changes are required in evaluating the operation of the economy. Similarly, normative concepts—about goodness and badness—are also required in such evaluations. Practical situations can be judged in terms of (1) not enough of one or more "goods," (2) too much of one or more "bads," or (3) combination of (1) and (2). Thus, normative information is required to evaluate, but as for nonnormative information, normative information alone is not enough. We need nonnormative as well as normative concepts.

By *normative concepts*, we mean concepts having as their meaning information about the goodness or badness of conditions, situations, and things. We regard "goodness" and "badness" as primitive undefined terms. By nonnormative concepts we mean concepts having as their meaning information about situations, conditions, and things other than information about their goodness and badness—i.e., information about what one refers to with such terms as weight, mass, volume, color, location, etc., primitive and undefinable as some of these terms are in such sciences as physics and chemistry. In both the normative or nonnormative cases, concepts deal with relationships among events and laws as well as with isolated events.

Whether we are dealing with the normative or the nonnormative, the evaluation of programs, policies, and performance requires objectivity and we must ask how we obtain objectivity with respect to, first, both normative and nonnormative information and, second, decisions as to "right actions." Knowledge is viewed as concepts, i.e., words and sentences with specifiable meaning. Our problem is to discuss the closely related subjects of the meaning of (1) objectivity of the concepts themselves and (2) objectivity of the process of carrying out research and investigations to establish concepts.

One way to understand the meaning of objectivity is to discover what objectivity does *not* mean. Some investigators hold that an objective concept is one which corresponds to reality, and at first blush, this seems to be a very acceptable meaning. According to this view, the objectivity of a concept is readily testable: all one has to do is compare the concept with reality to see whether or not it is, in fact, an accurate representation of reality. Some forthright people refer to this as the "snapshot" test. Somewhat deeper reflection on this point, however, indicates that the only things we have to compare one concept with are other concepts. Thus, the comparison of one concept with another does not provide a test of reality but rather a test of consistency among concepts.

Another meaning of objectivity is empirical truth, and the question becomes one of whether or not a sentence expressing a concept is true. When we ask what is meant by a "true" concept, the answer takes us back to the "snapshot" definition of objectivity discussed above.

In what follows, we argue that the essential meaning of the word "objective," when we use it to characterize a researcher's activity, is a willingness on the part of the researcher to refrain from identifying himself and his prestige with a concept, so that, in the absence of the pride or humiliation which comes with being identified with a concept, he is willing to subject the concept to various tests of objectivity. Among the commonly employed tests are those for consistency, clarity, and workability. Failure to meet any of these tests is reason enough to reject a concept, for certain purposes. Thus, more specifically, objectivity on the part of a researcher consists in detaching himself from a concept enough to submit it to tests for objectivity and willingness to reject and revise a concept which is, itself, not objective in terms of the tests of consistency, clarity, and workability. An objective concept, as contrasted to an objective researcher, is one which is subjected to the tests of consistency, clarity, and workability and does not flunk such tests for the purposes for which the concept is used.

We emphasize that those who hold a "snapshot" theory of objectivity believe that certain propositions are objectively true because they are outside the domain of evidence and justification, whereas the notion we defend here defines objectivity in terms of evidence and justification. To establish that a concept is objective is to show that it (1) has a clear and specifiable meaning; (2) is consistent with other acceptable concepts, laws, and theories; and (3) is useful in solving the problems with which one is confronted.

The test of consistency is both internal and external. Internal consistency is a logical or analytical matter. The internal test requires that a set of concepts must bear logical relationships to each other whether they pertain to the past, present, conditional future (if . . . , then . . .), or the unconditional future. There is also an external consistency test. This is the test of experience; as such, it is synthetic (derived from experience) as well as analytic (deduced by logic from propositions). Experience provides a basis for forming new concepts. To apply the test of external consistency, an existing concept is compared with concepts based upon new experience; while the new concept is synthetic, the process of comparison is likely analytic.

A new or independent experience (one which is outside a presently accepted body of knowledge) may involve observations of the operation of an ongoing system such as a farm, the universe of planets circulating around the sun, the chemical and physical activities going on in a cubic foot of soil, the operation of a biological organism, or the operation of the U.S. agricultural economy. Observations may also be generated by controlled experiments. In either case, observations or experience provide a basis for formulating new concepts which must be consistent with a given body of concepts if both they and that given body of concepts are to pass the test of external consistency.[1]

The test of clarity is both simple and difficult. One knows when a concept passes the test of clarity and can be communicated between people. Ambiguity and vagueness block such communication. It is difficult, however, to indicate the exact nature of the test of clarity. A concept is clear if it is understood and communicated from one person to another. For a concept to pass the test of clarity or communicability, two persons in possession of information derived from the same set of experience and with the same set of initial knowledge of that concept should both accept or reject the concept.

---

[1] Degrees of freedom in statistics can be regarded as "extra" observations whose consistency, or lack of consistency, with a fitted line of relationship is external to the line; we recognize the independence of these observations from the fitted line by referring to these extra observations as "degrees of freedom."

The test of workability is pragmatic. Concepts are used to solve both analytical and practical problems. Concepts are also often used to predict positivistically that a certain outcome will be forthcoming; if the outcome does not materialize, the concept has failed to pass the test of workability or usefulness. Similarly, if a normative concept of "goodness" is used in selecting a goal, the goal, when attained, must turn out as predicted or the normative concept flunks the workability test. Thus, the workability test is pragmatic and rather closely related to the test of external consistency.

A moment's reflection indicates that the meaning of objectivity just discussed is such that objectivity is not limited to the physical and biological sciences. It is as easy for concepts in the social sciences to be objective—in the sense that they possess internal and external consistency, clarity, and workability—as it is for concepts in the physical and the biological sciences to be objective. In either case, failure to pass any of the tests calls for reformulation.

Similarly, it is also obvious that objectivity is not confined to nonnormative as contrasted to normative concepts. Both types of concepts may or may not pass the tests of internal and external consistency, clarity, and workability. The test of external consistency with respect to a normative concept is more easily applied than is commonly supposed. For instance, I remember vividly one of my colleagues coming into my office after recovering from an unusually severe case of chicken pox. My colleague's comment simply was, "You're right. Chicken pox is bad." Quite simply, he had experienced chicken pox and thus knew it was bad.

Further reflection on the above meaning of objectivity will emphasize that "absolute" concepts, either nonnormative or normative, are not objective. Willingness to accept or reject concepts on the basis of workability tests indicates that the concepts are likely to work for some purposes but not for others. Thus, for purposes of sighting a rifle, we find the nonnormative concept that light travels in a straight line to be adequate. Yet Einstein found it necessary to modify this concept for his purposes. So it is with economic theories. In Chapter 3 we remarked that, for some purposes, it was sufficient to accept the concept that acquisition costs equal salvage values while for other purposes it was not sufficient. Neither normative nor nonnormative absolutes, then, are objective and neither are very helpful in "muddling" through the tough problems encountered while one is doing evaluative research in the presence of uncertainty.

One of the least objective arguments advanced is that of the positivistic absolutist who claims that there cannot be an objective normativism because there can be no absolute normative derived from observations of reality. And one of the more objective arguments which can be advanced is that any concept, normative or nonnormative, is tentative, relative, and likely to flunk the tests of external consistency and workability, however clear, internally consistent, and irrefutable it is if applied at any period in time.

Despite the relation of objectivity to purpose and despite the unacceptability of absolute knowledge, the criteria of objectivity in research and of conceptual objectivity require that concepts be divorced from their originators. Thus, to raise the question of "whose concept" is almost tantamount to raising the question of objectivity. The question can be raised with respect to either nonnormative or normative concepts and leads to wrong evaluations, whether the lack of objectivity occurs with respect to either type of concept.

THE ELEMENTS OF OUR EVALUATIVE METHOD

Briefly, our evaluative method consists in: (1) seeking objective, normative and nonnormative facts, laws, and theories; and (2) attempting to reach judgments as to the rightness and wrongness of past and proposed policies and programs while recognizing (a) those consequences of programs, policies, and the ongoing operation of the economy that simultaneously impose losses on some and benefits on others; (b) the lack of a common denominator in terms of which all goods and bads can be expressed as a basis for determining which policies, programs, and/or operations are right or wrong; (c) the likelihood that the second-order conditions do not hold which are necessary to guarantee the existence of a set of policies and programs that maximizes the difference between good and bad; and (d) the lack of a generally agreed-on basis for choice in making socio-politico-economic decisions concerning a right set of policies and programs.

In seeking objectivity, Chapter 3 placed heavy emphasis on the tests of both internal and external consistency. Long-standing, well-used assumptions (concepts) flunked the test of external consistency. The inconsistencies were with concepts (based on observations) about the characteristics of American agriculture as outlined in Chapter 2. Internal consistency checks were also important; thus, in Chapter 3, the acceptance of different concepts about the characteristics of American agriculture made it necessary to introduce substantial modifications in the assumptions for the theory of the firm. These modifications, in turn, led to the conclusion that a freely operating economy populated by imperfectly informed entrepreneurs would not reach a Pareto-optimal organization if (1) changes were continuous and (2) acquisition costs exceeded salvage values.

The process of applying the tests of internal and external consistency is continuous throughout this study. Also, as knowledge concerning institutional, technological and human changes is accumulated, the theoretical concepts originally developed in Chapter 3 are modified. For instance, stock/flow transformation rates are related to technical change, and the factor-share/lagged-adjustment technique for estimating MVP's is modified, etc.

Throughout the writing of background papers and theses by our several contributors, the test of clarity (or interpersonal communicability) was applied time and time again. Further, our rejection of absolute knowledge caused us to expect that the conclusions presented herein would need continual subjection to this (and the other tests for objectivity) and to be modified according to whether the tests are passed or failed. Further, the workability test is applied time and time again with respect to (1) theoretical, analytic, and descriptive (synthetic) concepts and (2) U.S. policies and programs, and (3) the ongoing operations of the national agricultural economy.

As a result of repeated application of objectivity tests in Chapters 1 to 10, we believe we have a considerably improved analytical and descriptive picture of how the U.S. agricultural economy operates and responds to policy and program changes. The new insights grow out of the theoretical reformulation presented in Chapter 3 and also out of the consequent empirical work on acquisition costs, salvage values, resource earnings, capital gains and losses, and price expectations. All of this has resulted in substantial reformulations of our original concepts about how the agricultural economy operates and responds to policy and program changes.

However, we still had serious problems. In addition to the likely remaining shortcomings in our analytical and descriptive (synthetic) concepts, we still faced the evaluative difficulties listed above—i.e., the lack of an interpersonally valid, common denominator of value, the possible absence of the necessary second-order conditions for the existence of an optimum, and the lack of an agreed-on basis for choice.

Our theoretical analysis (Chapter 3) and the empirical and historical chapters that follow this present chapter reveal that a competitively operating economy, characterized by imperfect knowledge and resource transfer costs, does allocate resource use so as to impose losses on many entrepreneurs and resource owners. This raises the question of an interpersonally valid common denominator of value among the different participants in the economy, a question that is intensified by the tendency of a free-enterprise economy to concentrate ownership of wealth. For the most part, our book does not address itself to the egalitarian problems of maintaining an acceptable degree of equality of resource ownership and of other rights. Instead, we focus more on the task of evaluating how effectively the economy allocates the use of its resources; however, we recognize that, in the final analysis, questions of equity and of allocative efficiency are not separable. Our empirical analysis also reveals that to order alternative institutional arrangements for controlling resources use, production, and prices so as to maximize the excess of "goods" over "bads" by choosing among them is difficult; i.e., no obvious initial order for taking subsequent actions to modify institutions permits us to maximize, whereas such permission is provided by the laws of diminishing returns for production and utility for consumption economics. Still further, even a superficial knowledge of the operation of agricultural lobbyists, agrarian politics, the farm block, and the changes caused in agrarian policies by the "one man-one vote" principle reveals some lack of consensus on what decision-making rule or basis for choice should be followed in changing the institutional structure of American agriculture and the influence of that structure on prices, resource use, and production.

Fortunately, however, this difficulty is neither complete nor uniform. There are substantial cases in which conclusions can be reached with respect to the rightness or wrongness of certain policies, programs, and operations; there are also substantial cases in which conclusions cannot be reached.

The theory presented in Chapter 3 provides some bases for evaluative conclusions. For instance, adjustments which permit farmers to cover acquisition costs on their resources can be adjudged to be superior to adjustments which do not. Thus, in Figure 1 in Chapter 3, point A represents the "right action" for an entrepreneur trying to maximize profits, the difference between the "good" of income and the "bad" of expense. When an entrepreneur makes a mistake and misses point A, his loss-minimizing adjustment is always in or on the edge of area 5. The subsequent act of moving to the edge of area 5 or of staying in area 5 is also a "right action" in view of what is possible, once the mistake is made with acquisition costs greater than salvage values. However, it would be better if the mistake of missing point A were never made, in which case one or both resources would not be producing less value than expected on its acquisition, resource MVP's would equal acquisition costs, production would not exceed that represented by the iso-product line passing through point A, and no losses would be imposed on the entrepreneur as the owner of L and V. Thus, an economic sector that forces a large proportion of its entrepreneurs to operate in or on the edge of area 5 other than at A is regarded as malfunctioning, i.e., it is using too much of resources L and/or V to produce output that must be sold at prices which make MVP's less than acquisition costs and, hence, imposes losses on both the entrepreneur and society at large. The loss to society results from having the resource(s) fixed in the production of a product that is less desirable than ones that can no longer be produced.

Designing right actions to correct such overcommitment is fundamentally difficult. Mistakes which hurt entrepreneurs benefit some consumers. Actions to ease the burdens of the entrepreneurs damaged would, as a minimum, hurt those consumers benefiting from lower product prices. In other words, any action has redistributive consequences.

Preventing errors of organizing other than at point A also involves these fundamental difficulties. This is true whether the prevention takes the form of public or semipublic action to (1) reduce imperfections of knowledge (extension) (2) regulate rates of entry and exit (acreage allotments, licensing by association of growers, etc.), or (3) reduce the difference between acquisition cost and salvage values (liquidation subsidies). Such public and semipublic programs almost invariably damage some people in benefiting others. It is difficult to order alternative actions in terms of descending net benefits per unit of effort, and the decision rules or basis for choice are not established. Most possible solutions involve redistributive aspects, despite the primary objective of making the allocative system function better, as contrasted with the objective of redistributing the ownership of resources. In efforts to improve the allocative efficiency of the price and marketing system, politicians and farm leaders may fail to recognize that a freely operating price system can (and should) be expected to malfunction. This lack of recognition can endanger the free price system, since its malfunctions are not corrected. Similarly, when economic theorists and advisors fail in this recognition, they lose the public's confidence in economics as a discipline.

With respect to the total evaluation of U.S. agricultural policies and programs and the operation of the economy, we are as a research group modestly constrained to regard ourselves as only one minor element in a complex socio-politico-economic evaluative process. Nevertheless, in the course of this study we sometimes have believed that we are capable of "getting on through" to conclusions about what is right or wrong and on occasion so state. In other instances, we regard ourselves as being helpful in (1) formulating certain new concepts and clarifying old concepts (both normative and nonnormative and both analytic and descriptive or synthetic) and (2) suggesting new and perhaps more appropriate institutional designs. We envision the total socio-politico-economic evaluative process as a creative, original, cooperative enterprise in which insights, new ideas, and new solutions emerge through the cooperative efforts of researchers, administrators, agricultural leaders, and lawmakers. The emergence of these insights, as we see it, is likely to be promoted by projections, speculations, and estimations of the consequences of following alternative policies, programs, and operations. Such quantitative work is most helpful if made with respect to situations of normative importance. As researchers, administrators, farm leaders, and lawmakers interact in originating and designing new policies, programs, and operating principles, such quantitative work can clarify the normative issues and nonnormative questions. It can even suggest bases for making choices even when common denominators and the necessary second-order conditions are missing.

PART II

Production and Resource Use

In setting forth the problems and theoretical basis for analysis and evaluation, Part I was a dress rehearsal for the analytical chapters in Part II. We now start at the beginning again, and with emphasis on product price expectations and specific input categories—capital, labor, and land—we analyze resource allocation in American agriculture and the impact of government action on that process. Chapters 5, 6, 7, 8, and 9 provide the link between theory and reality and, as such, provide the tests of objectivity discussed in Chapter 4. And, to the extent that tests of objectivity are met, new knowledge is provided about the chronic adjustment problems in American agriculture.

CHAPTER 5

Expected Product Prices

M. L. LEROHL

While expected rather than actual price has long been recognized as the relevant price variable for production planning, only in recent years has the concept aroused keen interest. In turn, the interest has led to attempts to obtain usable, empirical estimates of expected prices that will be susceptible to economic analysis, estimates that need not be, and usually are not, identical with observed prices in the marketplace.

Our study is concerned overall with production and the basis for production trends in a dynamic and unstable period of U.S. agricultural history. A basic ingredient in examining the sources of U.S. agricultural fluctuation is the explicit recognition of price, and the importance of expected prices for resource use. This chapter describes the techniques employed in developing the expected price series used, outlines the bases for the techniques, and undertakes a preliminary evaluation of the expected prices and, indirectly, of the concepts on which they are based. The objective is an improved understanding of the role of expected versus actual prices, an assessment of the use of future-oriented information in forming price expectations, and an evaluation of the prospect of developing explicit expected prices in economic analysis which incorporate elements of outlook-type information.

The expected price series used are designed to be those which reflect prices anticipated by reasonably well-informed farmers for explicit periods into the future. This concept represents a departure from the basis for some, but not all, previously developed price series, in that an attempt is being made to develop explicit estimates of an inexplicit variable, in which knowledge levels of farmers are involved. While attempts have been made to develop such series in the past, with indications of satisfactory preliminary results [Darcovich and Heady, 1956], an attempt has not yet been made to develop them on a broad base of commodities for an extended period, or to test them extensively in a variety of resource models and contexts concerning the history of the U.S. agricultural economy. An assessment of the methodology used is, therefore, one of the side-benefits of this study. More importantly, however, the overall study's incorporation of price expectations provides valuable evidence of the information input used by farmers, as well as tests of the adequacy of information services and the economic concepts employed by American farmers.

RECENT DEVELOPMENTS IN EXPECTED PRICES

Perhaps the most intriguing development in the recent history of expected prices is the work of Nerlove [1958], which has been a major factor in providing a wider appreciation of the difference between actual and expected prices. Briefly, Nerlove's distributed lag model of expected prices relies on an algebraic system of considerable simplicity and versatility. Where actual price in period $t-1$ is indicated by P_{t-1}, expected price in period t is indicated by $P_t^* = P_{t-1}^* + \beta (P_{t-1} - P_{t-1}^*)$, $0 < \beta \leq 1$. The case in which actual price in the previous period becomes expected price is then shown to be only a special case of the model, the one in which β, the coefficient of expectation, is equal to one.

The approach, while mathematically elegant, raises some concern because of its inability to specifically include future-oriented information. We know, for example, that considerable price outlook information is and has been provided to the agricultural community—from public as well as other sources—and that significant efforts have been made to communicate this information. In terms of the Nerlove model, the essence of this concern is whether β can safely be assumed to remain constant, even over fairly short periods of time. Glenn L. Johnson [January 1960, p. 26] has asked:

> Do we really believe that the next year's expected price is this year's expected price plus some proportion (constant from year to year) of the difference between last year's actual and last year's expected normal price regardless of wars, price-support activities, inflations, economic collapse, changing foreign demand, strikes, and institutional adjustments—all of which were important in the 1909–32 period studied by Nerlove?

The Interstate Managerial Survey (IMS), a seven-state survey in the north central United States, dealt with the models used by farmers to develop their expectations of future product and input prices, and the models used to develop expectations with respect to other variables important in the operation of their farms. The expectations part of the study [Glenn L. Johnson et al., 1961, pp. 85–104] pointed out that many farmers use more than one simple model, or use a combination of features of several simple models, to develop their price expectations. Similar results were found in an earlier Iowa study [Kaldor and Heady, 1954]. The value of outlook models in farmer decision-making has been shown as well [Darcovich and Heady, 1956], and provides evidence that farmers not only employ quite sophisticated decision-making models, but also suggests that information explicitly about the future is an input into those models. These conclusions are generally supported by Partenheimer, who provides evidence that farmers display substantial economic literacy in their decision making. Partenheimer [1959, p. 26] points out that farmers use more complex methods of decision making than the simple expectation models traditionally believed to be relevant.[1]

DEVELOPING THE EXPECTED PRICE SERIES

The work of Darcovich and Heady [1956] indicates that it is rational for farmers to incorporate outlook information in their expectation models. The IMS attests that farmers exhibit a large measure of economic literacy in their decision making. Nerlove's work and the results of the IMS agree that farmers appear to use expectation models which incorporate information about the past, the present, and the future, all based on a large measure of knowledge of the pertinent economic relationships. It appears important that all these types of information be incorporated if the objective in calculating the expected price series is to approximate prices *anticipated* by farmers rather than actual prices.

The method chosen in our study to include these three types of information in developing empirical estimates of farmers' expected prices is as follows: (1) a simple model is used to derive estimates ("own past price" estimates) of expected price on the basis of experience with past prices; (2) these "own past price" estimates are modified, where necessary, in the light of outlook information generally available at the point in time at which the expected price is being estimated. The result can be termed an "integrative" expected price, in that information from a variety of sources and concerning a variety of time periods is being incorporated.

Expected prices were developed for the United States for each of thirteen commodities. Three expected prices were developed for each year for each commodity: (1) a series indicating price expected at the beginning of year t for the year t (one-year expected price); (2) a series indicating average price expected at the beginning of year t for the year t and the following four years (five-year expected price); and (3) a series indicating the average price expected at the beginning of year t for the year t and the following nine years (ten-year expected price). Where P_t is actual price of a commodity in year t, P_{5t} is actual average price of a commodity for year t and the following four years, and P_{10t} is actual

---

[1] For examples of some simple expectation models, see Heady [1952, p. 479].

average price of a commodity for year t and the following nine years, three equations were fitted for each of the thirteen commodities:

$$P_t = f_1 (P_{t-1}, P_{t-2}, \ldots),$$

$$P_{5t} = f_2 (P_{t-1}, P_{t-2}, \ldots),$$

$$P_{10t} = f_3 (P_{t-1}, P_{t-2}, \ldots).$$

These equations were truncated in accordance with criteria concerning the level of $\overline{R}^2$ and the ability of the equations to reverse the trend of the dependent variable.

The estimated values of $P_t, P_{5t},$ and P_{10t} (respectively $\hat{P}_t, \hat{P}_{5t},$ and $\hat{P}_{10t}$) are the own past price estimates of expected price. These are altered, where necessary, to reflect opinions in available outlook information. The majority of the outlook information employed is from U.S. Department of Agriculture sources, and prominently includes *The Demand and Price Situation* and various situation reports for commodities. The final result is a series of prices, reflecting as far as possible pertinent outlook data, known as integrative expected prices ($EP_t, EP_{5t},$ and EP_{10t}) for each commodity. These estimates are based on *both* the past experiences of farmers with prices and generally available information about the future.

Aggregate expected price indexes for each of three horizons are also developed. These are overall indexes of the integrative expected prices for one year, five years, and ten years. Each of them is based on all of the thirteen integrative expected prices, one for each commodity. They are also designed to estimate expected average prices for aggregate U.S. farm output for one, five, and ten years in the future.[2]

THE EXPECTED PRICE OF CORN

While the concepts involved in developing the expected prices are not complex, the detail and commodity information input are a substantial and a significant part of our study. To illustrate the approach, data pertinent to the development of expected prices for corn are outlined here, to provide an improved appreciation of the method employed in developing the series, and a better understanding of the strengths and weaknesses of the final result. Corn is se-

---

[2] To the extent that thirteen commodities can adequately reflect price expectations for all U.S. farm commodities. For the weighting procedure employed, see Lerohl [1965, pp. 42–45]. Lerohl also presents empirical estimates of the expected prices, as well as the aggregate indexes for the period 1917–62.

lected for demonstration purposes both because it is an important commodity with a relatively fixed production period, and because the analysis for it is relatively straightforward.

Three expected price series for corn were developed, reflecting at planting time (1) the average price expected for the coming crop year (one-year expected price, EP_t), (2) the average price expected for the ensuing five crops (five-year expected price EP_{5t}) and (3) the average price anticipated for the forthcoming ten crops (ten-year expected price, EP_{10t}). In each case, a two-stage procedure was used: first the development of "own past price" estimates from a lagged model, and second the modification of the estimates where available outlook data suggested this to be appropriate.

Details of the Technique

An "own past price" estimate of expected prices for corn for one year was first developed from a generalized distributed lag model of the form $\hat{P}_t = a_o + \sum_{i=1}^{n} aiP_{t-i}$.[3] This was followed by "own past price" estimates obtained for five and ten years ahead, developed similarly from equations of the following nature:

$$\hat{P}_{5t} = [\frac{P_t + P_{t+1} + \ldots + P_{t+4}}{5}] = a_o + \sum_{i=1}^{n} aiP_{t-1} \, ,$$

$$\hat{P}_{10t} = [\frac{P_t + P_{t+1} + \ldots + P_{t+9}}{10}] = a_o + \sum_{i=1}^{n} aiP_{t-1} \, .$$

For corn, the following three equations were obtained reflecting the "own past price" estimates for one, five, and ten year horizons.

$$\hat{P}_t = 0.22 + 0.77 P_{t-1} \, ,$$

$$\hat{P}_{5t} = 0.43 + 0.55 P_{t-1} \, ,$$

$$\hat{P}_{10t} = 0.60 + 0.39 P_{t-1} \, .$$

These equations provide the "own past price" expected price estimates shown in columns 1 to 3 of Table 7. As a result of examining pertinent outlook informa-

---

[3] This form of generalized lag model, rather than the distributed lag form employed by Nerlove, is used, since concern is with overall predictions rather than the individual parameters, and because minimal emphasis is placed on the parameters as a result of concern that they do not remain stable [Lerohl, 1965, pp. 26 ff.].

TABLE 7. Calculated Expected Prices for Corn, United States, 1917–1962

(dollars per bushel)

Year	"Own past price" expected prices (not incl. outlook information)			"Integrative" expected prices (incl. available outlook information)		
	1-year (1)	5-year (2)	10-year (3)	1-year (4)	5-year (5)	10-year (6)
1917	$1.10	$1.05	$1.04	$1.25	$1.05	$1.04
1918	1.30	1.19	1.14	1.40	1.19	1.14
1919	1.34	1.22	1.17	1.34	1.22	1.17
1920	1.34	1.22	1.16	1.50	1.30	1.30
1921	.64	.73	.81	.50	.73	.81
1922	.58	.68	.78	.50	.60	.60
1923	.76	.81	.87	.76	.70	.70
1924	.81	.85	.89	.70	.75	.75
1925	1.01	.99	1.00	.80	.85	.85
1926	.73	.79	.86	.73	.79	.80
1927	.78	.83	.88	.78	.83	.80
1928	.84	.87	.91	.75	.78	.78
1929	.84	.87	.91	.75	.78	.78
1930	.81	.85	.90	.65	.70	.70
1931	.65	.73	.82	.45	.60	.65
1932	.45	.59	.72	.25	.45	.55
1933	.45	.59	.72	.40	.50	.55
1934	.60	.70	.79	.60	.60	.65
1935	.84	.87	.91	.70	.65	.70
1936	.71	.78	.85	.71	.78	.80
1937	1.02	.99	1.00	.90	.80	.80
1938	.60	.70	.79	.50	.65	.70
1939	.59	.69	.79	.59	.65	.70
1940	.64	.73	.81	.60	.65	.70
1941	.69	.76	.84	.69	.76	.84
1942	.80	.84	.89	.85	.95	.89
1943	.91	.92	.95	1.00	1.05	.95
1944	1.06	1.02	1.02	1.06	1.02	.95
1945	1.02	.99	1.00	1.02	.99	.95
1946	1.17	1.10	1.08	1.17	1.10	1.08
1947	1.41	1.27	1.20	1.55	1.27	1.20
1948	1.89	1.61	1.44	1.50	1.30	1.25
1949	1.21	1.13	1.10	1.40	1.25	1.20
1950	1.18	1.11	1.08	1.35	1.25	1.20
1951	1.39	1.26	1.19	1.65	1.30	1.30
1952	1.51	1.34	1.25	1.65	1.45	1.45
1953	1.39	1.26	1.19	1.39	1.35	1.35
1954	1.37	1.24	1.18	1.40	1.35	1.35
1955	1.32	1.21	1.16	1.35	1.30	1.30
1956	1.27	1.17	1.13	1.27	1.20	1.20
1957	1.22	1.14	1.10	1.22	1.15	1.12
1958	1.08	1.04	1.04	1.11	1.10	1.10
1959	1.09	1.04	1.04	1.05	1.04	1.04

TABLE 7. Continued

(dollars per bushel)

Year	"Own past price" expected prices (not incl. outlook information)			"Integrative" expected prices (incl. available outlook information)		
	1-year (1)	5-year (2)	10-year (3)	1-year (4)	5-year (5)	10-year (6)
1960	1.03	1.00	1.01	1.03	1.04	1.04
1961	1.00	.98	.99	1.05	1.08	1.08
1962	1.06	1.02	1.02	1.10	1.12	1.12

Source: Lerohl [1965].

tion, a series of integrative expected prices is obtainable and these are shown in columns 4 to 6 of Table 7.[4]

Similar information for additional commodities is also available [Lerohl, 1965]. While the series developed appear consistent with the state of knowledge concerning anticipations held by and information available to reasonably well-informed farmers, tests of their adequacy in explicit formal situations remains important. Substantive tests are found in other chapters of this book, employing the expected prices in more complete models focusing on the various resource sectors, but the preliminary tests and indications which follow here provide a base at least for use of the series, and outline conclusions obtained from other uses of the integrative expected price series.

TESTS OF THE EXPECTED PRICE SERIES

One of the tests of the integrative expected price series reported in this section compares results of the study with other expected prices which are available. Another makes a comparison of changes in land values, and a third discusses responses to a questionnaire sent to a number of agricultural economists. The incorporation of these prices into econometric models of other investigators is also discussed. In all cases, however, the criterion is not whether the expected prices of this study are good predictors of actual prices. The

[4] The equations above and the data of Table 7 indicate something of both the expected prices obtained and the process of obtaining them. It is shown, however, that the integrative estimates rarely concur exactly with the own past price estimates. An immediate question is whether the own past price series can be deleted, going directly to the integrative series. While to know with complete certainty whether this would produce equal results is impossible, it is clear that the own past price part of the process involves a formal way of bringing knowledge of the past to bear on expected prices. The development of both series also makes possible an assessment of the relative merits of the two types of expected prices, and both are thus included to provide evaluative methodological insights, although the overall goal remains the development of descriptively accurate expected price series integrating all pertinent information.

relevant criterion is that the estimates of expected price approximate the actual but unobservable ex ante price expectations of farmers.

Comparison Test

A study prepared by Glenn L. Johnson [1961] as a background paper for the Committee on Economic Development includes expected price estimates for the United States for eleven commodities. These expected price series were calculated for Johnson by USDA personnel and were designed to illustrate the prices expected by reasonably well-informed farmers during 1946–60. The estimates of expected prices "are really quantified opinions based on conferences with persons whose main business is to appraise the outlook and current situations for the commodities involved" [Johnson, ibid., p. 71]. These prices, like the expected prices developed under the criteria of this present study, assume considerable economic literacy on the part of farmers, and recognize a variety of factors which influence expected prices. The 1961 Johnson series, however, is not an adequate substitute for the later series. One difficulty is that the time span covered by the series is shorter than required by researchers interested in using this price variable. Nevertheless, as an independently developed set of estimates of expected price, the 1961 estimates can perform as checks on the prices developed in our present study.

Such a test was conducted for the one-year expected price series for ten commodities; a similar test for the five-year expected price series dealt with six of these commodities. The test was a modified (one-tail) sign test, and related expected price for year t (or, for the five-year expectations, expected price for year t and the following four years) to actual price in year $t - 1$. The null hypothesis (H_0) was that there exists no similar relationship between, on the one hand, the relative position of expected price in year t and the actual price in year $t - 1$ in the earlier Johnson study and, on the other hand, the relative position of expected price in year t and actual price in year $t - 1$ in this study. The alternate hypothesis (H_A) was that a similar relationship exists. For the one-year expected prices, H_0 was rejected at the following significance levels: 1 percent, one commodity; 5 percent, two commodities; 10 percent, three commodities; 15 percent, three commodities; none of these, one commodity. For the six commodities represented in the comparison of five-year expected prices, H_0 was rejected at the 1 percent level for four commodities, and at the 10 percent and 15 percent level each for one commodity.

The data thus indicate a large amount of similarity in the movement of expected price in the two series relative to actual price in the preceding year. The test supports the hypothesis that, despite the subjectivity involved in interpreting outlook data, different individuals can arrive at similar estimates of expected price, a hypothesis further strengthened because no one individual developed expected prices for more than one commodity for the Johnson study.

This test is not primarily a test of accuracy but rather an evaluation of the interpersonal comparability of the series.

Land Value Test

It is generally accepted that land values are based, in part at least, on capitalized expected rental incomes which, in turn, reflect price expectations held by farmers. Thus, changes in longer-term price expectations should be closely related to changes in an index of land values.

Table 8 compares the first differences of the ten-year aggregate expected price index with the first differences of the index of average value per acre of farm real estate in the United States. The latter is also compared with first differences of an index of actual prices received by farmers. The assumption in making the comparison with actual prices is that changes in them are a good indicator of changes in land values. Table 8 appears to provide scant support for this assumption. However, when the first difference of actual prices are lagged one year and compared with the first differences of the index of average value per acre of farm real estate, the value of the correlation coefficient is shown to be close to that obtained when the ten-year expected price is used. The comparison thus provides some support for the hypothesis that farmers' expected price can be approximated by last year's actual price (i.e., the hypothesis that farmers

TABLE 8. Comparison of Coefficients of Correlation *(r)* between Changes in Real Estate Values per Acre and Changes in Three Price Indices[a]

	Correlation coefficients obtained when average value per acre of U.S. farm real estate[a] is compared with			
Years	Actual price received by farmers	Actual price received by farmers lagged one year[b]	Own past price model of ten-year expected price[c]	Ten-year expected price[d]
1917–54	0.42^e	0.69	0.64	0.74
1917–62	$.36^f$	.60	.53	.61

Source: Lerohl [1965].

[a]Source of average value per acre of farm real estate: USDA, *Farm Real Estate Market Developments*, August 1963, p. 4.

[b]Actual price lagged one year corresponds to a "current-year" expected price model.

[c]The "own past price" model of ten-year expected price is based on the "own past price" estimates of expected price (P_{10t}).

[d]The ten-year integrative expected price (EP_{10t}) incorporating outlook information.

[e]Significantly different from the corresponding correlation coefficient for ten-year expected price at the 5 percent level.

[f]Significantly different from the corresponding correlation coefficient for ten-year expected price at the 15 percent level.

expect present prices to continue into the future). For example, Figure 5 indicates that the direction of change of the lagged actual and ten-year expected price is quite similar. However, it also indicates an important fact which a comparison such as that of Table 7 overlooks: Figure 5 shows that expected price is above actual for much of the 1917-62 period, and that the amount by which expected price has tended to be above actual is greater the longer the expectation horizon.

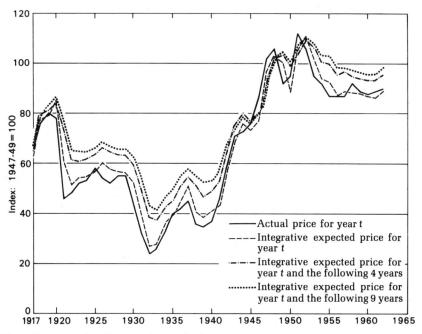

Figure 5. Comparison between index of prices received by farmers and integrative expected price series, United States, 1917-1962.

In Table 8, two correlation coefficients are presented for each of the four price variables, one for the period 1917-54 and another for the period 1917-62. The reason is that the relationship between real estate values and expected price becomes irregular in the years 1955 and following. The recent imprecision of the relationship appears to be due to a complex of factors, prominently including technological change. "There is some indication that farm land buyers . . . have capitalized a substantial part of the gains realized from new technology . . . into higher land prices" [USDA, 1963, "Farm Real Estate . . .", p. 45]. Larsen's study of land values in the United States [1966] also found technology to be a significant determinant of farm land values.

The above indicates that a comparison of changes in real estate values per acre and changes in expected prices provides a useful test of the latter series, although it is not especially helpful in deciding among the lagged, own past price, and outlook models of expected price. A more comprehensive empirical test, including an attempt to relate aggregate expected price indexes for specific states to real estate values in those states, is beyond the scope of this chapter. Larsen's study [1966] reports considerable success, however, in using expected prices in a model of U.S. farm land values.

Questionnaire

In a further attempt to evaluate the expected prices, we sent a questionnaire to thirty agricultural economists who are or have been associated with this discipline during some part of the period of time encompassed by our study. The respondents were asked to indicate, for each of about twenty annual observations, whether they believed expected price was above or below actual price in that year. Six usable questionnaires were obtained. The data from these six were evaluated by a modified sign test, similar to the one discussed previously. The relevant null hypothesis (H_0) was that there is no similar relationship between, on the one hand, the relative position of expected and actual prices (for the same year) in this study. The alternate hypothesis (H_A) was that a similar relationship exists, and the relative position of the expected and actual price is the same in the questionnaire responses and in this study.

The six questionnaires used suggest that the relative position of actual, versus expected, price is similar in these questionnaires and also to that in the estimates developed for this study. In all cases, H_0 is rejected at the 1 percent or 5 percent level. Nevertheless, the test has two main weaknesses: (1) the small number of observations obtained, and (2) —related to the first—the test relates only to the longer-term expected price series, since no usable data were obtained for any of the one-year expected price series. A third possible weakness is that several of the individuals sampled were (1) those who are also responsible for the material in the *Situation Reports* for commodities published by the USDA and/or (2) those who developed series of expected prices for the Johnson [1961] study. Thus, the amount of new information added by the completed questionnaires is difficult to assess, although it is corroborative.

Tests in Other Studies

Petit [1964] has developed models for feed-grain and beef and hog production based on data for the 1929–62 period. Each of the models was fitted using earlier versions of the expected-price series presented in this study. While Petit makes clear that his study is not concerned with the process of forming price expectations, he can also state "it can be viewed as a practical test of the hypotheses underlying . . . [these expected prices]. Generally speaking, it appears that these price expectations give reasonable results" [p. 214].

Comparing various expectation models, Petit notes [1964, p. 214] "in the explanation of the number of sows at the end of the year, current prices might have predicted better. For farrowings, we have not shown that these price expectations were superior to current prices for hogs at the time decisions to farrow were taken. However, the reverse is not true either as these price expectations have never proven inferior to any other price variable used and, in many instances, give fairly good results." He continues, "The performance of the '5-year' expected price for beef is surprisingly good. In many equations, it appears as the key explanatory variable. Therefore our results appear encouraging for the method employed" to estimate expected prices.

CONCLUSION

Valid and interpersonally comparable estimates of expected prices are obtainable. This chapter has outlined the method employed to obtain such estimates, and provides evidence concerning their usefulness and also their usefulness relative to an own past price model of expectations. The performance of the series and their logical foundations suggest that the estimates are useful and their foundations relevant in the context of the present study.

The price expectations developed are single-valued, however, and thus abstract from problems associated with the certainty with which a particular price is anticipated. While the results reported suggest that single-valued expectations are useful proxy variables for the expectations held by farmers, the farmers' true anticipations are probably more complex than a single measure of the central tendency of prices. Nevertheless, the results above, and the simplicity and applicability of single-valued expectations, suggest that the series developed do contain significant elements helping to explain and assess the changing fortunes of American agriculture in this century. The dynamics of prices and knowledge levels concerning prices appear key elements in the successes and failures of American agriculture since World War I.

CHAPTER 6

The Overall Pattern of Production, Disappearance, Income, and Resource Use

FRANCIS VAN GIGCH and C. LEROY QUANCE

This chapter sets the stage for the input-oriented chapters that make up the rest of Part II. Its three main sections—(1) agricultural production and disappearance, (2) the income picture, and (3) a summary of agricultural adjustments in the United States—provide overall information on agricultural patterns from 1917 to the late 1960's.

AGRICULTURAL PRODUCTION AND DISAPPEARANCE

During World War I, American agriculture was less responsive to stimuli in the short run than it was during World War II. Important factors behind the earlier relative inelasticity included: (1) the complex of labor-saving, land-saving, and output-expanding innovations had not yet been adopted and agriculture was still highly dependent on nature, labor, and farm-produced capital; (2) the war itself competed with farming for the use of some factors, notably manpower; and (3) massive additions to land were no longer possible through extension of the frontier.

During the period 1917–29 farm output increased by 13 percent with the total increase occurring after 1920 (Figure 6). There was no noticeable increase in production for the duration of World War I, despite the parity ratio—an expression of real farm prices—reaching its highest level of the century (Table 9). In addition to price stimuli, a series of programs to promote agricultural expansion existed during the war. The unusual war demand for agricultural products spent itself in high prices and appreciation of farm assets.

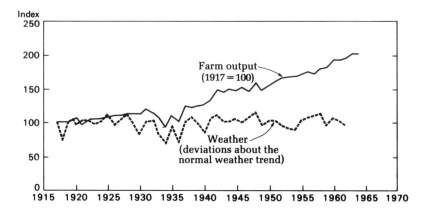

Figure 6. Indices of farm output and weather, United States, 1917–1964. (*Source*: USDA SB 233, June 1968, and Stallings, February 1960.)

Favorable wartime demand conditions were projected into bullish postwar long-run price expectations that reached their highest about 1920 when actual prices and the parity ratio reached their period low (Figure 6 and Table 9). The return of soldiers and overoptimistic expectations (plus the lagged effect of wartime efforts to expand output) accelerated the growth rate of farm output in all of the 1920's, although price expectations fell, again, late in the period.

The adverse economic conditions prevailing in 1930–33 were manifested by the lowest real agricultural prices since the turn of the century and by progressively depressed long-run price expectations; however, farm output showed no signs of slowing down. On the contrary, the average index of farm output in 1930–33 was higher than for any other prior four-year period despite rather mediocre weather conditions [USDA SB 233, June 1968, and Stallings, February 1960].

Changes in the output mix observed during the post-WWI period were a natural adjustment to a wealthier economy's changing consumption patterns. Consumption (and production) moved toward livestock products, vegetables, and fruits with relatively high-income elasticities of demand. This trend was not reversed during 1930–33 despite falling, rather than rising, incomes.

The upward trend in farm output momentarily reversed itself early in the recovery period of 1934–41. The index of output for 1934–36 (Figure 6) was lower than the average index of 1930–33 and resulted from a decrease in the production of both livestock and crops [USDA SB 233, June 1968].

Until 1935, long-run expected farm prices were falling (Figure 7), suggesting that the reduction of farm output was caused by (1) a reduction in the volume of resources devoted to agriculture and (2) government programs aimed at controlling output. But probably the primary cause was the onslaught of possibly

TABLE 9. Selected Indices of Agricultural Prices, United States, 1917–1970

(Index: 1947-49 = 100)

Year	Prices received by farmers	Prices paid by farmers	Parity ratio[a]	Ten-year average expected prices[b]	Ten-year average price received[c]	Ratio of expected to received
1917	66	59	112	67	–	
1918	76	69	110	78	–	
1919	80	79	101	81	–	
1920	78	86	91	86	–	
1921	46	62	74	76	–	
1922	48	60	80	65	61	107
1923	52	64	81	65	60	108
1924	53	64	83	64	58	110
1925	58	66	88	66	55	120
1926	54	64	84	69	52	133
1927	52	64	81	67	51	131
1928	55	65	85	66	48	138
1929	55	64	86	66	46	143
1917–29	59	67	89	70	54[d]	124
1930	46	60	77	68	44	150
1931	32	52	62	69	42	164
1932	24	45	53	67	41	163
1933	26	44	59	66	40	165
1930–33	32	50	63	67	42	161
1934	33	48	69	47	38	124
1935	40	50	80	50	36	139
1936	42	50	84	55	35	159
1937	45	52	87	58	36	161
1938	36	50	72	55	40	138
1939	35	49	71	52	44	118
1940	37	50	74	53	48	110
1941	46	53	87	57	52	110
1934–41	39	50	78	53	41	132
1942	59	61	97	67	57	118
1943	71	68	104	75	61	123
1944	73	73	100	79	67	118
1945	76	76	100	77	74	104
1946	87	83	105	82	80	103
1942–46	73	72	101	76	68	113
1947	102	76	106	84	71	128
1948	106	104	102	102	90	113
1949	92	100	92	105	94	112
1950	95	102	93	101	96	105
1951	112	113	99	106	97	111
1952	106	115	94	110	96	115
1953	95	111	86	108	96	113
1954	92	111	85	108	95	114
1947–54	100	106	95	103	94	110

TABLE 9. Continued

(Index: 1947-49 = 100)

Year	Prices received by farmers	Prices paid by farmers	Parity ratio[a]	Long-run prices		
				Ten-year average expected prices[b]	Ten-year average price received[c]	Ratio of expected to received
1955	87	110	79	103	94	110
1956	87	111	78	98	94	104
1957	87	115	76	98	91	108
1958	92	117	79	97	90	108
1955-58	88	113	78	99	92	108
1959	89	119	75	96		
1960	88	120	73	96		
1961	89	121	74	96		
1962	90	122	74	99		
1963	89	128	70			
1964	88	128	69			
1965	91	132	69			
1966	98	137	72			
1967	94	140	67			
1968	96	146	66			
1969	101	153	67			
1970	103	160	65			
1959-70	93	134	70			

Sources: Lerohl [1965, pp. 102-4]; USDA [Ag. Stat., 1967].

Note: Index (originally 1910-14 = 100) shifted to 1947-49 = 100.

[a]Ratio of the index of prices received by farmers to the index of prices paid by farmers.
[b]Price expectation formulated at time $t-5$ for a ten-year planning horizon of which t is the mid-period year.
[c]Average of prices actually received during years t and the nine subsequent years centered at $t + 5$.
[d]Average of years for which data were available.

the most severe and general drought in the history of American farming (Figure 6).[1] Government programs played an important role in keeping cotton and tobacco production in check but reductions in wheat and corn production were due primarily to weather [Benedict and Stine, 1956].

Except for the Southern Plains and Great Plains where adverse weather conditions continued until nearly 1940, the productivity of the farm sector regained momentum about 1937. The average index of output for 1937-41 was 126 (1917-19 = 100) [USDA SB 233, June 1968]. Even the farm depression had

[1] According to Stallings [1960], the weather index of farm output for the period 1934-41 was 7.5 percent below normal weather conditions; for the period 1933-36 it was 17 percent below average.

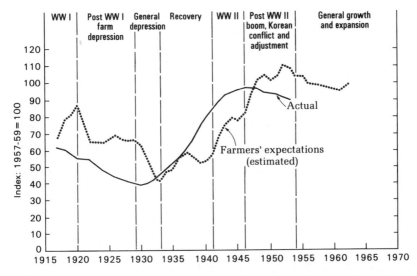

Figure 7. Indices of ten-year average actual and estimated farmers' expectations of average prices to be received for the current year and next nine years, Unites States, 1917–1962. (*Source*: Lerohl, 1965.)

not freed agriculture of resources previously overcommitted to farming during years of high-price expectations.

Despite adverse factors such as loss of manpower, relative scarcity of labor-saving, nonfarm-produced capital, and the need for many farmers to shift into unknown lines of production, agriculture responded well to incentives generated by World War II. The incentives were manifested through the highest real agricultural prices since World War I. High prices received by farmers reinforced the lagged impact of general recovery from the depth of the depression to the late 1930's and government programs committed to supporting farm prices, and resulted in an upward revision of long-run expected farm prices. According to Sherman Johnson [1949] farm supply response during World War II was enhanced by capacity which accumulated during the 1930's but was held in check by government restrictions and adverse weather of that era. Wartime policies replaced restrictions with price and other stimuli.

Sherman Johnson's 1949 study also compared changes in farm production during the two World Wars. In this present paragraph and the next we have drawn substantially from his analysis. During 1942–44, the three full years of World War II for the United States, the output index increased, on the average, 28 percent over 1935–39. Part of this increase was due to favorable weather, but, even if the index of output is deflated by Stallings's weather index [February 1960], the increase during 1942–44 is still remarkably high for such a short time interval—nearly 16 percent. Output responses were much greater during World War II than during World War I. Though the index of farm output in 1917-20 averaged 6.5 percent greater than in 1910-14, no output change is detected when the index of farm output is deflated by Stallings's weather index. During World War I most increases in farm production were due to weather.

Increases in output during World War II occurred across the board, with the exception of sugar and cotton. Lower cotton price incentives, relaxation of restrictions on corn acreage, and encouragement of peanut and soybean production help explain the relative decline in cotton production. Output increases for livestock were greater than for crops, with large gains in meats relative to dairy products. There were spectacular gains in the production of oil-bearing seeds with price support; the increase of 150 percent in oil seeds between 1935-39 and 1942-47 overshadows sustained gains in production for both food and feed grains.

During the 1948-54 period farm output rose by about 12 percent, an average rate of growth of 1.7 percent per year [USDA SB 233, June 1968]. Although both prices received and prices paid by farmers increased during the period, the latter grew faster than the former and the parity ratio decreased relative to the World War II period. But long-run price expectations tended to remain high relative to prices received. The optimistic outlook is attributed to the agricultural prosperity that had prevailed since the World War II years as well as to government programs. The Steagall Amendment of 1941 had provided for high price supports for a series of commodities whose production was stimulated for the war effort. The increase in demand for farm products generated by the Korean War kept price expectations at high relative levels throughout the 1947-54 interval.

The largest increases in farm output occurred in livestock products, which expanded 17 percent compared to 3 percent for all crops. Meats and poultry products led dairy products. Among crops, oil-bearing plants and hay and forages showed the largest production gains. Oil crops were good substitutes in production for various crops under acreage control and hay and forages fitted well into the soil conservation scheme. Substitution of livestock for cash crops is suggested by the expansion of hay and forages and feed grains. Production of food grains declined about 11 percent during the period; however this figure is misleading, in that production was exceptionally high at the period's beginning and exceptionally low at its end. Omitting the ending years of the period lowers the production decrease to 4 percent.

Farm output increased about 20 percent between 1953-55 and 1964-66 [USDA Ag. Statistics, 1941-67]. Its rate of increase was slightly higher than that of the U.S. population during most of the period, and the expansion happened despite relatively stable farm product prices, steadily rising prices paid by farmers, and falling long-run expected output prices.

Contrary to the pattern after World War I, crop production grew at least as fast as livestock production. Large gains were achieved in feed grains and also for hay, forage, and food grains. There was little change in tobacco output and a decrease in cotton production. Among livestock products, the largest gains were in poultry—nearly 4 percent per year. Government production controls of cotton, tobacco, and dairy products seemed to be fairly successful but efforts to control food and feed grains were less so.

Before the inauguration of price support programs in 1934, supply and disappearance were equated mostly through spontaneous price variations. After 1934, the federal government's power to accumulate stocks provided a demand which allowed only that part of supply that would secure some predetermined price to flow into regular markets.

World War I had provided a strong source of demand for U.S. agricultural products. Since farm output was not very responsive in the short run, wartime demand resulted in world farm price increases that encouraged diversion from domestic consumption into exports. The average index of the volume of exports between 1915 and 1919 was the highest of any five consecutive years from World War I to the mid-1950's [USDA FAS-M-76, 1960]. The war's termination and European reconstruction brought a dramatic decrease in demand for U.S. agricultural production.

The depression brought about a further decrease in the foreign demand for U.S. agricultural products. On the average, the United States exported during 1930-33 about 20 percent fewer agricultural products than during the 1925-29 interval and, of course, still less than during World War I [USDA FAS-M-76, 1960]. The decrease in the value of exports was larger than the decrease in volume: the value of exports was 44 percent lower, on the average, in 1930-33 than in 1925-29 [USDA Ag. Statistics, 1941-67].

During 1930-33, stocks of some agricultural commodities accumulated both on and off farms, but except for a short-lived experiment in price supports by the Federal Farm Board, stocks were held by the private sector. For example, the average total stock of wheat recorded on each July 1 during 1930-33 was two and one half times larger than the corresponding figures for the period 1925-29, despite rather mediocre yields [USDA Ag. Statistics, 1941-67]. These carry-overs in the early 1930's differed totally from those of later years. While carry-overs resulting from later price-support programs were a purposeful addition to the demand for farm products and were financed by the community at large, conditions of the early 1930's reflected a lack of demand that was almost completely absorbed by the farm sector through lower prices.

Domestic consumption of farm commodities was relatively stable from the mid-1920's to the mid-1930's at an index near 72 (1947-49 = 100), was exceptionally low in 1935, and thereafter increased steadily, reaching 82 in 1941 [USDA Ag. Handbook 62, 1962]. Per capita consumption decreased during the great depression and, although some gains were achieved in 1935-40, pre-depression levels were barely regained. Total consumption varied less than per capita consumption, owing to secular population growth.

The volume of U.S. agricultural exports was, on the average, lower in 1935-41 than during the depression years: exports decreased by nearly one-half with respect to the 1925-29 average [USDA FAS-M-76, 1960]. But the value of exports was only 7 percent lower during 1934-41 than in 1929-33 [USDA, Ag. Statistics, 1941-67]. Volume decreases reflected worldwide efforts for self-sufficiency, slow worldwide recuperation from the depression, and the widespread drought, which forced the U.S., traditionally a wheat exporter, to import wheat in excess of exports during 1934-36 for the first time since the Civil War.

Price-support legislation of the New Deal included loans on stored farm commodities. The major innovation in this context was the "nonrecourse loan" made available for corn and cotton as early as 1933 and generalized to other commodities in 1938. From the farmer's viewpoint, the federal government's power to build stocks became an additional source of demand. Stock changes in terms of net annual utilization of farm commodities were positive in every year between 1937 and 1941. By the end of 1941, the Commodity Credit Corporation (CCC), first organized in 1933, had accumulated substantial stocks of the three principal U.S. crops—wheat, cotton, and corn. Between 1934 and 1936, effective production controls and unfavorable weather had reduced cotton output, allowing the liquidation of some stocks held since 1932. However, high cotton price supports after 1937, not accompanied by strict production control, resulted in stock accumulation; between 1936 and 1939, nearly 10 million bales of cotton accumulated in CCC stocks, sufficient to provide normal consumption and exports for a year without any new crop [Benedict and Stine, 1956].

Between 1934 and 1936, wheat production was sufficiently affected by adverse weather conditions to require large imports, and the good harvest of 1937 was devoted to building normal carry-overs. Thus, between 1934 and 1937 there was no problem of overproduction of wheat and it was not covered by loan operations of the CCC. However, in 1938 a good domestic harvest and keen competition in world markets forced CCC into price stabilization operations for wheat. At year end, CCC owned 6 million bushels with an additional 21.5 million bushels under loan; during the following years, government programs failed to control, simultaneously, prices and output; and, at the end of 1941, 419 million bushels of wheat were either under loan or owned by CCC [Benedict and Stine, 1956].

Corn was (like cotton) one of the first crops placed under a nonrecourse loan program (1933) and a substantial quantity was pledged to CCC. When the very poor harvests of 1934 and 1936 eliminated corn surpluses, most corn placed as security under CCC was redeemed, but as weather conditions improved after 1936, attempts to support prices and control output so as not to accumulate carry-overs again became impossible. Although less acreage was planted, yields rose sufficiently to increase CCC holdings of corn to 403 million bushels at the end of 1941 [Benedict and Stine, 1956].

Between 1942 and 1947 carry-overs of all crops decreased, despite increased production. Two forces accounted for the large disappearances.

1. The volume of U.S. agricultural exports picked up momentum with the initiation of Lend-Lease arrangements in October 1941. The total volume of exports was no higher, however, than that of 1929-33 and clearly lower than during the earlier 1920's [USDA FAS-M-76, 1960]. USDA purchases for exports to fulfill Lend-Lease commitments accounted for between 2 and 5 percent of yearly food disappearances between 1942 and 1947. Together, commercial exports and USDA purchases for export amounted to about 5 percent per year of the total supply of United States food, a larger amount than at any time since 1925. The USDA contribution to these foreign deliveries was about 85 percent of the total.

2. Domestic consumption increased, owing to population growth, substantial increases in per capita consumption, and military needs. U.S. population, including our armed forces overseas, was about 7 percent larger in 1947 than in 1942, and had increased 16 percent from 1934 to 1947 [USDA FAS-M-76, 1960]. Per capita food consumption reached an average index of 104.4 in 1942-47 (1947-49 = 100), higher than for any other previous six consecutive years since 1917 [USDA Ag. Handbook 62, 1962]. The per capita consumption increase was principally in response to income redistribution toward sectors with higher propensity to consume farm products, a narrow range of choices open to consumers as a result of the diversion of resources to war production and the feeding of the armed forces.

This domestic and foreign demand had depleted carry-overs by the end of World War II: wheat carry-overs from 631 million bushels to 196 million; corn from 422 million bushels to 252 million; and cotton from 11 million bales to 3 million [USDA Ag. Statistics, 1941-67]. Further, the U.S. population increase continued—by about 10 percent between 1948 and 1954; this was almost the same rate as farm output's increase [Banks, Beale, and Bowles, 1963]. This and the increase in per capita incomes caused domestic disappearance to increase, although income growth is a weak force in that direction at high-income levels.

Exports of agricultural commodities were at unprecedented high levels between 1948 and 1951. The quantity index of agricultural exports reached 125 in 1950 (1952-54 = 100) and was an average 116 during 1948-51 [USDA FAS-M-76, 1960]. High exports during these four years resulted from Marshall Plan purchases and, beginning in 1950, from Korean War pressures.

Thus, until 1952, domestic and foreign disappearances absorbed the high production of U.S. farms. A few carry-overs, especially of corn, cotton, and wheat, developed between 1948 and 1950 when the earlier heavy need for postwar relief activities slowed, but between 1950 and 1952 carry-overs were mostly depleted. After 1952 they began to build rapidly, and, sometime between 1952 and 1953, total disappearance became insufficient relative to total supply at "acceptable" prices.

The phenomenal increase in carry-overs of the period immediately following the Korean War was brought under control during the second half of the 1950's. Carry-over costs, expressed as "investment in price-support loans and inventories as of end of fiscal year" remained around $7 billion per year between 1955 and 1964. Then, during 1965 and 1966, a trend toward depletion of carry-overs began to appear [USDA CCC Charts, 1967]. Data for 1967 show that "investments in price supports" were less than 3.5 billion dollars. Part of the credit is due to aggressive programs of foreign disposal to fill the international food gap.

The average quantity index of agricultural exports (1952-54 = 100) during 1948-53 was 70, increased to 105 in 1955-62 (a gain of 50 percent), and later rose to 137 in 1960-66 [USDA FAS-M-76, 1960]. Animal and animal products exports increased by more than 70 percent on the average during 1955-66 relative to 1948-53, with exports of poultry products doubling. Relative to 1948-53, yearly exports of grain and feed increased more than twofold during 1955-66. Exports during 1954-62 were a positive force in increasing disappearance; a substantial portion of the export increase is attributed to government policies. After the Korean War only about 45 percent of the value of U.S. agricultural exports moved through strictly regular channels [Menzie and Witt, 1962].

FARM INCOME

A comprehensive income picture, according to Hicks [1941], includes the amount that income recipients can consume without impoverishing themselves. This concept implies that, in addition to the rewards that resource owners receive for the use of their resources, income should include changes in asset values. Income is termed *conventional* if it does not include changes in the value of wealth due to price changes; if it does include such changes, it is referred to as *nonconventional* [Boyne, 1964]. Both conventional and nonconventional income are expressed in real terms by means of an appropriate deflator. Annual estimates of conventional and nonconventional farm income and government payments, both real and nominal, are shown in Table 10.

Nominal net income originating in agriculture for the period 1917-29 was at its highest value of $12,037 million in 1919.[2] By 1921, it had fallen to less than

---

[2] Net income is defined here as the sum of realized net income (excluding government payment), total farm wages, interest on farm mortgages, net rents (excluding government payment), and the net changes in crop and livestock inventories.

TABLE 10. Net Income Originating in Agriculture, Change in Asset Position of Agriculture, Government Payments and Total Farm Income, Nominal and Real, United States, 1917-1969

(millions of dollars)

Years	Net income Nominal	Real[a]	Changes in asset position Nominal	Real[a]	Government payments Nominal	Real[a]	Total farm income Nominal	Real[a]
1917	10,635	19,336	7,670	13,945	0	0	18,305	33,282
1918	11,525	18,008	5,756	8,994	0	0	17,281	27,002
1919	12,037	16,266	10,921	14,758	0	0	22,958	31,024
1920	10,663	12,399	−10,513	−12,224	0	0	150	174
1921	5,497	7,233	−10,377	−13,654	0	0	−4,880	−6,421
1922	6,518	9,053	− 287	− 399	0	0	6,231	8,654
1923	7,428	10,175	− 1,310	− 1,795	0	0	6,118	8,381
1924	7,270	9,959	149	204	0	0	7,419	10,163
1925	9,083	12,111	− 92	− 123	0	0	8,991	11,988
1926	8,290	10,908	− 1,999	− 3,630	0	0	6,291	8,278
1927	8,114	10,965	239	323	0	0	8,353	11,288
1928	8,357	11,448	417	571	0	0	8,774	12,019
1929	8,520	11,671	− 726	− 994	0	0	7,794	10,677
1917-29	8,764	12,272	− 12	537	0	0	8,753	12,808
1930	6,327	8,911	− 7,444	−10,485	0	0	−1,117	−1,573
1931	4,947	7,611	− 9,749	−14,998	0	0	−4,802	−7,388
1932	3,282	5,659	− 8,451	−14,571	0	0	−5,169	−8,912
1933	3,671	6,675	1,978	3,596	131	238	5,780	10,569
1930-33	4,557	7,214	− 5,916	− 9,114	33	59	1,327	−1,841
1934	3,842	6,740	2,449	4,296	446	782	6,737	11,819
1935	6,223	10,547	1,424	2,414	573	971	8,220	13,932
1936	5,645	9,568	1,875	3,178	278	471	7,798	13,217
1937	7,378	12,095	1,201	1,969	336	551	8,915	14,615
1938	5,532	9,220	− 1,626	− 2,710	446	743	4,352	7,253
1939	5,323	9,022	− 704	− 1,193	763	1,293	5,382	9,122
1940	5,529	9,215	1,091	1,818	723	1,205	7,343	12,238
1941	8,126	12,898	5,470	8,683	544	863	14,140	22,444
1934-41	5,950	9,913	1,397	2,307	514	860	7,861	13,080
1942	11,996	17,137	6,511	9,301	650	929	19,157	27,367
1943	14,408	19,470	6,561	8,866	645	872	21,614	29,208
1944	14,404	19,205	5,619	7,492	776	1,035	20,799	27,732
1945	15,154	19,681	5,337	6,931	742	964	21,233	27,575
1946	18,448	22,226	11,729	14,131	772	930	30,949	37,288
1942-46	14,882	19,544	7,151	9,344	717	946	22,750	29,834
1947	19,563	20,378	12,342	12,856	314	327	32,219	33,561
1948	21,999	21,358	1,655	1,607	257	250	23,911	23,215
1949	16,751	16,423	− 4,158	− 4,076	185	181	12,778	12,527
1950	17,698	17,183	16,190	15,718	283	275	34,171	33,176
1951	20,281	18,271	13,197	11,889	286	258	33,764	30,418
1952	19,372	16,993	− 5,628	− 4,937	275	241	14,019	12,297
1953	17,170	15,061	− 5,829	− 5,113	213	187	11,554	10,135
1954	16,372	14,237	2,380	2,070	257	223	19,009	16,530

TABLE 10. Continued

(millions of dollars)

Years	Net income		Changes in asset position		Government payments		Total farm income	
	Nominal	Real[a]	Nominal	Real[a]	Nominal	Real[a]	Nominal	Real[a]
1947–54	18,650	17,488	3,768	3,752	259	243	22,678	21,482
1955	15,309	13,429	2,235	1,961	229	201	17,773	15,590
1956	15,082	13,002	8,543	7,365	554	478	24,179	20,844
1957	14,554	12,128	11,014	9,178	1,016	847	26,584	22,153
1958	16,935	13,657	14,611	11,783	1,089	878	32,635	26,319
1959	15,237	12,190	407	326	682	546	16,326	13,061
1960	15,820	12,457	2,347	1,848	693	546	18,860	14,850
1961	16,139	12,609	8,216	6,419	1,484	1,159	25,839	20,182
1962	16,191	12,551	5,888	4,564	1,736	1,346	23,815	18,461
1955–62	15,658	12,753	6,658	5,431	935	750	23,251	18,932
1963	16,391	13,369	na	na	1,686	1,375	na	na
1964	15,039	12,267	na	na	2,169	1,636	na	na
1965	17,645	13,090	na	na	2,452	1,819	na	na
1966	17,906	12,900	na	na	3,277	2,361	na	na
1967	17,005	11,917	na	na	3,079	2,158	na	na
1968	17,269	11,613	na	na	3,462	2,328	na	na
1969	18,668	11,913	na	na	3,794	2,421	na	na
1963–69	17,132	12,439	na	na	2,846	2,014	na	na

Source: USDA [1962, 1965, 1967, and 1970, *Farm Income Situation*]; G. L. Johnson [1961, "An Evaluation of U.S. Agricultural Programs"].

na = Not available.

[a]Corresponding nominal figures deflated by the Consumer Price Index (1947–49 = 100).

50 percent of that peak. After 1921, and for the rest of the 1917-29 period, money income recovered somewhat, but, by 1929, it was still only 77 percent of the 1919 high. In real terms, net income originating in agriculture did not fluctuate as much as the nominal counterpart, indicating that this portion of income retained its purchasing power, but in 1920 and 1921 it fell considerably, relative to the rest of the period.

Nonconventional farm income fluctuated widely during the 1917-29 period. The value of durables in agriculture in current prices doubled between the censuses of 1910 and 1920. Appreciation was responsible for most of the increase, as the real growth in the volume of durables was only 10 percent in that period [Tostlebe, 1954]. Land that remained essentially unchanged in quantity was worth twice as much in current prices in 1920 as in 1910. Owners of land and other farm resources felt, and were, wealthier at the turn of the 1920's. Those who bid the price of assets up expected returns commensurable with the prices they were sanctioning. The collapse of farm prices in the early 1920's was followed by the collapse in the value of farm assets. In 1925, the value of farm durables in current dollars fell to $60.7 billion, a decline of about 28 percent from 1920 [ibid.]. Naturally, these sharp changes in the value of assets generated, alternatively, capital gains and losses. Glenn L. Johnson [1961] estimated that the capital gains that accrued to agriculture between 1917 and 1919 were about the same magnitude as the capital losses generated between 1920 and 1929; extending the comparison back to 1915, however, there were net capital gains during the 1915-29 interval.

Changes in the asset position of agriculture were positive in only six of the thirteen years of the 1917-29 period. In 1921 losses in the value of assets were larger than conventional farm income. About 95 percent of all positive changes in the value of farm assets occurred in 1917-19 during the war boom. In only three years after 1919 (during the 1917-29 period) were changes in the real values of farm assets positive. And in all three cases, gains were small.

Total farm income was negative during all but one year of the 1930-33 period.[3] More often than not, farmers were not able to consume without depleting their wealth. Negative total income resulted from large capital losses coupled with exceptionally low net farm income originating in agriculture.[4]

Prior to 1933, the burden of adjustment to changing economic conditions fell heavily on prices. During 1930-33, a 4 percent shrinkage in the physical volume of durables was accompanied by a depreciation of 33.2 percent in the value of the total stock [Tostlebe, 1954]. As a consequence, producers suffered large capital losses. Although capital gains and losses partially offset each other during 1917-29, in the overall 1917-33 period capital losses outweighed capital gains by over $23.5 billion.

Conventional gross farm income fell during 1930-33 as a direct consequence of a fall in the demand for agricultural commodities relative to their supply. Since the price elasticity of demand for agricultural products is low, the relative decrease in demand resulted in a greater proportionate fall in prices than in quantity taken. Thus, gross farm income fell. Prices paid by farmers did not fall in proportion to prices received. Therefore, net farm income decreased more than gross farm income. Since net farm income fell, while the total amount of resources engaged in agriculture remained fairly stable, resource earnings decreased and their values were lowered. Thus, holders of farm wealth received capital losses.

After many years of depression, farm incomes recovered somewhat in the 1934-41 period. Both "conventional" and "nonconventional" income increased

[3] The events occurring during 1933 are considered pre-"New Deal," since little if any of the new legislation had yet made impact during the calendar year of 1933.

[4] Net income originating in agriculture was lower relative to earlier years in both nominal and real terms. Further, 1930-33 was a period of net population inflow to agriculture, and thus per capita income must have fallen faster than total income.

nominally, as well as in real terms. Yearly real net income originating in agriculture was, on the average, 37 percent larger during 1934-41 than at the bottom of the great depression.

With the exception of 1938 and 1939, farm resource owners received capital gains during 1934-41; net changes in the current value of assets in agriculture in that period amounted to $8.8 billion, or a yearly gain of $1.3 billion. Glenn Johnson has reported [1961] that the highest appreciation rate took place in productive livestock. The value of "land and buildings" also increased, despite decreases in their physical stock. Small changes in the value of land and buildings led to substantial changes in farm wealth, since real estate typically represents more than 80 percent of all farm wealth.

Increases in land values in general are attributed not only to improvements in business expectations, but also to the inauguration of government programs. Larsen [1966] concluded from his study of the sources of changes in land values that a large part of the increase in land values was caused either by conservation expenditures or by factors strongly correlated with a conglomerate of expenditures related to conservation.

The "New Deal" brought a new element into the structure of farm income. Government payments grew from slightly over $100 million in 1933 to over $700 million at the end of 1940, or nearly 10 percent of net farm income. An expected stream of government payments represents wealth, the value of which is the present value of the stream of future payments.

In 1940-46, larger output and sustained demand for farm products resulted in a net income originating in agriculture that was higher than that in any previous period: it averaged $14.8 billion per year. Nominal income increased faster than the price level and thus resulted in real income gains.

The development of a favorable outlook for farming, coupled with inelasticities in the supply of factors of production and government payments, resulted in an upward revaluation of agricultural assets and consequently in capital gains to asset owners. When expressed in real terms the capital gains, however, were not as large on the average as during World War I, due primarily to a greater supply response during World War II.

Total income, i.e., the sum of conventional and nonconventional income, was higher than ever before. In real terms, average yearly total income in the 1934-41 period just matched the corresponding figures for the World War I period. But farm population decreased drastically during the interwar period, and per capita real farm income was substantially higher during 1942-47 than during 1917-19.

Average total income over 1947-54 was lower in both nominal and real terms than the average for the preceding period but particularly in real terms. Average total real income over the period, including conventional and nonconventional income plus government payments, was 35 percent lower than during 1942-46.

Beginning in 1947, farm income originating in agriculture decreased or increased at a slower pace than the general price level. Hence, during 1947-54, net income originating in agriculture fell in real terms. Government payments were smaller on the average during 1947-54 than during any previous period since 1933. Although product prices were a powerful force in determining land values, they were not the only force, nor apparently the most important. Larsen's analysis [1966] indicated that farm programs were a powerful influence on land values, particularly after World War II. The slowing of increases in land values in 1949, 1953, and 1954 coincided with decreases in government conservation expenditures, a variable that Larsen found particularly significant. Thus, smaller government payments were partially responsible, directly and indirectly via non-conventional income, for deterioration of total farm income.

Large capital gains in 1950 and 1951 were caused at least in part by the Korean War, but negative changes in asset values occurred in 1949, 1952, and 1953. Farmers were beginning to suffer the consequences of phenomenal over-investments made at the end of the depression and accentuated during the post World War II period. The downward re-evaluation of farm assets indicates that these investments were not capable of supporting earnings expected at the time they were committed to farm production.

Real farm income from all sources was lower on the average during 1955-62 than during 1947-54. Nominal income grew at a lower rate than the price level. Net income originating in agriculture was smaller on the average than in the previous period both in current and constant dollars, being 25 percent lower in terms of constant dollars. This loss was partially offset by larger government payments (which increased threefold relative to the yearly average of 1947-54). About 85 percent of the change in the value of assets in this period originated with real estate. And there is evidence that changes in the value of real estate are associated with government payments. Thus, the income position of farming in the late 1950's and early 1960's was very dependent upon government help. And recent estimates by Quance and Tweeten [1971] indicate that net farm income would fall to 50 percent of its 1969 level by 1980 if government diversion programs and payments were terminated.

ADJUSTMENTS IN RESOURCE USE

The changes in agricultural production, disappearance, and income discussed above are the visible results of more fundamental changes in resource use in American agriculture from 1917 to the present.

Changes in resource use in agriculture generally involve an increasing use of capital resources on a fairly constant land base and much less labor. Increases in total capital inputs, both absolutely and relative to labor and land, received a great deal of attention, but significant changes also occurred within the capital structure itself. Some inputs, such as horses and mules, declined from a position of great importance (26.7 million head in 1917) to such a level of insignificance that the USDA has discontinued including them in their farm input series. Pesticides as an input increased in importance from almost nil in 1917 to a sizable 770.9 million pounds in 1964. Many adjustments in the capital input mix within these extremes reflect the technological revolution in agriculture. Input changes involve shifts from durable to expendable, farm-produced to nonfarm-produced, labor-using to labor-saving, and generally a move to input supply specialization.

Rapid increases in the use of fertilizer, petroleum products, chemicals, and pesticides paced a large increase in expendable inputs as indicated by the index of operating expenses in Figure 8.[5] Prior to World War II, the stock of durable inputs remained fairly constant with mechanical power replacing horsepower.

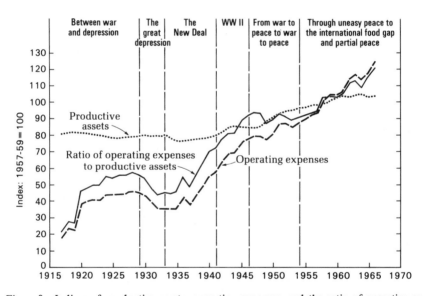

Figure 8. Indices of productive assets, operating expenses, and the ratio of operating expenses to productive assets, United States farm sector, 1917–1966. (*Source*: Operating expenses are from USDA Ag. Handbook 62, 1962. Productive assets were computed from data supplied by the Farm Production Economics Division, Economic Research Service, U.S. Department of Agriculture.)

Tractors on farms increased from 51,000 in 1917 to 1.02 million in 1932, while the number of horses and mules on farms decreased 8.9 million during the same period. Increased use of mechanical power caused the index of operating expenses (1957–59 = 100) to increase from 17.6 in 1917 to 57.1 in 1941 as

[5] Operating expenses include expenditures on feed, seed, livestock, fertilizer, and miscellaneous production inputs.

petroleum products and automotive supplies were required to fuel and maintain mechanical power and machinery. Expenditures on petroleum fuel and oil rose from $49.3 million in 1917 to $153.5 million in 1932 (1910–14 dollars).

Expendable inputs are more responsive to economic change than durables are. During the depression years, the index of productive assets remained fairly constant while the index of operating expenses decreased from 44.4 in 1929 to 34.7 in 1934. And when the economy began to recover from the depression, farmers were much quicker to expand operating inputs than durables. Part of the rapid increase in expendables was required to bring the stock of durables back to a high state of maintenance after considerable neglect during the depression.

With World War II came a general increase in both durables and expendable inputs. The increase in durables was no longer so much required to replace horses and mules as to replace the dwindling farm labor force and to increase output. Farm labor decreased by 31 index points from its 223 level in 1917 to 192 in 1941, but then decreased by 122 index points to a level of 70 in 1966 (1957–59 = 100); while the index of farm output increased from 55 in 1917 to 73 in 1931 and to 113 by 1966 [USDA SB 233, June 1968, pp. 16, 17].

Specialization between the farm and nonfarm sectors and within the farm sector has resulted in the substitution of purchased for nonpurchased inputs. The nonfarm sector exerted its comparative advantage in producing mechanical power and machinery, electricity, chemicals, fertilizers, and marketing and processing services. Within the farm sector, specialization took place along commodity lines. Grain producers now tend to specialize in grain, and livestock producers are specializing in some phase of livestock production. Some farmers produce feed grain, others with cow-calf operations produce calves, another group buys calves and produces stocker calves, and still another group purchases both the feed and calves and feeds the calves to slaughter weights. Rather than one farmer producing the calf and carrying it all the way to slaughter weight, the calf may be marketed two or three times before reaching the slaughter house. These and other kinds of specialization have resulted in farmers purchasing a greater share of total inputs. Only during the depressions of the early 1930's when earnings were low and during World War II when inputs were scarce did the ratio of purchased to nonpurchased inputs reverse its upward trend (Figure 9).

The rapid increase in labor-saving technology and the corresponding decrease in farm labor resulted in an increase in output per man hour from an overall index of 25 in 1917 to 182 in 1968 (1957–59 = 100). In the production of some formerly labor-intensive enterprises the production of which is now mechanized, the increase in output per man hour was fantastic. Total man hours used for farm work decreased from 23.75 million hours in 1917 to 7.0 million in 1968 [USDA SB 233, June 1969, p. 14] with farm output more than two times larger in 1968 than in 1917.

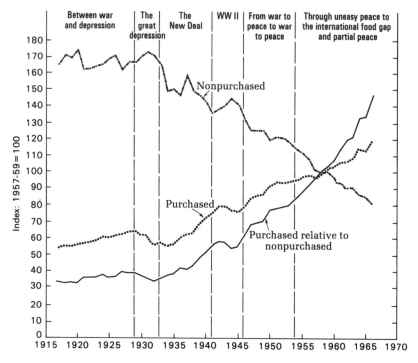

Figure 9. Indices of the use of purchased, nonpurchased, and ratio of purchased to nonpurchased inputs, United States farm sector, 1917–1966. (*Source*: USDA SB 233, June 1968, p. 16.)

The farm sector is an economic subsystem with many variables interacting simultaneously and it is difficult to separate causes of resource adjustments from impacts of the adjustments. However, most economists agree that decreasing acquisition costs of capital inputs relative to their productivity, rising wage rates, scarcity of land, and the availability of land substitutes encourage capital intensification of American agriculture.

Because traditional research in agricultural economics is oriented around the usual neoclassical economic theory of the firm, data on resource prices are not specific as to whether they represent acquisition costs or salvage values. And with much price data representing farm values, it is unclear as to whether prices are acquisition, salvage, or use values. But available price data, illustrated in Figure 10, indicate that, since 1934, the prices of capital inputs decreased relative to prices received by farmers. Correspondingly, the index of total capital used increased from 78 in 1917 to almost 500 in 1964 (1917 = 100).[6] De-

[6] Estimates of capital inputs were aggregated by Quance [from data in USDA, July 1967, Farm Income Situation]. The total includes: (1) farm depreciation and other capital con-

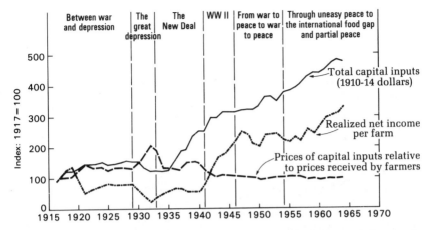

Figure 10. Indices of total capital inputs and prices of capital inputs relative to prices received by farmers, United States, 1917–1964. (*Source*: See footnote 7, this chapter.)

clining capital prices relative to product prices and productivity encourage increased use of capital inputs in output-increasing adjustments and an upward trend in realized net income per farm.

Land in farms increased only 150 million acres from 956 million acres in 1920 to 1,106 in 1964. The value of farm real estate, however, although fluctuating in the short run, more than tripled from $48.81 per acre in 1917 to $157.00 in 1966. The rapid substitution of capital for land, illustrated in Figure 11, is an output-increasing adjustment that began about 1935 during the big depression. The increasing price of land relative to prices paid for capital inputs since World War II greatly encouraged capital land substitution. And, as is pointed out in Chapter 9, farm enlargement is a force pushing land values up.

Off-farm opportunities for farm labor and the declining farm labor force are studied in detail in Chapter 8. Total man-hours required for all farm work declined from 23,751 million hours in 1917 to 6,998 million man-hours in 1968

---

sumption expenditures, with the exception that those changes for farm operator's dwellings and automobiles were excluded; (2) current farm expenditures on fertilizer, lime, and operation and repairs of capital items, with the exception that repairs and operation of farm operators' dwellings are excluded; (3) government payments for conservation practices (government payments were doubled to account for matching expenditures by farmers); (4) expenses for purchasing livestock, and (5) expenditures for feed and seed. Prices of capital inputs are the index of prices paid by farmers for all commodities bought for use in production [USDA Ag. Statistics, 1965, Table 684, and 1957, Table 681]. Prices received by farmers are from USDA Ag. Statistics, 1965, Table 683, and 1957, Table 680. Land inputs are from USDA SB 233, June 1968, p. 6. Land prices are from USDA, December 1964, Ag. Finance Review, Table 35, page 63. Data on the labor input are from USDA SB 233 1965, Changes in Farm Production ..., Table 17, p. 31. The farm wage rate is from USDA Ag. Statistics, 1965, Table 649, and 1957, Table 681.

Figure 11. Indices of price of farm land relative to prices paid for capital inputs and capital use relative to land input, United States, 1917–1964. (*Source:* See footnote 7, this chapter.)

Figure 12. Indices of farm wage rate relative to prices paid for capital inputs and capital inputs relative to labor input, United States, 1917–1964. (*Source:* See footnote 7, this chapter.)

[USDA SB 233, June 1969, p. 14]. Figure 12 illustrates the rapid increase in capital relative to labor inputs, a trend that began about 1933 when the U.S. economy began to recover from the depression and wage rates began to increase absolutely and relative to prices paid for capital inputs. The replacement of capital for labor in farm production was both an output-increasing and labor-substituting adjustment.

The ability of U.S. farmers to more than double farm output from 1917 to 1968 on about the same land area—with one-third the amount of labor—indicates the magnitude of increased use of land substitutes on American farms. Figure 13 indicates that while the index of farm output increased from 55 in 1917 to 120 in 1968, the index of production inputs increased only 22 points from 89 in 1917 to 111 in 1966. The resulting productivity index almost doubled from 1917 to 1968. It was with increases in labor-saving and land-saving capital inputs that American farmers could continue to increase production on limited land and with much less labor.

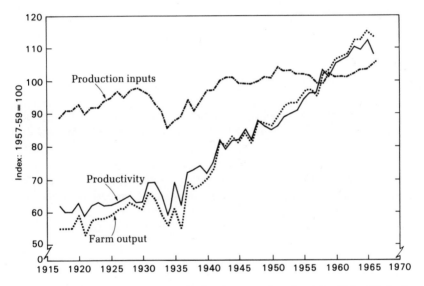

Figure 13. Indices of farm output, production inputs, and productivity, United States farm sector, 1917–1966. (*Source*: USDA SB 233, June 1968, p. 17.)

The above discussion of changes in the farm sector's input structure and the causes and impacts of these changes is a general overall view. In the following three chapters, causes and impacts of adjustments in capital, labor, and land categories are studied in detail.

CHAPTER 7

Capital

C. LEROY QUANCE

The overall view of agriculture in Chapter 6 indicated that, in general, resource adjustments from 1917 to 1968 involved the use of additional and different capital inputs such that farm output more than doubled from about the same land area but with less than one-third the labor required in 1917. And within the capital structure itself, changes involved shifts from durable to expendable, from farm-produced to nonfarm-produced, and from labor-using to labor-saving inputs. Overall trends were discussed in Chapter 6; here we examine causes and/or impacts of adjustments in the productivity and use of specific capital inputs.

Whereas relative input prices were given in Chapter 6 as market incentives for adjustments in the farm input mix, relative productivities are offered here as the technological incentive and/or impact of increased use of capital inputs, both absolute and relative to land and labor. Resulting capital earnings and capital gains or losses are the end result of an imperfect adjustment process. There is a significant, but differing over time, correspondence between the estimated results of these imperfections and the characteristics of American agriculture that were discussed in Chapter 2.

A NOTE ON EMPIRICAL TECHNIQUES

A fundamental problem in studying adjustments in the use of farm capital is that physical capital assumes meaning only within a given set of prices and for a given technological and institutional framework. And, in the progressive U.S. economy, this meaning undergoes constant change. This point was amply illustrated by Alvin S. Tostlebe [1957] in his groundbreaking study of durable capital in the U.S. farm sector. Data series developed by Tostlebe provide the basis for many current series on capital inputs in the farm sector.

Concerning the measuring of capital inputs, Griliches [December 1960, p. 1411] chastises the USDA for using commodity definitions in such vague general terms as "most commonly bought by farmers." He estimates, for example, that "quality change" accounts for between one-third and two-thirds of the actual change in list prices of some automobiles in the periods 1937–50 and 1950–59.

Our study avoids the index problem so critical in measuring capital inputs in deflated expenditure series by measuring inputs where possible in numbers on farms, thus making the quality problem more explicit. In estimating machine numbers, for example, all machines, large or small, new or old, those used 1,000 hours and those not used at all, count as one. Some have attempted to measure such farm machinery as tractors in horsepower units, but progress in this direction is slow.

Although Griliches endorses the declining balance method of depreciating capital inputs used by the USDA, he believes the rates of depreciation (trucks, 21 percent, tractors, 18.5 percent, and other farm machinery and equipment, 14 percent) are too high. Rather than rates derived from used machinery prices, as Griliches suggests, the USDA decided on rates by the arbitrary criterion that the resulting rate depreciates the item to 5 percent of its original value by the time its "useful" life is up [Griliches, p. 1421]. Griliches believes that the USDA underestimates stocks of tractors by about 75 percent, and underestimates other classes of machines by varying smaller percentages. But with census data to use as bench marks, it is not likely that USDA figures err as much as Griliches estimates.

The changing quality of capital inputs is not as critical as might be expected in our study. Each year is, in effect, a separate study with production elasticities estimated on an annual basis. Inasmuch as the underlying Cobb-Douglas production function involves constant elasticities over all combinations of inputs, annual differences in elasticities serve to shift the production function owing to changing technology and input quality. And because each year of the analysis is essentially a separate study with a particular input of one year of different quality from the same input in name of another year, nominal input prices reflecting quality changes are used.

Production Elasticities

A Nerlove-type adjustment model is employed to estimate equilibrium factor shares which are used as parameters in assumed underlying Cobb-Douglas production functions in lieu of the more conventional direct least-squares method of obtaining production parameters. The adjustment-equilibrium factor share model lends itself to implementing modifications of neoclassical theory that recognize the divergence between input acquisition costs and salvage values.[1]

MVP's, Present Values, Economic Rents, and Capital Gains or Losses

Given the production elasticity estimates, usual procedures are followed in estimating annual marginal value products (MVP's), both gross and net of overhead costs. Net MVP's over the lifespan of durables are then discounted to obtain ex post present values. But farm managers base investment and utilization decisions on comparisons between (1) acquisition costs and salvage values of inputs and (2) expected MVP's and hence ex ante present values. Thus, estimates of expected or ex ante present values are useful in understanding overcommitment or undercommitment of durable inputs to the farm sector.

In obtaining estimates of ex ante present values, we assume that farmers expect constant production elasticities and input stocks over the life of inputs. It then follows that expected output remains constant and all that remains to estimate expected MVP's and present values is to employ Lerohl's concept (see Chapter 5) of expected future product prices and overhead costs rather than their actual values.

In keeping with the economic theory outlined in our Chapter 3, economic rent and capital gains or losses are defined with respect to the relationship between the marginal factor flow and acquisition costs. For *expendable inputs*, the difference between MVP's and acquisition costs yields estimates of economic rent per unit. If MVP's are greater than acquisition costs, positive rents ensue and it is profitable to expand use of the input. When MVP's are less than salvage values, inputs earn negative rents, part of which are eliminated by selling the input at its salvage value.

Durable inputs with ex post present values greater than acquisition costs represent capital gains which are expected to disappear as stocks of the inputs are profitably increased. When ex post present values are less than acquisition costs but greater than salvage values, owners of such durables sustain unavoidable capital losses. Durables with ex post present values less than salvage values are salvaged to minimize capital losses.

[1] Fred H. Tyner and Luther G. Tweeten [1965] advocate using adjustment models in estimating production parameters. For a more detailed explanation of the technique as applied in our study, see Quance [1967]. Briefly, the assumption is that each year farmers adjust the use of an input by a constant proportion of the desired adjustment if use of the resource were to reach that level equating the ex post present value with the input acquisition cost, or salvage value, depending on whether expansion or contraction is under consideration. The validity of this assumption is more critical to the intensive than to the extensive aspects of our measurements. The term "present value" is used to represent the discounted present value of future marginal value products net of overhead costs.

The capital gain or loss for a durable input is the excess or deficiency of the durable's ex post present value over its acquisition cost. To estimate capital gains or losses to purchasers of a durable of a specific type in a specific year, the capital gain or loss per unit of the durable in a specific year is multiplied by the total quantity acquired in that year.[2] However, in accordance with the assumption of linear depreciation over n years, $100/n$ percent of the stock of durables is assumed replaced each year. Thus, if the capital gain or loss per unit of a durable is first multiplied by the total number of that type of durable on farms and then divided by the expected life of the durable, a rough estimate is obtained of the capital gains and losses eventually incurred, ex post, on the quantity of the durable acquired in that year.

These empirical techniques involve many mathematical abstractions which are, of course, imperfect representations of reality; we cannot correctly specify mathematical equations that will reflect the true production relationships and accurately measure prices, quantities, expectations, impact of weather, and other important variables. Nevertheless, mathematical abstractions used in conjunction with the economic theory presented in Chapter 3 furnish the best available indicators of the causes and impacts of continuous adjustments in dynamic U.S. agriculture.

TECHNOLOGICAL INCENTIVES

Because agriculture is an economic subsystem with many variables interacting simultaneously, it is difficult to separate causes of adjustments from impacts. However, corresponding to the relative input prices discussed in Chapter 6—i.e., the market incentives and/or the results of changing the input mix—there are corresponding technological aspects.

Land-Saving Capital

Prior to World War II, the increase in capital inputs was primarily a labor-saving adjustment. But the rapid increase in land values since World War II was accompanied by the addition of land substitutes to the relatively fixed supply of land. The most direct substitution of capital for land was through increased use of fertilizers.

Fertilizer use had remained relatively low until World War II. On the average during the war, the acquisition cost of a ton of fertilizer nutrients (elemental N, P, and K) could purchase the service of 11 acres (Table 11). But a land investment equivalent to only 10.73 acres was required to replace a ton of fertilizer in

_____

[2]To validate this procedure of aggregating economic rents and capital gains or losses across all inputs in a particular category, the estimated MVP's must be viewed as MVP's for the average input unit in the farm sector.

TABLE 11. Ratios of Acquisition Costs and Marginal Physical Products (MPP's) of Selected Capital Inputs to Acquisition Costs and MPP's of Selected Substitute Inputs, Averages for Specified Periods, U.S. Farm Sector, 1917–1964

Period	Relative acquisition costs (P) and MPP's for:[a]							
	P (tractor): P (horse)	MPP (tractor): MPP (horse)	P (tractor): P (labor)	MPP (tractor): MPP (labor)	P (corn): P (milk cow)	MPP (corn): MPP (milk cow)	P (fert.): P (land)	MPP (fert.): MPP (land)
From WWI to the crash (1917–29)	5.60	83.70	0.32	4.79	1.96	2.14	6.38	6.25
From 1930 to the bottom (1930–33)	7.50	29.80	.49	1.74	1.59	1.82	5.64	5.82
The New Deal (1934–41)	5.60	6.70	.51	.68	2.17	3.42	9.04	8.40
WWII (1942–46)	9.70	11.50	.34	.48	1.70	2.16	11.00	10.73
From war to peace to war to peace (1947–54)	14.70	19.20	.26	.49	1.35	1.54	6.25	5.79
Through uneasy peace to the international food gap and partial war (1955–64)	14.90	10.60	.25	.32	1.05	1.15	3.05	2.82

Source: Quance [1967].

[a]The price (P) is the acquisition cost of the *service* of one tractor, one horse, 1,000 hours of labor, one ton of corn, one milk cow, one ton of fertilizer, or one acre of land. Marginal physical products (MPP's) are based on the same units as acquisition costs.

production. Thus, it was slightly profitable for farmers to substitute land for fertilizer. With limited land, the acquisition cost of land was bid up rapidly while fertilizer acquisition costs decreased. By 1955-62, the acquisition cost of a ton of elemental nutrients relative to the acquisition cost of land decreased to an average 3.05. But continual use of fertilizer in lieu of more land in output-increasing adjustments caused the MPP of a ton of fertilizer to decrease, relative to the MPP of land investment, to an average 2.82 during 1955-62. Thus, fertilizer was apparently overcommitted relative to land in the short run, al-though, since World War II, decreasing fertilizer costs relative to land costs have encouraged increased use of fertilizer, at least on private account. The apparent short-run overcommitment of fertilizer relative to land probably resulted from (1) acreage allotments restricting the number of acres a farmer could plant but not the amount of fertilizer he could use, and (2) insufficient land available at recorded market prices in the vicinity of individual farmers' current holdings.

Labor-saving Capital

Total man hours required for all farm work declined from 23,751 million in 1917 to 593 million in 1966 [USDA, June 1970, SB 233]. A linear projection of the farm labor force indicates the United States would not have any farmers by 1982!

Estimated MPP's of the services of one tractor in aggregate farm production relative to the MPP's of 1,000 hours of labor decreased from an average 4.79 in the 1917-29 period to an average 0.32 in the 1955-64 period as tractors were substituted for more expensive labor (Table 11). As the nonfarm economy ex-panded and forced farm wages up, the acquisition cost of the services of a tractor relative to the acquisition cost of 1,000 hours labor decreased from an average .32 during 1917-29 to an average .25 during the 1955-64 period. Since tractors remain a relatively cheaper source of labor services than workers whose acquisition cost and salvage value continue to increase, the substitution of tractors for labor will likely continue. But the substitution of tractors for labor is now becoming such that larger tractors are substituted for both labor and smaller tractors. Estimates of prices and MPP's of other types of farm machinery relative to labor indicate a similar incentive to substitute labor-saving capital for labor. (Off-farm opportunities for farm labor and the declining farm labor force are considered in detail in Chapter 8.)

Increasing Productivity

Production elasticities and annual percentage changes in them for selected capital inputs are averaged over specified periods in Table 12. The estimates generally reflect the greater productivity of new forms of capital embodying new farm technology. Production appears more responsive to expendable inputs than

TABLE 12. Elasticities of Production and Percentage Changes in Elasticities of Production for Specified Inputs, Averages for Specified Periods, U.S. Farm Sector, 1917–1964

Classification and input	From WWI to the crash (1917–29)		From 1930 to the bottom (1930–33)		The New Deal (1934–41)		WWII (1942–46)		From war to peace to war to peace (1947–54)		Through uneasy peace to the int'l food gap to partial war (1955–64)	
	Elast. of prod.	% Δ in elast.	Elast. of prod.	% Δ in elast.	Elast. of prod.	% Δ in elast.	Elast. of prod.	% Δ in elast.	Elast. of prod.	% Δ in elast.	Elast. of prod.	% Δ in elast.
Durables												
Nonfarm-produced												
Specialized												
Tractors	.020	23.4	.046	-9.1	.020	40.2	.029	11.3	.041	62.0	.043	-2.5
Grain combines	.001	42.9	.002	44.0	.004	3.1	.004	1.8	.100	19.4	.016	.4
Pickup balers[a]	–	–	–	–	–	–	.001	26.7	.006	65.4	.003	5.3
Forage harvesters[b]	–	–	–	–	–	–	–	–	.013	73.7	.005	-7.4
Buildings	.098	14.9	.177	15.3	.094	-4.4	.050	7.5	.070	5.5	.072	-1.8
Tractors in wheat prod.	.023	43.6	.126	42.5	.082	2.6	.032	18.4	.044	35.0	.059	9.1
Grain combines in wheat prod.	.001	60.6	.007	48.7	.011	5.9	.011	-6.3	.020	21.1	.046	5.6
Tractors in corn prod.	.032	39.5	.122	62.2	.052	30.4	.040	-19.9	.066	94.9	.081	-.6
Corn pickers	.001	46.3	.005	29.7	.006	3.0	.005	3.1	.018	30.9	.044	4.6
Unspecialized												
Motor trucks	.007	14.4	.021	9.5	.014	1.5	.013	7.1	.025	12.6	.033	.4
Farm-produced												
Specialized												
Horses and mules	.350	0.02	.308	7.2	.198	-9.7	.084	-11.2	.034	-8.1	.025	-7.7

Unspecialized												
Beef cows	.129	−.9	.164	4.4	.153	−.9	.184	4.2	.193	−.2	.204	−.6
Milk cows	.257	2.0	.210	−10.8	.196	3.5	.234	−2.4	.233	2.2	.190	−.6
Expendables												
Nonfarm-produced												
Specialized												
Fertilizer	.022	1.1	.022	−5.5	.023	4.9	.024	−.5	.028	5.4	.035	.7
Unspecialized												
Gasoline	.018	15.2	.033	13.1	.035	−.8	.027	−5.3	.038	7.9	.045	−1.6
Electricity^c	–	–	.006	23.9	.007	6.1	.007	−1.6	.011	12.8	–	–
Farm-produced												
Specialized												
Hay in beef prod.	.101	−4.0	.092	13.2	.099	−2.1	.154	16.1	.152	−.01	.170	−2.6
Hay in milk prod.	.515	.2	.232	−24.7	.202	9.4	.262	8.4	.328	−1.2	.272	6.0
Unspecialized												
Corn in beef prod.	.072	−2.4	.076	22.2	.097	−2.0	.112	6.8	.110	−3.9	.090	−2.6
Heifers in beef prod.	.132	−1.2	.150	1.3	.185	−2.0	.193	3.4	.213	−2.2	.216	.2
Steers in beef prod.	.312	−3.1	.323	−.8	.315	−2.0	.322	4.3	.312	−4.6	.325	1.8
Corn in milk prod.	.095	62.7	.068	54.9	.111	54.4	.134	8.9	.100	−2.6	.101	3.4
Dairy heifers in milk prod.	.154	5.1	.129	−12.5	.133	8.9	.168	−1.8	.198	2.1	.176	2.3
Corn in pork prod.	.768	15.0	.622	66.4	.700	20.9	.459	10.2	.492	−4.1	.492	1.8
Sows in pork prod.	.266	−9.5	.203	4.8	.149	.6	.138	4.6	.166	−1.1	.146	−.8
Feeder pigs in pork prod.	.105	−5.0	.097	−1.3	.100	−3.2	.099	3.0	.094	2.2	.107	2.8
Corn in poultry prod.	.305	−1.6	.275	−31.5	.249	25.4	.248	15.2	.200	14.6	.189	−6.0
Chickens in poultry prod.	.297	2.4	.351	2.7	.272	−2.5	.205	3.11	.183	−1.6	.133	−.6

Source: Quance [1967].

[a]Available data permit estimates for pickup balers beginning in 1945.

[b]Available data permit estimates for forage harvesters beginning in 1948.

[c]Available data permit estimates for electricity from 1929 to 1955.

to durables and also more responsive to livestock inputs than to machinery, feed, gasoline, fertilizer, and buildings. This latter phenomenon generally reflects the intensification of farm production with respect to nonlivestock inputs. (One exception is the high response of milk production to hay fed.) Production response to mechanical power and machinery generally increased after 1917, while response to horsepower decreased. Production elasticities with respect to livestock generally remained stable over time, while elasticities with respect to farm machinery and expendables increased. This reflects the rapid technological advances in machinery and complementary expendables compared to more conventional livestock inputs. Elasticities with respect to livestock, feed, and nonfarm-produced expendables fluctuate as their use is varied in response to economic conditions. And the more important an input is in production in terms of its factor share, the more responsive is output to changes in its use.

But just as labor-saving and land-saving capital inputs are extending available supplies of land and replacing labor, newer and more productive capital inputs are replacing less efficient capital inputs. One great phenomenon in the farm sector was the virtually complete transition from horsepower to tractor power. After reaching a peak of nearly 27 million head in 1918, the number of horses and mules continually declined; by 1960 there were about 3 million head. Average estimates in Table 11 for 1917 to 1929 indicate that the services of one tractor cost the equivalent of the services of 5.6 horses and/or mules. But estimated MPP's indicate that one tractor could replace 83.7 horses and mules in aggregate farm production without altering output. As tractors were substituted for the animal power, their relative prices increased and relative MPP's decreased. However, with relative MPP's of tractors generally larger than their relative prices through the 1947–54 period, it is evident that horses and mules could not profitably substitute for tractors as a source of power.

The substitution of mechanical power for horsepower on U.S. farms was a type of specialization. The nonfarm sector produced mechanical power units at a lower cost relative to productivity than the farm sector could produce horses and mules. Thus, farmers were provided with a more profitable source of power which, at the same time, freed 77 million acres of cropland for producing food and fiber for human consumption.

Developing new inputs which profitably substitute for older inputs and labor was more dramatic in crop production than in livestock production. There is a strong need for feed crops to produce livestock for which demand increases with increases in per capita income and population. Feed prices decreased relative to acquisition costs of livestock inputs, thus providing incentives to breed livestock that are more efficient at converting feed to livestock products and to feed *fewer* animals *more* feed. In comparing MPP's and prices of corn relative to MPP's and prices of livestock inputs, the incentive was to substitute corn for livestock in beef, milk, hog, and poultry production (the estimates in Table 11 are, however, only for the substitution of corn for milk cows in producing milk). By 1964 the number of milk cows had decreased 24 percent from their World War II level, and corn fed to dairy animals increased 35 percent over the same period.

IMPACT OF THE CHANGING
CAPITAL STRUCTURE

In the paragraphs above we have documented the incentives for farm operators to replace relatively higher-priced labor and land with various forms of farm and nonfarm produced capital. But characteristics of the farm sector and its environment, as discussed in Chapter 2, result in imperfect adjustments. For example, farmers allocate resources under conditions of imperfect knowledge and foresight. Adjustments are likely made in the right direction, but due to erroneous expectations—either from imperfect knowledge of prices and production functions existing at the time of investment or from failure to foresee changes in technical and economic productivity of inputs over their productive life—capital resources committed to farm production earn MVP's and present values that often fall short of acquisition costs. The economic fixity of resources which result from such imperfect knowledge and foresight provides further incentive to use more land-saving and labor-saving capital as a loss-minimizing adjustment.

Usual methods of imputing returns to farm labor and management indicate that if investments in land and capital were paid a going rate of return, residual returns to labor and management would be low and often negative on typical farms. Our study provides substantial evidence that in many cases investments in farm capital do not earn a going rate of return, and this situation, in turn, accounts for much of the negative rent, capital losses, and low income in the farm sector. Important characteristics determining resource adjustability are durability, source of supply, the differential between acquisition cost and salvage value, degree of specialization, and technical relationships with labor and land.

Durables

Durable inputs are subject to considerable adjustment rigidities because (1) they last more than one production period; (2) durables are committed to farm production on the basis of expected product prices and input earnings which usually either fall short of, or exceed, realized product prices and input earnings; and (3) characteristics of durables, the farm sector, and the farm sector's environment cause divergencies between acquisition costs and salvage values.

Prices of certain farm-produced durables such as breeding stock are closely correlated with prices received by farmers, while prices paid for nonfarm-produced durables are fairly independent of prices received. Estimates for three farm-produced durables are averaged over specified periods in Table 13. These estimates indicate that from World War I to 1929, expected present values of

TABLE 13. Farm-Produced Durable Capital: Annual Average Employment and Earnings for Specified Inputs and Periods, United States, 1917–1964.

Period and Input	Animals on farms		Acquisition cost		Average level of Present values				Capital gains
					Expected		Actual		
	No.	Δ in no.	Cost[a] per animal	Δ in cost[a]	Value per animal	Δ in value[a]	Value per animal	Δ in value[a]	
	million head		$		$		$		mil. $
From WWI to the crash (1917–29)									
Horses and mules	24.4	–.58	90	–	252	+ –	71	+ –	–.11
Beef cows[b]	10.8	–.41	43	+	76	+ –	74	+ –	.06
Milk cows[b]	22.2	.14	32	– +	64	+	69	+ –	.15
From 1930 to the bottom (1930–33)									
Horses and mules	18.2	–.60	62	–	383	+	66	+	–.04
Beef cows	10.2	.58	22	–	64	–	47	–	.05
Milk cows	24.4	.88	23	–	57	–	43	–	.13
The New Deal (1934–41)									
Horses and mules	15.5	–.40	91	–	218	+	83	+	–.02
Beef cows	11.0	.01	26	+	65	+	74	+	.10
Milk cows	25.3	–.06	7	–	49	+	60	+	.27

WWII (1942–46)

Horses and mules	12.5	−.60	85	+ −	96	−	89	−	.01
Beef cows	15.0	1.25	47	0	124	+	136	+	.27
Milk cows	27.1	.22	30	+	101	+	109	+	.43

From war to peace to war to peace (1947–54)

Horses and mules	7.4	−.79	63	+ −	133	+	85	+	.03
Beef cows	19.1	1.08	131	+ −	180	+	188	+ −	.22
Milk cows	24.0	−.32	104	+ −	163	+ −	158	+ −	.26

Through uneasy peace and the international food gap to partial war (1955–64)

Horses and mules	3.6	−.28	82	−	285	−	99c	c	.03
Beef cows	26.9	.68	110	+ −	178	− +	188	+d	.43
Milk cows	20.7	−.58	113	+	163	+ −	166	+d	.32

Source: Quance [1967].

aThe discounted salvage value of the canner-cutler was subtracted from the acquisition cost of beef and milk cows.

bAvailable data permitted estimates for beef and dairy cows beginning in 1923.

cAvailable data and the discounting technique permit MVP estimates for horses and mules only through 1960 and estimates of capital values and capital gains through 1956.

cAvailable data and the discounting technique permit MVP estimates through 1964 and actual capital value and capital gains estimates through 1960.

dAvailable data and the discounting technique permit MVP estimates through 1964 and actual capital value and capital gains estimates through 1960.

farm-produced durables were decreasing but did exceed (except for milk cows) decreasing ex post present values. Present values exceeded acquisition costs (except for horses and mules), and modest capital gains resulted for beef and dairy cows while owners of horses and mules received capital losses. From 1930 to the bottom of the depression, present values continued to lag expectations, and capital gains on beef and dairy cows were low. After the depression and through World War II, rising present values began to exceed expectations and owners of beef and milk cows began to receive significant capital gains (according to our estimates). Following World War II, present values and acquisition costs of beef and milk cows fluctuated considerably.

When there is a competing demand for farm-produced durables in the nonfarm sector, ex ante present values in farming are compared to off-farm salvage values and input use is adjusted accordingly. Thus, ex post present values of unspecialized durables are kept more in line with acquisition costs and a reasonable rate of return.

The responsiveness of acquisition costs and salvage values of unspecialized farm-produced durables to changing conditions tends to shift the incidence of capital gains or losses to land, buildings, farm and operator labor, and such specialized farm-produced durables as orchards, terraces, fences, etc.

Two inputs that fall in the unspecialized classification—beef and milk cows— have tended (according to estimates presented in Table 13) to earn more over their productive life than their acquisition cost. Although trending upward, cattle numbers have continued to cycle, and the opportunity to sell unproductive cows in the nonfarm sector as canners and cutters tends to place a floor under the profitability of beef and milk cows. However, in some years during the depression and also in the early 1950's, estimated ex post present values of beef and milk cows were not sufficient to cover acquisition costs, and the capital losses in these periods were probably more numerous and severe than the estimates indicate. Underutilization and capital gains for owners of beef and milk cows tend to increase during periods of high consumer demand—for example, during World War II and in the nonfarm expansion since the early 1950's.

Farm-produced durables specialized to the farm sector often have long productive lives, remaining in production many years despite ex post earnings less than acquisition costs. Farmers often minimize losses by keeping the durables in production rather than salvaging them, because present values in use, although less than original acquisition costs, are greater than salvage values. A durable in this situation can contribute significantly to producing more output than can be sold at prices which equate earnings with acquisition costs. Due to lack of data, some interesting inputs in this category (fruit trees, for example) were not studied.

Horses and mules are one input category qualifying as a farm-produced durable specialized to the farm sector. As anticipated, estimated ex post present values of horses and mules were usually less than acquisition costs. As noted earlier, farmers continuously decreased the number of horses and mules on farms after World War I; but, given inaccurate expectations, their specialization in farm production, and the durable nature of horses and mules, estimates indicate that horses and mules were a source of capital losses from 1917 to 1941 except for the depression years when draft power was a loss-minimizing substitute for purchased inputs (Table 13). After World War II, our estimates indicate that horses and mules earned ex post present values in excess of acquisition costs; by this time, however, horses and mules were so insignificant that the use of our estimating technique is highly questionable. Omitting the carcass value of horses and mules in the present values may have more than offset the upward bias in present values caused by the low PCA interest rates used for discounting, and thus capital losses may be overestimated.

Farmers must base decisions concerning the purchase of farm machinery, motor trucks, buildings, and other nonfarm-produced durables on long-run expectations about product prices and other important variables. Since farmers cannot forecast future product prices with a large degree of accuracy, they encounter considerable adjustment problems with nonfarm-produced durables. Acquisition costs of these durables are generally independent of prices received by farmers. This causes wide variation in the divergence between acquisition costs and salvage values, on one hand, and present values, on the other, of nonfarm-produced durables, thus increasing adjustment problems for these important inputs.

Farmers may purchase new or used nonfarm-produced durables such as motor trucks, which have employment opportunities in the nonfarm sector. If ex ante present values of these durables in farm production drop below their net salvage values in the nonfarm sector, the inputs are sold to that sector. Thus, unspecialized, nonfarm-produced durables are less subject to adjustment problems than are durables, which do not have competing demands in the nonfarm sector. In our investigation of the use and earnings of motor trucks on farms (Table 14), limited data prevented estimating ex post values of used trucks. But estimates of ex post and expected MVP's of motor trucks in aggregate farm production tended to justify the continual increase in the number of motor trucks on farms from 1917 to 1964, except during a few years in the general depression and after 1957 when the number appeared to stabilize. While average estimates in Table 14 indicate that usually actual, and often expected, present values of new motor trucks fell short of acquisition costs, a large proportion of the trucks are purchased used. And MVP estimates indicate that a used motor truck would need to remain in production only five or six years to cause present values to cover acquisition costs.

Nonfarm-produced durables such as farm machinery and buildings which are specialized to the farm sector are more susceptible to asset fixity and capital

TABLE 14. Nonfarm-Produced Durable Capital in Aggregate Farm Production: Annual Average Employment and Earnings for Specified Inputs and Periods, United States, 1917–1964

	Machines on farms		Average level of						Capital gains
			Acquisition cost		Present values				
					Expected		Actual		
Period and Input	No.[a]	Δ in no.[b]	Cost[a]	Δ in cost[b]	Value	Δ in value[b]	Value	Δ in value[b]	
	1,000 mach.		$/mach.		$/mach.		$/mach.		mil. $
From WWI to the crash (1917–29)									
Tractors	385.0	65.0	1,011	–	13,730	–	4,630	–	96.60
Grain combines	17.4	3.4	1,786	–+	1,872	+–	1,648	+	–.20
Buildings[a]	6,415.7	80.8	1.78	–	1.42	+–	1.24	–	–.33
Motor trucks	295.6	52.0	1,001	–	1,742	+–	1,218	–	c
From 1930 to the bottom (1930–33)									
Tractors	989.5	48.0	931	–	4,880	–	1,513	–	55.60
Grain combines	80.5	11.2	1,646	–	2,530	+–	1,570	–	–.70
Buildings	8,169.0	–226.0	1.37	–	1.97	+–	1.03	–	–.27
Motor trucks	898.8	6.2	772	–	1,745	+–	683	–	c
The New Deal (1934–41)									
Tractors	1,308.3	80.8	1,020	0	1,524	+–	1,488	+	60.80
Grain combines	160.5	15.6	1,719	+	2,188	+	1,423	0	–4.90
Buildings	7,131.4	–47.1	1.46	+	1.62	+	1.27	+	c
Motor trucks	985.3	28.8	827	+	1,015	+	736	+	–.36
WWII (1942–46)									
Tractors	2,181.8	163.0	1,664	+–	2,377	–	1,959	–+	66.4
Grain combines	347.0	39.0	1,959	+	1,710	–	1,827	+	–4.2
Pickup balers[a]	40.3	7.7	1,286	+	1,869	+	4,626	+	16.2

Buildings	7,159.0	246.6	+	1.89	+	1.21	+	1.66	+	-.17
Motor trucks	1,373.0	91.0	+	1,231	+	994	- +	1,259	+	c
From war to peace to war to peace (1947–54)										
Tractors	3,484.9	220.4	+	1,862	+	2,949	+ -	2,486	+ -	199.7
Grain combines	740.8	68.1	+	3,142	+	2,774	+	2,906	+	-19.8
Pickup balers	220.5	42.6	+	1,994	+	7,255	+ -	4,912	-	50.3
Field forage harvesters[e]	95.6	18.8	+	1,615	+	42,005	-	16,545	+	n.a.
Buildings	6,820.6	-131.1	+	3.24	+	2.80	+	2.66	+	-.40
Motor trucks	2,221.5	132.5	+	1,900	+	1,863	+	1,853	+	c
Through uneasy peace and the international food gap to partial war (1955–64)										
Tractors	4,608.9	41.4	+	2,441	+	2,625	-	2,199	f	74.60
Grain combines	1,020.5	4.5	+	4,193	+	3,835	+	3,237	f	-28.60
Pickup balers	641.3	38.0	+	2,656	+	3,815	-	3,216	f	43.70
Field forage harvesters	278.0	17.0	+	2,075	+	5,956	-	5,131	f	n.a.
Buildings	6,866.8	34.8	+	3.84	+	3.36	0	2.75	f	-.58
Motor trucks	2,806.8	30.5	+	2,413	+	2,178	+	1,886	f	c

Source: Quance [1967].

n.a. = Not available.

[a] Buildings are measured in constant 1910–1914 dollars and thus the acquisition cost of the value of a 1910–1914 dollar invested in buildings is the purchasing power of a 1910–1914 dollar in current dollars.

[b] A plus sign indicates the variable was increasing over the specified period while a negative sign indicates the variable was decreasing. A negative sign following a plus sign indicates the variable increased over the first part of the specified period and decreased over the latter part of the period and vice versa for plus signs following negative signs. Zero indicates that the variable was generally stable over the specified period.

[c] Capital gains or losses were not estimated for motor trucks, as explained in the text.

[d] Available data permitted estimates for pickup balers beginning in 1945.

[e] Available data permitted estimates for field forage harvesters beginning in 1948.

[f] Actual capital values were estimated only through 1955 so the direction of changes in capital values in the 1955–1964 period are not available.

losses than are nonfarm-produced durables that have employment opportunities in the nonfarm sector. And the more specialized a durable is within the farm sector, the more likely that its ex post capital value will fall short of its acquisition cost for the farm sector.

Versatile tractors in aggregate farm production usually have estimated ex post present values greater than acquisition costs (Table 14), while more specialized machines such as corn pickers and grain combines were often subject to economic fixity and capital losses, even considering apparent biases in the estimates (Tables 14 and 15). On the other hand, estimates for pickup hay balers and field forage harvesters indicate that these machines are so labor-saving that their actual present values, while in recent years not equaling expectations, continually exceeded acquisition costs.

In the rapidly changing structure of the farm sector, there is perhaps no more pronounced example of economic fixity at work than farm buildings. Estimates indicate that ex ante present values of investments in farm buildings seldom covered acquisition costs from 1933 to 1964 (Table 14). The constant dollar value (1910–14 = 100) of buildings on farms decreased slowly from $8,799 million in 1931 to $7,188 million in 1964, despite an expanding farm sector in terms of productive capacity. With the exception of buildings, nonfarm-produced durables specialized to the farm sector generally increased in use from 1917 to the late 1960's.

Estimates of employment and earnings statistics for some nonfarm-produced durables employed in the production of specific commodities (see Table 15) generally indicate that the more specialized an input, the greater the possibility of ex post present values falling short of acquisition costs. Thus, tractors in corn and wheat production generally earned capital gains, but owners of grain combines in wheat production and corn pickers received capital losses.

Expendables

Expendable inputs are "used up" in one production period when committed to farm production, and farmers base utilization decisions on expectations of one year or less. These factors tend to make expendables from the nonfarm sector that are used in farm production less susceptible to economic fixity and rents. But when changes occur in acquisition costs and salvage values of expendables, present values of parent durables can change significantly. In contrast to the situation of expendables from the nonfarm sector, severe adjustment problems for farm-produced expendables may exist, depending largely on (1) whether or not the inputs have employment opportunities in the nonfarm sector, (2) transportation costs for the inputs, and (3) resource fixities involved in their production.

Fourteen categories of expendables were studied, and for them, estimated employment, MVP's, and economic rents are averaged over specified periods in Table 16. As in the case of farm-produced durables, acquisition costs and MVP's of expendables tended to fluctuate from World War I to 1929, then to decrease until 1933, fluctuate but trend upward until 1941, strongly increase during World War II, and continue to increase with more fluctuations since World War II.

Major economic disturbances cause the prices, use, and MVP's of farm-produced expendables to fluctuate and increased demand for livestock products (and therefore for feed inputs) caused the use of farm-produced expendables to trend upward over time. But prices of these expendables are closely correlated with prices received for farm products. This tends to lessen the occurrence of imbalance and rents for farm-produced expendables.

Estimated rents on farm-produced expendables are usually quite small, especially on a per unit of input basis, and are sometimes caused by computational error. When estimated rents are real, they may be of a sizable amount when small per unit rents are multiplied by the total quantity of the input. But their impact is small compared to the capital losses which can occur on economically fixed durables used to produce the expendables.

Steers, heifers, sows, feeder pigs, and chickens generated estimated ex post discounted MVP's that generally fell short of market prices by not more than the cost of discounting or marketing charges. These inputs all have employment opportunities in the nonfarm sector which tend to keep their farm earnings at or above slaughter market prices. Use of expendable livestock inputs trended upward as nonfarm demands for livestock products increased due to rising per capita income and population increases. Expendable inputs in beef and pork production fluctuate over their respective cycles, while dairy heifers and chickens on farms decreased in number since World War II due to the substitution of feed for heifers, broilers, and laying hens.

Inputs such as hay and corn are storable and quite specialized to production.[3] Use, MVP's, and prices of these inputs are more dependent upon quantities produced than are the use, MVP's, and prices of other farm produced expendables. Generally, fluctuating MVP's and rents for farm-produced expendables specialized to the farm sector support this conclusion. Whether nonfarm-produced expendables are specialized to farming (such as with fertilizer) or have competing nonfarm opportunities (such as with gasoline), our estimates indicate that these inputs are not subject to large adjustment problems or rents.

SUMMARY

Rising farm wages and land values provided incentives for developing and substituting capital inputs to extend the fixed land base and to replace labor in farm production. The capitalization of farming constitutes the technological

---

[3] This ignores the demand for corn for food and industrial uses, which is relatively minor, and the export demand for corn, which was rather minor until after World War II.

TABLE 15. Nonfarm-Produced Durable Capital in the Production of Specified Products: Annual Average Employment and Earnings for Specified Periods, United States, 1917–1964.

Period and input	Mach. on farms		Average level of							Capital gains
			Acquisition cost		Present value					
					Expected		Actual			
	No.	Δ in no.	Cost	Δ in cost[a]	Value	Δ in value[a]	Value	Δ in value[a]		
	1,000 mach.		*$/mach.*		*$/mach.*		*$/mach.*			*mil. $*
From WWI to the crash (1917–29)										
Tractors in wheat production	63.4	13.2	1,011	–	2,624	– +	1,840	– +		4.80
Grain combines in wheat prod.	3.2	.5	1,786	+ –	2,594	+	1,433	+		–.11
Tractors in corn production	98.2	17.1	1,011	– +	11,131	–	3,757	–		21.1
Corn pickers	18.5	3.0	696	– +	614	– 0	547	+		–.22
From 1930 to the bottom (1930–33)										
Tractors in wheat production	204.6	33.3	931	–	3,000	–	1,216	–		5.10
Grain combines in wheat prod.	14.0	2.2	1,646	–	1,944	–	1,453	–		–.26
Tractors in corn production	328.5	32.7	931	–	4,696	+	1,755	–		26.2
Corn pickers	59.0	5.5	643	–	878	+ –	585	–		–.34
The New Deal (1934–41)										
Tractors in wheat production	294.3	–6.7	1,020	0	1,183	+	935	+		–2.5
Grain combines in wheat prod.	28.0	2.5	1,719	+	1,742	+	1,462	0		–.74

Tractors in corn production	412.0	18.5	1,020	0	1,422	+ –	1,229	+	8.4
Corn pickers	95.5	6.5	670	+	673	+	555	0	-1.14
WWII (1942–46)									
Tractors in wheat production	245.9	10.1	1,664	+ –	871	+ –	1,273	+ –	-8.8
Grain combines in wheat prod.	55.8	5.5	1,959	+	1,480	–	1,682	+	-1.5
Tractors in corn production	578.0	17.7	1,664	+ –	1,181	+ –	1,720	+	3.4
Corn pickers	157.0	16.6	762	+	523	–	637	+	-1.92
From war to peace to war to peace (1947–54)									
Tractors in wheat production	330.4	-.2	1,862	+	1,648	+ –	1,984	+ –	4.0
Grain combines in wheat prod.	111.3	10.0	3,142	+	1,852	+	2,619	+	-6.0
Tractors in corn production	703.8	26.2	1,862	+	2,309	+ –	2,509	–	43.8
Corn pickers	470.4	57.1	1,227	+	683	+	1,031	+	-9.63
Through uneasy peace and the international food gap to partial war (1955–64)									
Tractors in wheat production	337.4	7.9	2,441	+	2,013	0	2,091[b]	b	b
Grain combines in wheat prod.	167.0	2.8	4,193	+	2,816	+	3,061[b]	b	b
Tractors in corn production	827.6	-7.8	2,441	+	2,293	+ –	2,274[b]	b	b
Corn pickers	772.3	17.8	1,630	+	1,214	+ –	1,219[b]	b	b

Source: Quance [1967].

[a]A plus sign indicates the variable increased over the specified period; a negative sign indicates the variable decreased; a negative sign following a plus sign indicates the variable increased over the first part of the period and decreased over the latter part of the period and vice versa for plus signs following negative signs. Zero indicates the variable was generally stable over the specified period.

[b]Due to the discounting technique, actual capital values and therefore capital gains were estimated only through 1955.

TABLE 16. Expendable Capital: Annual Average Employment and Earnings in Farm Production for Specified Inputs and Periods, United States, 1917–1964

		Average level of:								
		Input		Acquisition cost		Marginal value product[a]				
						Expected		Actual		
Period and input	Units	Quantity used	Δ in quantity used[b]	Cost	Δ in cost[b]	Value	Δ in value[b]	Value	Δ in value[b]	Economic rent
		mil. units		$/unit		$/unit		$/unit		mil. $
From WWI to the crash (1917–29)										
Aggregate farm prod.										
Fertilizer	Ton	1.065	+	300	–	290	–	274	–	–28.20
Gasoline	Gal.	1,078.6	+	.18	+ –	.16	+	.16	+	–28.50
Electricity[c]	Kw-hr	1,283.3	c	.03	c	.03	c	.03	c	–9.00
Beef production										
Hay	Ton	9.937	–	15.33	– +	14.70	– +	14.21	– +	–13.43
Corn	Ton	3.218	+ –	33.18	– +	34.40	– +	33.57	– +	1.67
Heifers[d]	Head	3.057	– +	66.40	+	60.32	+	62.39	+	–10.35
Steers[d]	Head	6.868	–	69.40	+	65.27	+	67.58	+	–9.98
Milk production										
Hay	Ton	35.975	+ –	15.33	– +	23.61	– +	23.90	– +	303.69
Corn	Ton	4.481	+ –	33.18	– +	29.20	– +	30.38	– +	–12.37
Dairy heifers[d]	Head	4.166	+	62.14	+	60.69	+	59.50	+	–10.76
Pork production										
Corn	Ton	30.310	+ –	33.18	– +	28.81	+ – +	27.30	+ – +	–174.68
Feeder pigs[e]	Head	25.318	+ –	5.70	+ –	6.02	+ –	5.73	+ –	–.49
Poultry production										
Corn	Ton	8.191	+	33.18	– +	54.29	– +	60.40	– +	212.68
Chickens	Bird	402.1	+	.90	– +	.80	+ –	.86	– +	–.02
From 1930 to the bottom (1930–33)										
Aggregate farm prod.										
Fertilizer	Ton	1.114	–	160	–	186	–	163	–	–1.49
Gasoline	Gal.	1,840.7	–	.16	–	.16	–	.14	–	–34.00
Electricity	Kw-hr	1,719.8	–	.03	0	.03	0	.03	0	–8.00
Beef production										
Hay	Ton	8.361	+	8.53	–	8.99	–	7.66	–	–7.37

Item	Unit									% change
Corn	Ton	4.130	+	15.72	-+	15.60	-+	15.46	-+	-9.29
Heifers	Head	3.085	-+	39.75	-	40.87	-	34.85	-	-14.92
Steers	Head	5.683	0	42.00	-	47.51	-	40.41	-	-8.96
Milk production										
Hay	Ton	40.101	+	8.53	-	10.59	-	9.82	-	45.17
Corn	Ton	4.008	+	15.72	-+	21.15	-+	20.24	-+	29.57
Dairy heifers	Head	5.021	+	43.00	-	44.17	-	41.13	-	-9.54
Pork production										
Corn	Ton	29.534	+	15.72	-+	21.87	-+	15.52	-+	-5.73
Feeder pigs	Head	26.520	+	3.23	-	4.46	-	3.17	-	-1.95
Poultry production										
Corn	Ton	8.697	+	15.72	-+	35.08	-+	30.51	-+	114.72
Chickens	Bird	449.9	-	.68	-	.73	-	.63	-	-.02
The New Deal (1934–41)										
Aggregate farm prod.										
Fertilizer	Ton	1,292	+	201	+	200	+	188	+	-17.06
Gasoline	Gal.	2,344.5	+	.16	0	.17	+-	.16	-+	-7.00
Electricity	Kw-hr	2,611.8	+	.03	0	.03	0	.03	0	-13.00
Beef production										
Hay	Ton	9.789	+	8.71	-+	9.02	-+	9.38	-+	6.80
Corn	Ton	4.012	+	24.42	-+	23.84	-+	24.50	-+	-1.45
Heifers	Head	3.385	-+	52.38	+	49.08	+	50.98	+	-4.76
Steers	Head	5.563	-+	54.88	+	51.63	+	53.55	+	-7.93
Milk production										
Hay	Ton	44.866	+	8.71	-+	8.67	-+	8.52	+-+	-26.83
Corn	Ton	4.946	-+	24.42	-+	38.53	-+	38.55	-+	82.65
Dairy heifers[d]	Head	5.147	-+	48.13	+	48.39	+	47.09	+	-4.96
Pork production										
Corn	Ton	25.152	+	24.42	-+	29.21	-+	26.77	-+	40.86
Feeder Pigs[e]	Head	23.346	+	4.52	+-+	4.58	+-+	4.51	+-+	-1.37
Poultry production										
Corn	Ton	8.692	+	24.42	-+	32.33	-+	30.58	+-	32.43
Chickens	Bird	415.1	+	.64	+	.65	+	.64	+	.00
WWII (1942–46)										
Aggregate farm prod.										
Fertilizer	Ton	1,679	+	336	-	321	-+	332	-+	-9.93
Gasoline	Gal.	3,490.3	+	.18	+	.17	0	.18	0	11.00
Electricity[c]	Kw-hr	5,485.0	+	.04	0	.03	0	.03	0	-35.00

TABLE 16. (Continued)

Period and input	Units	Input		Acquisition cost		Marginal value product[a]				Economic rent
		Quantity used	Δ in quantity used[b]	Cost	Δ in cost[b]	Expected		Actual		
						Value	Δ in value[b]	Value	Δ in value[b]	
		mil. units		*$/unit*		*$/unit*		*$/unit*		*mil. $*
WW II (1942–46) Continued										
Beef production										
Hay	Ton	19.302	+	19.34	+	16.77	+	18.00	+	−24.32
Corn	Ton	6.602	+	41.64	+	35.48	+	38.32	+	−22.98
Heifers[d]	Head	4.700	+	94.80	+	85.07	+	92.03	+	−13.53
Steers[d]	Head	7.572	+	97.40	+	88.87	+	96.22	+	−8.33
Milk production										
Hay	Ton	59.649	+−	19.34	+	14.30	−+	15.66	+	−218.33
Corn	Ton	9.047	+−+	41.64	+	47.12	+−	51.11	+	86.64
Dairy heifers[d]	Head	6.075	+	97.20	+	88.77	+	96.16	+	−5.95
Pork production										
Corn	Ton	35.782	−	41.64	+	33.19	+	37.31	+	−157.31
Feeder Pigs[e]	Head	33.820	+−	8.56	+	7.71	+	8.62	−+	−2.56
Poultry production										
Corn	Ton	12.645	−	41.64	+	54.71	−	56.38	+−	178.06
Chickens	Bird	528.2	+−	1.11	+	1.07	+	1.08	+	−.02
From war to peace to war to peace (1947–54)										
Aggregate farm prod.										
Fertilizer	Ton	3.182	+	323	−	300	−	300	−	−76.35
Gasoline	Gal.	5,923.1	+	.23	+	.21	+	.21	+	−101.00
Electricity	Kw-hr	15,061.0	+	.03	0	.03	0	.03	0	−63.00
Beef production										
Hay	Ton	29.312	+	23.23	−+	22.00	−+	22.68	−+	−22.50
Corn	Ton	8.840	+	54.86	−+	52.93	−+	54.93	−+	−3.87
Heifers	Head	5.320	+	181.25	+−	170.13	+−	177.05	+−	−23.49
Steers	Head	7.583	+	184.13	+−	174.40	+−	182.16	+−	−16.94
Milk production										
Hay	Ton	61.798	+−	23.23	−+−	25.99	+−	25.52	+	134.73

	Unit								
Corn	Ton	8.951	+-	54.86	-+-	54.78	-+-	54.35	-+-	-4.93
Dairy heifers	Head	5.594	+	168.88	+-	171.17	+-	168.20	+-	-3.45
Pork production										
Corn	Ton	31.758	+-	54.86	-+-	55.87	-+-	59.09	-	133.95
Feeder pigs	Head	29.737	+-	12.33	-+	11.34	-+	11.96	-+	-11.61
Poultry production										
Corn	Ton	12.761	+-	54.86	-+-	53.81	-+-	54.17	+-	9.16
Chickens	Bird	437.6	-	1.47	+-	1.44	+-	1.44	+-	-.01

Through uneasy peace and the international food gap to partial war (1955–64)

	Unit								
Aggregate farm prod.										
Fertilizer	Ton	5.782	+	235	-	226	-	226	-	-57.17
Gasoline	Gal.	6,440.0	+	.26	+	.26	+	.26	+	-34.00
Electricity[c]	Kw-hr	21,646.0	c	.03	c	.03	c	.02	c	-45.00
Beef production										
Hay	Ton	43.532	+	21.73	-+	19.78	-+	21.03	-+	-30.34
Corn	Ton	12.071	-+	40.53	-+	19.51	-+	40.68	+--+	-7.93
Heifers[d]	Head	6.890	-+	176.00	+-	165.33	+-	170.39	+-	-37.35
Steers[d]	Head	10.361	+	178.90	+-	167.20	+-	172.38	+-	-64.66
Milk production										
Hay	Ton	65.730	+	21.73	-+	20.40	-+-	20.62	+-	-85.10
Corn	Ton	12.237	+	40.53	-+	40.25	-+	40.75	-+	8.71
Dairy heifers[d]	Head	5.131	-	175.60	+-	169.14	+-	170.81	+-	-25.86
Pork production										
Corn	Ton	37.499	+-	40.53	-+	40.86	-+	40.27	-+	-15.22
Feeder pigs[e]	Head	35.770	+	9.61	+-	9.44	+-	9.25	+-	-13.07
Poultry production										
Corn	Ton	13.358	+	40.53	-+	47.38	-+	47.49	-+-	79.52
Chickens	Bird	376.3	-	1.18	+-	1.14	+-	1.16	+-	-.01

Source: Quance [1967].

[a] MVP's net of overhead were discounted for six months.

[b] A plus sign indicates the variable increased over the specified period; a negative sign indicates the variable decreased; a negative sign following a plus sign indicates the variable increased over part of the period and then decreased and vice versa for plus signs following negative signs. Zero indicates the variable was generally stable over specified period.

[c] Estimates for electricity were made for the period 1929–55.

[d] Estimates for heifers in beef and dairy production and steers were made beginning in 1925.

[e] Estimates for feeder pigs cover the period 1923–63.

revolution in the U.S. farm sector and involves shifts from durable to expendable inputs, from farm-produced to nonfarm-produced inputs, from labor-using to labor-saving inputs, to land substitutes, and generally a move to input supply specialization in farming.

Given the characteristics of farm production and the farm environment, farmers operating with imperfect knowledge and foresight commit to farm production capital inputs that earn MVP's and present values that often fall short of, or exceed, expected MVP's, present values, and acquisition costs. Economic fixity often resulting from such imperfect adjustments provides incentive to further adjust the capital-labor, capital-land, and capital-output ratios as loss-minimizing or profit-maximizing adjustments are made. Such adjustments are usually output-increasing, thereby further depressing product prices and lessening the probability of ex post present values of new investments covering expected present values and acquisition costs.

Our estimates generally substantiate theoretical hypotheses presented earlier concerning the chronic adjustment problem in the farm sector. More specifically with respect to capital inputs, expendables are adjusted toward rates of use which equate relevant ex post MVP's or present values with acquisition costs more rapidly than durables, farm-produced durables more rapidly than nonfarm-produced durables, nonfarm-produced expendables more rapidly than farm-produced expendables, and inputs which are not specialized to the farm sector more rapidly than specialized inputs.

And estimates of marginal rates of substitution of various kinds of capital inputs for land and labor indicate that, despite the phenomenal adjustment which has taken place in the farm sector and despite the capital losses often resulting from these adjustments made under conditions of imperfect knowledge and foresight, incentives still remain to continue substituting capital for land, labor, and obsolete capital.

In this chapter, we have largely taken the supplies and acquisition costs of land and labor as given. Chapter 8 contains an analysis of how labor has fared under the capitalization of farming, and rising land values and use are studied in Chapter 9.

CHAPTER 8

Labor

VENKAREDDY CHENNAREDDY
and
BOB F. JONES

Rapid growth in both rural and urban sectors of America is associated with substantial movement of farm people to the nonfarm sector of the economy. In fact, if the out-movement over the next 20 years were to be as great as that experienced in the past 20 years, there would presumably be no farm population by about 1985. Despite this tremendous out-movement, there remains chronic and continuing overcommitment of labor in American agriculture.

The first section of this chapter sketches the historical flow of labor between the farm and nonfarm sectors for the 1917-69 period. The five successive sections deal with farm operator mobility as related to expected earnings; analysis of the impact of labor-saving technology on the labor resource; marginal value products (MVP's), acquisition costs, and salvage values of labor; institutional on-farm training for war veterans; and finally, analysis of the impact on farm labor of federal credit programs for farm development.

THE GROSS HISTORICAL PICTURE, 1917-69

Table 17 shows the changes in farm labor from 1917 to 1969. The decline was slow at first, and sometimes halted, but in recent decades became dramatic. The changes summarized in the table include those in farm population, farm labor force, and farm labor requirements.[1] In 1917, farm population was 32.4

---

[1] Since there is no single series measuring the labor input which fully meets all criteria desired, these three measures were chosen, as they provide useful insights into the differential flows over time. See Jones [1964, Appendix A] for discussion of these and other available labor series.

TABLE 17. Number and Changes in Farm Population, Farm Labor Force, and Farm Labor Requirements, United States, Selected Years, 1917-1969

Year and interval	Farm population			Farm labor force			Farm labor requirements		
	Number	Change		Number	Change		Number	Change	
	1,000	*1,000*	*%*	*1,000*	*1,000*	*%*	*mil. hr.*	*mil. hr.*	*%*
1917	32,430			13,568			23,751		
1917-19		−1,230	−3.8		−325	−2.4		−122	−0.5
1919-25		10	−		−207	−1.5		171	.7
1925-29		−610	−2.0		−273	−2.1		−642	−2.7
1929	30,580			12,763			23,158		
1917-29		−1,850	−5.7		−805	−5.9		−593	−2.5
1929-30		−51	−		−266	−2.1		−237	−1.0
1930-31		316	1.0		248	2.0		506	2.2
1931-32		543	1.8		71	−		−822	−3.5
1932-33		1,005	3.2		−77	−		−51	−
1933	32,393			12,739			22,554		
1929-33		1,813	5.9		−24	−		−604	−2.6
1933-34		−88	−.2		−112	−.9		−2,322	−10.3
1934-35		−144	−.4		106	.8		820	4.0
1935-36		−424	−1.3		−402	−3.1		−612	−2.9
1936-37		−471	−1.5		−353	−2.9		1,657	8.1
1937-38		−286	−.9		−356	−3.0		−1,520	−6.9
1938-39		−140	−.4		−284	−2.4		98	.5
1939-40		−293	−.9		−359	−3.2		−203	−1.0
1940-41		−429	−1.4		−310	−2.8		−426	−2.1
1941	30,118			−10,669			20,046		
1933-41		−2,275	−7.0		−2,070	−16.2		−2,508	−11.1
1941-42		−1,204	−3.9		−165	−1.5		537	2.6
1942-43		−2,728	−9.4		−58	−.5		−286	−1.3
1943-44		−1,371	−5.2		−227	−2.1		−134	−.6
1944-45		−395	−1.5		−219	−2.1		−1,325	−6.5
1945-46		983	4.0		295	2.9		−758	−4.0
1946	25,403			10,295			18,080		
1941-46		−4,715	−15.7		−374	−3.5		−1,966	−9.8
1946-47		1,426	1.6		87	.8		−884	−4.8
1947-48		−1,446	−5.5		−19	−		−363	−2.1
1948-49		−189	−.7		−399	−3.8		−631	−3.7
1949-50		−1,146	−4.7		−38	−.3		−1,065	−6.5
1950-51		−1,158	−5.0		−380	−3.8		72	.4
1951-52		−142	−.6		−397	−4.1		−767	−5.0
1952-53		−1,874	−8.6		−285	−3.1		−572	−3.9
1953-54		−855	−4.3		−213	−2.4		−621	−4.4
1954	19,019			8,651			13,249		
1946-54		−5,384	−21.2		−1,644	−16.0		−4,831	−26.7
1954-55		59	.3		−270	−3.1		−454	−3.4
1955-56		−366	−1.9		−529	−6.3		−733	−5.7

TABLE 17. Continued

Year and interval	Farm population			Farm labor force			Farm labor requirements		
	Number	Change		Number	Change		Number	Change	
	1,000	*1,000*	%	*1,000*	*1,000*	%	*mil. hr.*	*mil. hr.*	%
1956-57		-1,056	-5.6		-252	-3.2		-900	-7.4
1957-58		-528	-2.9		-97	-1.2		-450	-4.0
1958-59		-536	-3.1		-161	-2.1		-193	-1.8
1959-60		-957	-5.7		-285	-3.9		-545	-5.1
1960-61		-832	-5.3		-138	-2.0		-386	-3.8
1961-62		-490	-3.3		-219	-3.2		-528	-5.5
1962	14,313			6,700			9,060		
1954-62		-4,706	-24.7		-1,951	-22.6		-4,189	-31.6
1962-63		-946	-6.6		-182	-2.7		-396	-4.4
1963-64		-413	-3.1		-408	-6.3		-470	-5.4
1964-65		-591	-4.6		-500	-8.2		-419	-5.1
1965-66		-768	-6.2		-396	-7.1		-394	-5.1
1966-67		-720	-6.2		-311	-5.8		-112	-1.5
1967-68		-421	-3.9		-154	-3.1		-264	-3.6
1968-69		-147	-1.4		-153	-3.2		-154	-2.2
1969	10,307			4,596			6,851		
1962-69		-4,006	-27.0		-2,104	-31.4		-2,209	-24.4

Sources: Banks, Beale, and Bowles [October 1963, p. 23]; USDA [SB 334, 1970, p. 7 and SB 233, 1963 and 1970].
— = negligible.

million; by 1929 it had decreased to 30.6 million. A large decrease occurred between 1917 and 1919, principally under war pressure. With the return of soldiers from overseas, an increase took place until 1921-22, after which a steady decrease set in until 1930-31, when a new set of forces began affecting labor movements.

Overall, the farm labor force decreased from 13.6 million in 1917 to 12.8 million in 1929, as Table 17 indicates. In relative terms the decrease was only slightly greater than the decrease in farm population. About 23.8 million hours of man-labor were used in agriculture in 1917, of which 2.5 percent was no longer needed by 1929.

From 1929 to 1933 farm population increased, principally in the latter half of the period. In fact, the 1917-29 decrease was almost completely offset by the increase in the depression years, with farm population in 1933 nearly equaling the 1917 figure.

There was essentially no change between 1929 and 1933 in the size of the farm labor force. However, to reconcile the relatively large increase in farm population with a stationary labor force is difficult. One possibility is that the labor service required in 1929-33, while remaining almost unchanged, was supplied by a larger farm labor force. Given the general unemployment and underemployment in the entire economy, each laborer probably worked fewer hours per year during the depression.

The period 1933-41 marks the resumption of the farm population's downward trend that was interrupted by the events of 1929-33. Between 1933 and 1941, farm population decreased by 2.3 million persons, or 7 percent. The average yearly decrease was larger during this time interval than during 1917-29. The change in the farm labor force, which decreased by over 16 percent, was larger than the 11 percent decrease in farm population. The disproportionate decrease in the farm labor force represented a drain on underemployed farm labor which built up between 1930 and 1933.

Between 1941 and 1946, the farm population decreased 4.7 million persons—almost 16 percent of the 1941 population—with an increase beginning in 1946. Population outflow in 1941-45 was pressed by armed forces manpower needs and plentiful off-farm job opportunities. Regional changes in farm population indicated that relative decreases were clearly smaller in industrialized areas such as New England and larger in areas where pockets of underemployment existed [Jones, 1964, pp. 267 ff.].

The labor force declined only 3.5 percent during 1941-46 compared with a 15.7 percent decrease in farm population. The large difference was due mainly to rural women and children joining the labor force in response to need and to patriotic appeals when men left for war. Labor requirements fell at about two-thirds the rate of farm population, hence much faster than the quantity of farm labor. The decrease in labor requirements appears at first slightly paradoxical since labor-saving inputs were in short supply. However, a backlog of farm capacity had built up during the 1930's and overcommitted labor was suppressed, in part, by output restrictions which were unleashed with the outbreak of war. A closer examination of labor requirements shows that, until 1944, the change in labor requirements was small and that almost all the decrease occurred during 1944-46.

The decrease in farm population continued during 1946-54; although varying greatly from year to year, outmigration was at a high level. Net population outflow was 14 percent larger during 1946-54 than during 1941-46. However, the labor force decreased less during the period than labor requirements did. All three series show very large decreases during 1954-62 and 1962-69. Farm population and farm labor force declined at about the same rate, 24.7 and 22.6 percent respectively, from 1954 to 1962, but labor requirements declined at an even greater rate—about 32 percent. In the 1962-69 period, the decrease in farm population and farm labor force accelerated to 27 and 31.4 percent respectively, but the decline in labor requirements eased slightly to 24.4 percent. Apparently, a continuing need for downward adjustment in labor use remains.

"Cohort analysis" provides another way of looking at the flow of labor [Kanel, May 1961; Clawson, 1963, pp. 14-19]. A "cohort" of farm operators includes all operators who were born during a specified time period, and cohort analysis concerns changes in cohort size over time. This analytical technique is somewhat limited in that it concentrates solely upon farm operators, because similar age data are not available for family and hired labor. However, farm-operator labor comprises more than one-half the total labor input; also, changes in family-labor use follow changes in farm-operator labor fairly closely. Thus, cohort analysis permits examination of a substantial segment of the labor input.

For this study, cohorts were adjusted for differences in life survival rates. Thus, an adjusted rate of change in the number of farm operators in a cohort is the difference between the number of operators in an age group at the beginning of the decade who are expected to survive (live) to the end of the decade and the number of farm operators actually surviving at the end of the decade expressed as a percent of the expected number. These calculations show high rates of entry for younger age groups during 1910-20 (see Table 18).[2] The data do not permit us to determine when, during the decade, entry rates increased, but there is reason to believe that this occurred during latter parts of the decade as a result of a favorable economic environment for agriculture and availability of draft deferments for agricultural workers [Jones, 1964, p. 189].

TABLE 18. Net Percent Change in Number of Farm Operators Adjusted for Life Survival Rates, United States, Selected Periods, 1910-1959

(percent)

Age at beginning of decade	1910-20	1920-30	1930-40	1940-50	1945-55	1950-59
Under 25	261.4	189.8	169.1	260.9	320.6	145.4
25-34	22.2	12.5	22.3	30.8	30.0	1.5
35-44	3.5	.4	7.6	2.5	-9.4	-15.1
45-54	-11.9	-9.5	-3.4	-13.4	-24.3	-22.7
55-64	-8.1	-1.5	8.2	-9.1	-12.0	-16.1

Source: Jones [1964, p. 272].

Entry rates for the three younger groups were lower in the 1920-30 decade than in the immediately preceding decade. This is not surprising considering that agriculture was in a state of depression while the rest of the economy enjoyed relative prosperity. Rates of withdrawal for older groups, however, were higher during the 1910-20 decade than during 1920-30.

Comparing the two periods for total changes, there was a net increase in the number of farm operators of about 1.4 percent during 1910-20, in contrast to a net decrease of about 2.5 percent during 1920-30. The decrease in the rate of

―――――――――――

[2] The following comments should be helpful in interpreting Table 18. The number of farm operators who were 25 years of age or under during the decade 1910-20 increased by 261.4 percent with respect to their number at the beginning of the decade. This cohort (which would be between 25 to 34 years of age the following decade) increased by 12.5 percent during 1920-30 (reading on the diagonal).

entry of the 1920's relative to the teens was larger than the decrease in the withdrawal rate [Jones, 1964, p. 177].

For 1930-40, cohort analysis indicates (1) exceptionally low farm entry rates for younger age groups and (2) exceptionally low withdrawal rates in older age groups. Low entry rates for younger workers is the result of the relative unattractiveness of agriculture as an occupation. For older workers, lack of off-farm job opportunities slowed the withdrawal rate.

Based on census data, estimates in Table 18 do not provide specific information for the five years which include World War II. However, comparing data for 1940-50 with data for 1945-55 and 1950-59, it is possible to make inferences about changes occurring during the first and second halves of the 1940's.

The entry rate of age groups under 34 during 1940-50 is exceptionally large, particularly for the 25-34 age bracket, when entry rates exceeded any other period. Comparing data for 1945-55 with those of 1950-59, the first of these two periods shows overwhelmingly higher rates of entry for farmers below age 34 than the second does. It follows that the large entry rates of 1940-49 occurred mostly during the second half of the decade. Percent changes in number of farm operators by age groups indicate that, contrary to the case for farmers under age 34, much of the exceptionally high entry rate of the age group 35-44 occurred before 1945. Figures on average annual changes in number of farm operators indicate that the under-25 age group of farmers decreased much more than the 25-34 age group in the early 1940's and early 1950's when the United States was at war. Younger persons were more subject to induction than older groups. Unusually large increases in operators of less than 25 years of age and also between 25-34 are observed in 1945-55.

EXPECTED EARNINGS AND
FARM OPERATOR MOBILITY

Although actual labor earnings are useful as a welfare index, an important factor in labor mobility is the expected earnings in farming relative to expected earnings in alternative occupations. Our discussion centers on comparing (1) the present values of expected earnings in manufacturing with those in farming for 25-year-old workers and (2) expected earnings in laundry and farming for the 45-year-old workers.[3] These comparisons are useful in explaining the mobility patterns of "younger" and "older" men faced with the decision to enter or depart the farm sector.

The selection of alternative employment opportunities for farm operators singled out in this study was dependent upon the age and skill differentials of

---

[3] Present values are defined as the sum of expected income streams discounted to the given (present) year. The average rate of interest on farm mortgage loans was used as the discount rate.

farm operators in light of theoretical considerations discussed in Chapter 3. Access to farm and industrial employment is fairly open to *young* men whether reared on farms or not. Skill requirements are different, but accumulated experience and knowledge of the job are not significantly great enough to prohibit mobility between the two alternatives at this point in a worker's career. But the situation is different with respect to a 45-year-old, for whom, if he lacks accumulated skills and knowledge specific to the job, an unskilled job in a laundry is a better proxy for types of jobs available than manufacturing is. Thus, wages in manufacturing represent opportunity or acquisition costs for young farmers and laundry wages represent opportunity costs or salvage values for older farmers.

Chennareddy's estimates of expected labor earnings on-farm and off-farm for 25- and 45-year age groups are presented in Table 19. The estimates suggest that (1) expected earnings for "younger" and "older" operators moved synchronically and (2) expected earnings in laundry work were more variable than expected earnings in manufacturing.

TABLE 19. Present Value of Expected Income Streams for 25- and 45-Year-Old Workers in Selected Occupations, United States, 1917–1962

(thousand current dollars)

Year	Present value of a 25-year-old		Present value of a 45-year-old	
	In farming	In manufacturing	In farming	In laundries
1917	19	27	13	13
1918	21	33	15	15
1919	22	34	16	15
1920	24	35	18	20
1921	12	25	8	18
1922	17	31	12	18
1923	20	37	14	20
1924	19	33	13	21
1925	19	36	13	22
1926	20	36	14	24
1927	20	35	13	24
1928	20	35	13	24
1929	20	36	14	24
1930	18	30	12	23
1931	14	26	9	22
1932	13	22	8	19
1933	15	27	9	20
1934	19	34	12	23
1935	19	34	12	23
1936	21	39	13	26
1937	23	43	13	27
1938	21	36	13	26
1939	22	42	13	28

TABLE 19. Continued

(thousand current dollars)

	Present value of a 25-year-old		Present value of a 45-year-old	
Year	In farming	In manufacturing	In farming	In laundries
1940	23	45	14	29
1941	26	53	17	30
1942	32	66	21	31
1943	38	73	26	36
1944	40	74	28	39
1945	42	71	29	41
1946	44	70	30	45
1947	48	83	32	49
1948	50	86	35	50
1949	48	81	33	48
1950	47	90	31	49
1951	55	97	39	53
1952	43	97	38	51
1953	53	100	38	52
1954	51	95	36	52
1955	53	108	38	54
1956	56	108	40	55
1957	56	106	42	54
1958	55	101	41	54
1959	57	112	43	55
1960	56	107	43	55
1961	54	105	42	54
1962	56	118	44	57

Source: Chennareddy [1965].

Study of earnings estimates and cohort data for 1917–29 generally indicates that, as wages for laundry work increased relative to farm wages, the ratio of these two wages, regarded as guiding employment decisions of "older" farmers, also increased, persuading many "older" farmers to leave agriculture. The exit of older farmers caused farm wages to increase above what they would have been otherwise, resulting in a decrease in expected earnings in some urban occupations relative to those in farming. At the same time, increases in expected earnings in farming relative to expected earnings in manufacturing encouraged the entry of young men into farming. The decrease in the number of 45-year-old farmers was larger than the increase in the number of 25-year-old farmers, and the total number of farm operators decreased.

Table 18 indicates, for the 1930–40 decade, a relatively low entry rate of younger farmers and a low exit rate of older farmers. Generally, a low entry rate means that young postulants decided to take their chances in occupations other than farming. There is, however, an alternative interpretation which seems more plausible in explaining the events of the Great Depression. The likelihood of finding off-farm jobs was small, while it was extremely difficult to get started in farming under the then prevailing financial conditions.[4] Thus, young men of farm extraction were unlikely either to find industrial employment or to get started as independent farmers. Instead, many farm youths were simply forced to remain in agriculture as low-paid family workers. As such they likely received near the average value product of labor in the family operation, which was higher than the near-zero marginal value product of their labor in off-farm alternatives when returns in such alternatives were adjusted for the unemployment probability. In short, many younger persons were forced to postpone making a long-run career choice. Low rates of withdrawal were consistent with the then-existing nonfarm economic conditions.

Data of Table 18 are not very helpful in explaining farm labor flows during the period 1930-33, since the data available for cohort analysis covered the wider (1930-40) interval. Changes in farm operator numbers in different age brackets for 1930-40 were likely more typical of the 1934-40 period than 1930-40. Thus changes in cohort sizes during 1930-40 were consistent with expected earnings for 1934-40.

Table 19 indicates that during 1934-40 expected earnings in manufacturing increased faster than expected earnings in laundry and that the ratio of manufacturing to farm wages increased. As this ratio increased, more young farmers were persuaded to take nonfarm jobs in preference to farming; thus the number of entering young farmers decreased. As fewer young people entered farming, the total number of farmers decreased, causing farm earnings to rise. Higher farm earnings relative to earnings in such industries as laundries induced more "older" farmers to remain in farming. Thus, for the period 1930-40, cohort analysis shows low entry rates for younger age groups and low exit rates for older age groups.

For 1942-47, expected earnings on and off farms for the two age groups indicated that opportunity costs of young farmers (as reflected by expected earnings in manufacturing) increased less, relative to expected earnings in farming, than the opportunity cost of older farmers (as reflected by the expected earnings in laundries). Exected earnings in laundry relative to farming decreased slightly, encouraging more older farmers to remain in farming. The greater number of farmers drove farm labor earnings down, raising expected earnings in manufacturing relative to farming, and, in response to this raise, fewer young farmers chose farming as a career. We might expect the *total* number of farmers to increase, since the number of marginal older farmers deciding to remain in farming would have more than offset the number of young

[4] Unemployment measures as "percent of Civilian Labor Force" increased from 1929 to 1933 and decreased thereafter except for a brief relapse in 1938-39. In 1933 one-fourth of the labor force was unemployed. See U.S. Dept. of Commerce [Historical Statistics of U.S., p. 73].

farmers leaving agriculture. But this did not happen, primarily because two important factors had been at work during this period, which were not considered in the above analysis.

The first factor was a direct allocation of workers through nonmonetary means, i.e., draft deferments and, later, vocational education programs for veterans. The second factor related to changes in job availabilities. Over the longer run, laundry wages are a proxy for off-farm opportunity cost for older farm workers. However, during World War II many semiskilled and unskilled workers were needed to man defense production lines. This need provided opportunities for older farm workers at higher manufacturing wages. Although expected farm earnings rose relative to manufacturing earnings, many 45-year-olds, having suffered through twenty years of farm depression, grasped the opportunity to shift to nonfarm employment.

For 1948-54, expected nonfarm earnings increased at a greater rate than expected farm earnings for 25-year-olds. Thus, fewer young farmers were attracted into farming, and this reduced entry caused farm wages for 45-year-olds to maintain their relative but lower position with respect to expected earnings in laundering. The net change was a reduction in the total number of farmers.

During 1955-62, the pattern of expected earnings duplicated that of 1948-54 (Table 19). The same consequences resulted. Fewer young people entered farming and thus farm wages were higher than otherwise. This increased the expected earnings of 45-year-olds in farming. But expected earnings in laundering were still greater than expected farm earnings for 45-year-olds and so the total number of farmers decreased. If we overlap the rates of entry and withdrawal as determined by cohort analysis for 1940-50, 1945-55, and 1950-59 (Table 18), the entry rates are seen to be the lowest on record during 1950-59, and particularly low in the latter part of that period. And exit rates of farmers over 34 years of age were higher than ever before during both 1945-55 and 1950-59, indicating that they were probably high during the latter part of the period.

LABOR-SAVING TECHNOLOGY AND ITS
IMPACT ON LABOR RESOURCE FLOWS

One phenomenon of U.S. agriculture is the reduction in the number of farm operators from 6,448,000 in 1920 to 3,933,000 in 1960. This is attributed to "pull-and-release" factors that usually affect the flow of farm labor. The nonfarm sector exerts "pull" on, and the farm sector "releases," farm labor. The pull factor is identified as the increased demand for labor in the nonfarm sector, and the release factor is the introduction of labor-saving technology in the farm sector.

As the United States became more industrialized, an enormous increase in demand for labor in the nonfarm sector increased nonfarm wage rates. This, in turn, induced further movement of farm labor to the nonfarm sector, causing scarcity of labor in the farm sector at existing farm wage rates. The next turn of the sequence was that the scarcity of farm labor created the necessity for labor-saving and capital-intensive farm technology, and the rapid growth in farm technology contributed to further decline in the demand for labor. In sum, rapid industrialization in the nonfarm sector and tremendous advances in labor-saving farm technology are two reasons for the decline in the use of farm labor. A third reason is the price inelasticity of demand for farm products. The tremendous labor-saving and output-increasing farm technology made larger-scale farms more feasible and economical (in terms of capital and land but not in terms of labor). Thus, farmers increased their size of operation and output. The increase in farm output and an inelastic demand for farm products held down farm product prices, which, in turn, further depressed the MVP of farm labor and discouraged its use.

Results of release-and-pull factors are observed more specifically in changes over time in the index of farm inputs and its components. And the changes can be related to empirical estimates of changing marginal physical products of factors.

Although the total index of inputs used in farm production has not changed much from 1917 to 1970, major shifts occurred in the composition of inputs. The index of farm labor decreased from 223 in 1917 to 64 in 1969, while the index of mechanical power and machinery increased from 28 in 1917 to 115 in 1969 (1957-59 = 100).

The shift from horse and mule power to tractors indirectly contributed to a significant part of the substitution during the first part of the period. After the shift to tractor power was nearly completed, further labor was released as farmers shifted from small tractors to larger ones.

Labor is complementary to both horse power and tractor power but in different proportions. Over time, the shifts from hand to horse cultivation and then from horse to tractor cultivation led to substituting labor-saving capital for labor. Thus a shift from horses to tractors reduced the MVP of labor combined with horses. The adjustment consisted of forming new complementary relationships between tractors and labor. In the process older complementaries were broken and labor was released from agriculture.

The strength of these economic forces is indicated by Quance's estimates, in Chapter 7, of marginal physical products of factors and relative factor costs. He calculated the cost of the services of one tractor relative to the cost of the services of one horse or mule and compared this to the marginal physical product (MPP) of one tractor relative to the MPP of one horse or mule. These data estimate that the MPP of one tractor was 83.7 times as great as one horse or mule during the 1917–29 period but the cost was only 5.6 times as great. These relatives changed substantially and tended to decline during the periods considered up to 1946, but the ratios continued to favor substitution of tractors for horses. Actually the substitution was largely completed by 1946; by that time the ratios had reversed and the substitution took the form of larger tractors being substituted for smaller tractors. Since larger tractors combined one man with greater tractor horse power, the MVP of former combinations of labor was again reduced and the overall effect was a further substitution of labor-saving capital for labor.

Coincident with the shift to tractor power was the shift to tractor-drawn complementary equipment. During the latter part of the period mechanical corn pickers, cotton harvesters, and forage equipment were substituted for hand methods. These substitutions led to decreased MVP's for given quantities of labor in agriculture and further contributed to the release of certain kinds of labor from agriculture.

Pull-and-release factors usually have differential impacts on flows of farm operators in various age groups to the nonfarm sector. General evidence to date is that the average age of farm operators increased from one census to the next. The number of young adults entering farming was not large enough to replace older farm operators who retire or die. Waldo [1962] writes: "The prospects of low earnings in agriculture and the difficulties of becoming established in farming, along with the alterations of nonfarm employment and urban living, caused a large outmovement of young adults from the farm population." This situation encouraged remaining farm operators to enlarge the sizes of their farms, thereby tending to eliminate inefficient farms and discourage young and/or inexperienced persons from entering farming. Factors in the nonfarm labor market which reduce the expected incomes of older farm operators considering a shift are: discrimination on the basis of age, low levels of education, and lack of previous nonfarm job experience [Waldo, 1962]. Factors mentioned earlier clearly support the observation that the size of each group and the rate of withdrawal of the older farm operators in relation to the entry rate for young adult farm operators is changing the age composition of the farm operator group. Clawson [1963, p. 13] writes: "Normal aging processes will greatly reduce the number of farmers in another generation, but for the next two decades the proportion of older farmers will rise considerably." The aging of farm operators is seen clearly in Table 20, which gives the percentage of operators by age group in the census years 1920–64, according to the 1950 U.S. Census definition of a farm.

The number of farm operators under 25 decreased from 6.06 percent in 1920 to 1.65 percent in 1960. For those 25 to 34 years old, the respective change was from 20.38 percent to 10.89 percent. Thus, the number of young people committed to farming decreased steadily and rapidly. On the other hand, the per-

TABLE 20. Percentage Distribution of Farm Operators by Age Group in the
Census Years 1920-1964, United States

(percent)

	Age					
Year	Under 25	25-34	35-44	45-54	55-64	65 and over
1920	6.06	20.38	25.12	23.46	15.73	9.25
1930	6.11	17.25	23.91	24.04	17.54	11.15
1940	4.07	16.54	20.13	24.86	19.98	14.42
1950	3.25	15.69	23.54	22.94	19.82	14.76
1960	1.65	10.89	21.82	26.63	21.64	17.37
1964		11.5[a]	20.7	27.0	23.5	17.4

Source: U.S. Census of Agriculture, 1950 and 1964.

[a] Under 35 years.

centage of farm operators aged 55 to 64 and over 65 increased rapidly from
1920 to 1964. The proportion of farm operators aged 55 to 64 increased from
15.73 percent in 1920 to 23.5 percent in 1964, and from 9.25 percent to 17.4
percent for those over 65.

LABOR PRODUCTIVITY AND
EARNINGS IN AGRICULTURE

The particularly high prices received for farm products during World War I
reflected favorably on factor earnings. During the war years, the average annual
farm income per worker[5] grew faster than the annual wage per employed
factory worker. Even so, the absolute level of farm income per worker remained
below the wage per employed factory worker. Table 21 contains information
with regard to residual returns to labor (all labor and family labor) in U.S.
agriculture for selected years between 1910 and 1962 which are compared with
the hourly earnings of factory workers. Data in Table 21 show that residual
returns per hour to all labor and to family labor are consistently below the
average wage for factory workers. Furthermore, the gap between the rewards to
labor service in and out of farming increased between the years 1910 and 1930.
The MVP of labor decreased during the period as a consequence of a decrease in
both the MPP of labor and product prices. The decrease in the MPP of labor
would logically result from the availability of a relatively larger labor force.
Residual earnings to family labor computed on typical commercial family-
operated farms were generally negative from 1930 through 1933 [Goodsell and
Jenkins, 1961]. The smaller reward to human effort made leisure cheaper in
terms of what work would fetch and, hence, more leisure was probably taken.

[5] Realized net income of farm operators plus total farm wage. See USDA [July 1970,
FIS, p. 41].

TABLE 21. Residual Returns to Labor in Agriculture (All Labor and Family Labor) and Related Data, United States, 1910–1969

Year	Net income originating in agriculture	Capital invested in agriculture	Farm-mortgage interest rate (all lenders)	Interest on capital invested in agriculture	Labor income	Wage bill	Family's labor income	Man-hours of labor used for farm work	Man-hours of family labor used for farm work	Returns per hour of work		Average hourly earnings of factory workers
										All labor	Family labor	
	million dollars	*million dollars*	%	*million dollars*	*million dollars*			*million hours*	*million hours*	*dollars/hour*		
1910	5,436	43,293	6.0	2,598	2,838	755	2,083	22,547	16,924	0.13	0.12	0.20
1920	10,663	83,846	6.1	5,115	5,548	1,790	3,758	23,995	17,936	.23	.21	.55
1925	9,083	60,711	6.3	3,825	5,258	1,267	3,991	23,800	17,736	.22	.23	.55
1930	6,327	60,493	6.0	3,630	2,697	1,177	1,520	22,921	17,069	.12	.09	.55
1935	6,223	40,392	5.5	2,222	4,001	775	3,226	21,052	16,294	.19	.20	.54
1940	5,529	43,902	4.6	2,019	3,510	1,029	2,481	20,472	15,477	.17	.16	.66
1941	8,126	46,000	4.5	2,070	6,056	1,249	4,807	20,046	15,063	.30	.32	.73
1942	11,996	52,400	4.4	2,306	9,690	1,631	8,059	20,583	15,576	.47	.52	.85
1943	14,408	61,200	4.4	2,693	11,715	2,027	9,688	20,297	15,558	.58	.62	.96
1944	14,404	69,400	4.4	3,054	11,350	2,202	9,148	20,163	15,761	.56	.58	1.01
1945	15,154	76,100	4.5	3,424	11,730	2,299	9,431	18,838	14,846	.62	.64	1.02
1946	18,448	82,400	4.6	3,790	14,658	2,532	12,126	18,080	14,236	.81	.85	1.08
1947	19,563	92,800	4.5	4,176	15,387	2,783	12,604	17,196	13,441	.89	.94	1.22

Year												
1948	21,999	103,400	4.5	4,653	17,346	2,990	14,356	16,833	13,037	1.03	1.10	1.33
1949	16,751	109,700	4.5	4,936	11,815	2,806	9,009	16,202	12,540	.73	.72	1.38
1950	17,698	108,000	4.5	4,860	12,838	2,811	10,027	15,137	11,585	.85	.87	1.44
1951	20,281	125,700	4.6	5,782	14,499	2,921	11,578	15,209	11,646	.95	.99	1.56
1952	19,372	140,100	4.6	6,445	12,927	2,857	10,070	14,442	11,058	.89	.91	1.65
1953	17,170	137,700	4.7	6,172	10,698	2,736	7,962	13,870	10,601	.77	.75	1.74
1954	16,372	134,300	4.7	6,312	10,060	2,596	7,464	13,249	10,062	.76	.74	1.78
1955	15,309	137,600	4.8	6,605	8,704	2,615	6,089	12,795	9,689	.68	.63	1.86
1956	15,082	141,100	4.8	6,773	8,309	2,641	5,668	12,062	9,063	.69	.63	1.95
1957	14,554	149,900	4.7	7,045	7,509	2,734	4,775	11,162	8,313	.67	.57	2.03
1958	16,935	157,600	4.8	7,565	9,370	2,842	5,528	10,712	7,882	.87	.83	2.11
1959	15,237	173,500	4.9	8,501	6,736	2,882	3,854	10,519	7,722	.64	.50	2.19
1960	15,820	175,600	5.0	8,780	7,040	2,864	4,176	9,974	6,683	.71	.62	2.26
1961	16,139	176,900	5.1	9,022	7,117	2,918	4,193	9,588	6,520	.74	.64	2.32
1962	16,191	185,000	5.2	9,620	6,571	2,902	3,669	9,060	6,161	.73	.60	2.39
1963	16,391	193,000	5.3	10,229	6,161	2,990	3,171	8,664	5,816	.71	.55	2.46
1964	15,039	201,800	5.3	10,695	4,344	2,913	1,431	8,194	5,497	.53	.26	2.53
1965	17,645	210,100	5.4	11,345	6,300	2,849	3,451	7,775	5,276	.81	.65	2.60
1966	17,906	226,800	5.4	12,247	5,659	2,889	2,770	7,381	5,032	.77	.55	2.72
1967	17,005	240,300	5.4	12,976	4,029	2,878	1,151	7,269	5,105	.55	.23	2.83
1968	17,269	252,900	5.6	14,162	3,107	3,045	1,213	7,005	4,890	.44	.25	3.01
1969	18,668	266,500	5.7	15,190	3,478	3,192	286	6,851	4,831	.51	.06	3.19

Sources: USDA [FIS, July 1970 and earlier; Ag. Handbook 118, 1957; SB 334; Agri. Stat., 1970; AIB 290, 1965]. U.S. Bureau of Labor Statistics [Employment and Earnings, 1961–63]. Tostlebe [1954].

127

Increasing returns to human effort in 1934-41 relative to the immediately preceding period indicated increasing productivity of farm labor. Residual returns to operators and family labor computed on typical commercial farms were low, but, with few exceptions, were positive for the period. This represented substantial progress over 1930-33 when residual returns to labor were as a rule negative. Increased value productivity of farm labor was consistent with higher prices received by farmers, increased use of cooperating factors, and important technological changes.

Almost without exception, residual returns to operator and family labor computed on typical farms were substantially higher during 1942-47 than during 1934-41. Considering the farm sector as a whole, residual hourly earnings to all farm labor and to family labor trebled. These relative changes compare favorably with relative changes in the average hourly earnings of factory workers during the same period and the absolute difference in labor earnings between farm and off-farm work narrowed during the period. And residual earnings to farm labor grew faster than the general price level and thus part of the gains were real.

To assess the direction in which labor value productivity moved from 1947 to 1954 is difficult. Labor requirements falling faster than the farm labor force, substantial investment in machinery (mostly labor-saving investment), and a small increase in land input suggests that the physical productivity of labor decreased. However, prices received by farmers were improving. Since the two elements making up MVP may have moved in opposite directions, the end result is uncertain. Residual labor earnings, both those computed on typical commercial farms and those computed for the sector (Table 21), increased relative to prior periods. Assuming that labor earnings fluctuate with labor's value productivity, it follows that the forces making for a larger MVP prevailed. However, as stated before, the absolute labor earnings in agriculture are not as significant in explaining labor mobility as earnings in agriculture relative to those in other occupations.

As in the previous period, it is difficult to establish with any degree of precision the direction of changes in the productivity of labor for 1955-69. The presumption is that value productivity decreased. Indications that the MPP of labor decreased are that (1) complementary land decreased, (2) substitute capital increased, and (3) labor requirements fell faster than the farm labor force. It appears that the decrease in land input relative to labor coupled with labor-saving technological change, partly embodied in capital replacement, decreased the MPP of farm labor. The fall in product prices reinforces the presumption of a decrease in labor MVP.

Information on residual earnings of farm labor computed for the sector (Table 21) and for typical commercial farms [Goodsell and Jenkins, 1961] indicates a decrease in labor value productivity relative to the preceding period. While residual returns per hour of work in agriculture were decreasing, the average hourly earnings of factory workers increased greatly (Table 21). Evidence from the typical commercial farm's computations is less conclusive. Residual returns to labor on typical farms decreased in about half of the cases.

INSTITUTIONAL ON-FARM TRAINING
FOR WAR VETERANS

Government labor and manpower policy affect labor use in agriculture indirectly through policy applicable to the general economy and directly through policy specific to agricultural labor. Our study has made no attempt to specifically evaluate impacts of general labor policy in the nonfarm sector. However, policies such as attitude toward unionization, bargaining assistance, minimum wages, and workers' benefits affect earnings, expected earnings, and employment in agriculture. For example, to the extent that unionization in a given industry negotiates above-equilibrium wages, thereby reducing the number of nonfarm jobs, the number of persons seeking work in the farm sector increases and acquisition costs for agricultural laborers are lowered.

The importance of employment opportunities, unemployment rates, and the general tempo of business activity as factors in migration from the farm sector is clearly established by various researchers, for example, C. D. Bishop [1961].

Most discussion and analyses of farm labor legislation center on only one segment of the farm labor force, i.e., hired farm workers. Perhaps this is for good reason, as Rich states, "The history of farm labor legislation was one largely of attempts to bring hired farm workers—those working for wages—under the protection of the federal labor, health, and welfare laws already covering employees in nonfarm employment" [Congressional Quarterly Service, 1963]. In addition, some studies have dealt with the Federal Mexican Labor Program, a program whose impact was felt primarily in a limited number of states and on certain crops.

In this section we present a partial analysis of the impact of veterans' on-farm training on acquisition costs, entry rates, and productivity of veterans in the farm sector. Characteristics of the program as it operated for World War II veterans, as contrasted to Korean veterans, decreased acquisition costs of young farm workers, encouraged employment in agriculture, reduced migration from agriculture, and contributed to "trapping" of young farm operators in the agricultural sector.

The basic provisions for the education and training of World War II veterans were contained in Title II of the Servicemen's Readjustment Act of 1944, commonly called the GI Bill of Rights.[6] The law specified eligibility for education and training, the period of education, and payment rates. Two points stand out with respect to choice of education for veterans and hence occupational mo-

---

[6] U.S. Statutes at Large, 1944, Vol. 58, Part 1, pp. 284–301.

bility: (1) essentially there were no limits placed upon the type of education the veteran could receive, except that certain "frills" were excluded, and (2) an effort was made to provide educational guidance to all veterans taking training.

In contrast to university and college training where guidance centers were established by the Veterans Administration (VA), there is no evidence that participants in GI On-Farm Training received guidance other than that received from supervisors of the program. Because supervisors had vested interests in the program, it is unlikely that trainees were advised against taking farm training or against entering agriculture despite historically unfavorable relative incomes in agriculture. In fact, teachers and supervisors urged veterans to enroll in the program and did a certain amount of recruiting.

As a result of administrative cuts made by the VA in the original program as established by the GI Bill, hearings were held, and Public Law 377 was passed in 1947 to establish institutional on-farm training as a specialized program. A full-time course was defined as organized group instruction of at least 200 hours per year. Full-time status provided for payment of full tuition and a monthly subsistence allowance. Payment of the maximum subsistence allowance was conditional on individual farm earnings. However, reported earnings were low and the ceiling did not prevent most trainees from receiving the maximum permitted allowance. Of those in training on May 31, 1949, some 87 percent were drawing the maximum subsistence allowance [Chief of Investigations of the General Accounting Office, 1951].

Although the law specified that the veteran must operate an "adequate" farm to qualify for training, there is clear evidence that this was not always the case. The supervisor of the Mississippi program, under questioning, indicated two major sources of funds important for getting started in farming: (1) loans from the Farmers Home Administration and other lending agencies, and (2) the subsistence allowance. In fact, he stated, "We have required in our state that . . . the veteran . . . would have to invest at least the amount of his subsistence into improving his farm, his livestock, his machinery, the buildings or buying land" [U.S. Congress, House Committee on Veterans Affairs, Hearings, 1952, p. 290].

Analysis of entry and withdrawal rates presented in Table 18 and further discussed above led to the following conclusions: (1) despite availability of draft deferments for farm workers, entry rates for the two groups under 35 years of age were below rates for previous periods; (2) availability of deferments probably increased entry rates for the 35- to 44-year-old group; and (3) entry rates during 1945–50 for the two groups under 35 were unusually high in comparison to previous or subsequent periods. Thus economic factors, coupled with characteristics of the educational program, encouraged veterans to return to the farm and in effect subsidized workers back into agriculture, thereby lowering their acquisition costs to the agricultural sector.

About 700,000 nondisabled veterans of World War II took institutional on-farm training under P.L. 346. This represented over one-half of all farmers and farm laborers who had entered the armed services. Of veterans returning to the farm, about three-fourths enrolled in the program. A larger proportion of pre-service farmers and farm laborers enrolled in the program in those regions where farm opportunities were poorest. For example, 62 percent of pre-service farmers in the South Atlantic region enrolled in the program in contrast to 32 percent in the Pacific region. Where farm incomes were smaller, the subsistence allowance was relatively more attractive. This, coupled with industrial development and availability of nonfarm jobs, which also show similar regional variation, en-couraged returning veterans to return to farming in areas where farm opportu-nities were poorest.

An additional factor is important in understanding why such a large propor-tion of farm veterans took farm training. If we assume that the returning veteran was interested in additional education or training per se, the prior level of education he had attained was important in explaining the type of education selected. Only about 25 percent of all veterans of World War II of farm origin were educationally equipped to enroll in training above the high school level. Although nonfarm vocational training was available, only a very small propor-tion of men with farm background took advantage of it; in fact, only about 3.9 percent of all farm veterans entered *any* type of nonfarm training.

Two other aspects of the on-farm training concern (1) the impact of training on the productivity of farm labor involved, and (2) the impact of the program on keeping workers in agriculture. There is little information available on a national level to evaluate productivity effects. Reports of adoption of improved practices indicate substantial increases in yields and animal output per produc-tion unit [U.S. Congress, House Committee on Veterans Affairs, Hearings, 1952, pp. 1650-51]. Fragmentary evidence (in addition to the logical connection between new knowledge and supervision of practices supplied by trained in-structors) strongly suggests that the training did increase labor productivity.

Participation in farm training prohibited what is often the initial step in movement from the farm: off-farm work was not encouraged. For World War II veterans there is, in fact, evidence that nonfarm work was considered in violation of regulations pertaining to participating in the training [ibid., 1952, p. 1664].

Cohort analysis and examination of changes in the size of an age group of farm operators for 1945-50, as contrasted to 1950-55 and 1955-59, detect no increase in entry rates possibly connected to farm training following the Korean War. Changed circumstances—including a less optimistic agricultural outlook and a new law governing educational programs—appear responsible.

World War II veterans who took on-farm training received a full-time sub-sistence allowance for part-time training. Nonfarm trainees received equivalent subsistence allowances. Although benefit levels were raised for Korean War veterans, the allowances for taking farm training were smaller than for other training.

Veterans of the Korean War had more pre-service education than veterans of World War II. Consequently, Korean veterans had a wider choice of educational welfare benefits from which to choose. However, although Korean War veterans exceeded World War II veterans in their farm backgrounds, a smaller proportion of them availed themselves of on-farm training. By 1955, 4.5 percent of all veterans of World War II had availed themselves of institutional on-farm training in contrast to only 1.7 percent of Korean veterans. However, the smaller participation of Korean veterans in farm training undoubtedly in part resulted from the fact that farming was relatively less attractive as an occupation in the 1950's than in the 1940's.

FEDERAL CREDIT PROGRAMS
FOR FARM DEVELOPMENT

Since the early days of the New Deal, the federal government has engaged in various types of subsidized and/or supervised farm credit programs. By the end of World War II, these activities centered in three federal agencies: (1) the Farm Security Administration (FSA), which was responsible for various programs designed to aid individual farm development as well as programs for small watershed development; (2) the Rural Electrification Administration (REA), which provided low interest rate loans for construction of electrical facilities to serve rural areas; (3) the Farm Credit Administration (FCA), which was designed to give farmers access to moderate-cost private credit from central money markets.

The REA and FCA have been concerned with the infrastructure serving agriculture and are thus of less interest to this study than the activities of the FSA and its successor agency, the Farmers Home Administration (FHA), which have been more concerned with individual farmers and the development of their farms. Hence, our analysis here is limited to the FSA and FHA, and more specifically to those parts of their programs concerned with individual farmers and the development of their farms.

The argument here is that extension of public credit to low-income farm operators involves them in programs that further commit the borrowers to farming and thereby reduce mobility of labor from agriculture. This argument is based on the belief that persons who receive farm operating loans and, to a lesser extent, those who receive ownership loans are on the margin of leaving or entering farming.[7] And since these people presumably cannot get credit else-

---

[7] Farm operating loans are funds extended for purchase of working capital items, in contrast to ownership loans, which are made for purchase of real estate.

where, the credit tips the scales in favor of remaining in the farm sector. In view of the characteristics of economic development leading to relative declining demand for farm products, a program which facilitates entry into farm employment may increase the cost to the individual of occupational adjustments which are eventually made. Also, facilitating entry into agriculture affects the income and asset position of farm operators already in agriculture.

Providing supervised credit to low-income farmers to aid them in farm development began as an anti-depression measure. Gradually, the policy was directed more toward assisting anyone to remain in agriculture who wanted to do so and could not get credit elsewhere. Initially, emphasis was on subsistence farming and maintaining people on the land; this later gave way to assisting low-income farmers to become commercial farmers.

From the beginning of the program in 1935 through fiscal 1962, over 2.2 million farm operating loans were made (Table 22). On September 30, 1943, the number of initial loans that had been made was equal to 11.4 percent of all farm operators reported in the 1940 census. In terms of persons involved, the program became less important during the 1950's. For the 1955–59 period, loans were made to 3.2 percent of all operators reported by the 1959 census.

TABLE 22. Initial Farm Operating Loans as a Percent of All Farm Operators at End of Period, United States, for Selected Periods, 1936–1962

Period	Total initial loans made	Total farm operators at end of period	New loans as a percent of all operators
	number	thousand	percent
1936–39	505,626	6,097	8.3
1940–44	319,271	5,859	5.4
1945–49	318,056	5,379	5.9
1950–54	192,411	4,783	4.0
1955–59	126,536	3,934	3.2
1960–62	81,997	–	–
1936–43	695,661	6,097	11.4
1936–62	2,239,558	–	–

Source: Jones [1964, p. 213].

Operating loans involve a considerably larger proportion of all farm operators in some states and regions than in others. From the beginning of the rural rehabilitation program through September 1943, 20 percent or more of all operators in Florida, New Mexico, Utah, Colorado, and Wyoming received loans [Larson et al., 1947, p. 354]. In addition, over 15 percent of all operators in nine other states in the South or the Great Plains areas received loans during the period.

A more recent study of three irrigation projects in Idaho and Washington indicated that the FHA provided from 32 to 57 percent of all credit obtained by farm operators [Franklin et al., 1959, p. 23]. A survey of the Columbia Basin Irrigation Project in 1955 showed that the FHA was an important source of credit in that area [ibid., p. 25].

In addition to its regional selectivity, the program was age selective, a relevant fact for evaluating its effects on entry rates and mobility of labor. For the period 1936–39, 60 percent of all standard loan receivers were under age 45, compared to 41 percent of all farm operators under 45 in 1940. In 1956 the proportion of borrowers under 35 years of age was almost twice as great as the proportion of all farm operators under 35.

It is argued elsewhere that monetary circumstances alone do not completely explain variations in entry and exit rates for farm operators. This is particularly true for the 1940–50 period. In the previous section we suggested that operation of institutional on-farm training for veterans contributed to increased entry rates during the 1945–50 period. This was also a period when the FHA made large numbers of loans for farm development. Thus, we focus our interest on the magnitude of loans related to changes in entry rates for various periods. Under the extreme assumption that all operators who received loans would have left agriculture if they had not received loans, we can obtain one measure of the possible impact of the program on entry rates. This calculated difference represents an upper limit to the impact of loans on entry and exit rates.

Entry rates would have been substantially lower and exit rates higher if all persons receiving loans left agriculture. For example, during the 1936–40 period, the 35 to 54 age group actually increased 2.4 percent, but, if all persons receiving loans were excluded, it would have decreased 5.8 percent. For 1940–50 the two figures show an actual 5.5 percent decrease versus a calculated 14.5 percent decrease for the 35 to 54 age group when loan receivers are excluded. But we cannot conclude from these data that loans actually increased entry rates or reduced withdrawal rates because the assumption itself needs testing.

An alternative method for measuring the impact of loans on entry rates is a single-equation multiple-regression approach. Variables found relevant by Heady and Tweeton [1963, Chap. 9] in explaining family labor employment on farms were used in combination with a variable measuring the number of persons involved in loan programs. Two general functions with variations were fitted. The first one specified farm employment as a function of the following variables:[8]

$$N = -R + UR + E_{t-1} + L - T$$

[8] See Jones [1964, pp. 228–36] for specification of variables and discussion of results.

where

N = average annual family labor employed on farms,
R = relative sector income,
UR = the average proportion of the industrial labor force unemployed during the year times R,
E = the aggregate farm equity ratio,
L = the number of initial farm operating loans made during the fiscal year,
T = time.

A second specification replaced R and UR with R' where R' represented a composite value constructed to represent the expected salvage value of farm labor.

All coefficients had expected signs and statistical results were acceptable within usually acceptable limits. Results show a positive relation between the number of initial farm operating loans made and average annual farm employment. Depending on which function is accepted, an increase of 1,000 initial farm operating loans increases employment by 1,580 to 2,810 persons. Although the upper limit is somewhat higher than expected from knowledge of the labor force on family farms, the coefficient is plausible within usual confidence limits.

Given this statistical relationship, a link appears between the unusually high entry rates of the 1945–50 period and loan activity. Previously it was concluded that institutional on-farm training contributed to those higher rates of entry; therefore, this finding is not inconsistent. The FHA made almost 110,000 loans in 1947, a number exceeded only in 1936 and roughly equaled in 1939. In 1947 the program was expanded to enable veterans to get back into farming; in fact, from then on, preference among loan applicants was granted to military service veterans.

Another relevant aspect of the loan program is the impact of supervised loans on productivity of labor involved. Farm records kept by borrowers and summarized by the FHA in annual progress reports show substantial increases in gross output and net income on borrowers' farms. A major proportion of loan funds was spent on inputs complementary to labor and thus would increase productivity. Therefore, purchase of complementary inputs tended to more fully employ labor that had frequently been underemployed.

We have made an attempt to measure the impact of this increased product on aggregate output and prices of farm products. The admittedly crude estimates suggest that the increased inputs due to federal credit programs in agriculture had a relatively small impact on price. However, the impact was larger for aggregate net farm income. Credit extended for operating loans in any one year probably increased aggregate output less than 1 percent. The impact on product prices was probably in the neighborhood of a 1 to 3 percent decrease as a result of credit extended during a given year; this is magnified to a 2 to 6 percent decrease in net farm income. Also, the cumulative effect of increased inputs, to the extent that inputs have life of more than one year, probably was somewhat greater than the above estimate.

SUMMARY

The index of labor used in farming decreased from 223 in 1917 to 70 in 1967. Labor-use data in agriculture indicate that declining farm labor use, whether measured by farm population, farm operators, hired and/or family labor resulted more from declining entry rates for younger farmers and less from increased exit rates for older farmers. Out-migration of various age cohorts over the time periods studied was quite consistent with estimated lower expected present values of future lifetime earnings in agriculture compared to higher expected present values in manufacturing for young farmers and expected present values of employment in laundries for older farmers. Older workers (over 35) often become "trapped" on farms because the marginal value product of their labor is greater than their salvage value off the farm. The labor exodus is also consistent with estimated residual returns to labor in agriculture which were consistently lower than nonfarm earnings.

As the United States became more industrialized, increased demand for labor in the nonfarm sector exerted "pull" on farm labor which was "released" from agriculture as the introduction of labor-saving technology decreased the marginal value productivity of farm labor. But despite the drastic contraction of labor use in agriculture, labor remains more productive relative to its cost, in the nonfarm economy, and less productive, relative to its cost, than labor-saving capital inputs in the farm sector. Thus, some continued exodus of farm labor is expected.

Study of institutional on-farm training for war veterans and of federal credit programs for farm development indicate that both programs contributed to the economic fixity of labor in agriculture. Persons involved in loan programs represent a relatively small proportion of all farm operators. Credit programs probably slowed the reduction in family labor employment in the short run, but in the long run loans of this type probably had a small impact on farm employment. On-farm training taken by the large majority of World War II veterans with farm backgrounds probably hindered occupational mobility.

CHAPTER 9

Land

GEORGE E. ROSSMILLER
and
ARNE LARSEN

This chapter explores the various economic and policy factors contributing to changing land use and value patterns, capital gains and losses on land, and the influence of land on output in the United States between 1917 and 1970. Land is treated separately as a factor of production because of its unique qualities, which derive from a relatively fixed aggregate physical supply, immobility, heterogeneity, and spatial characteristics. Throughout both time and space, land is combined with such other productive factors as labor and capital in agricultural production. Some capital serves the same purpose as land, either as a substitute for, or as an extender of, the fixed supply of land. Other capital complements land, and some combines with land as an imperfect substitute or, viewed alternatively, as an imperfect complement.

The first century and a half of U.S. agricultural technological advance was concentrated on the creation, production, distribution, and adoption of labor-saving capital, first to extend and later to replace labor. In recent years an added dimension has characterized advances in agricultural technology: a relatively fixed land base dictates that our innovative efforts should also concentrate on the creation, production, distribution, and utilization of land-saving capital to extend our fixed land base. Like labor-saving capital, land-saving capital can be overcommitted. And, when it is, it influences land values as well as its own value. At the individual farm level, land can also be overcommitted in two senses—too much physically and too much monetarily.

LAND USE 1917 TO 1964: THE HISTORICAL PICTURE

General land policy in the United States has progressed through four distinct phases since 1784. The first phase began with sales from the public domain to encourage national economic growth and to provide cash receipts to the federal treasury. To augment cash sales and to provide for more rapid settlement of the public domain for agricultural purposes, the Homestead Act was passed in 1862. This second phase lasted until 1891, although full settlement was not accomplished until the second decade of the 1900's. Farm population reached its peak in 1916 (in part due to the federal land disposal policies), declined up to 1930, rose again through 1933 with a "back to the farm" movement during the depression, and has declined since.

Between 1891 and the beginning of the New Deal in 1933, land policy emphasis was on reservation and conservation implemented through various legislation including the Forest Reserve Act (1891), the Newlands National Reclamation Act (1902), the federal Water Power Act (1920), and the Clarke-McNary Forest and Watershed Improvement Act (1924). The present phase of policy began in 1933 with the New Deal and has been characterized by public land management of the remaining public domain and legislative assistance to agriculture through various commodity, trade, production control, price support, and credit policies.

Table 23 presents the gross picture of land use in agriculture for the census periods 1910–64. Land in farms increased from 879 million acres in 1910 to a peak of about 1,160 million acres in the early 1950's and then declined to 1,106 million acres by 1964. For the most part, the increase was accounted for by the transfer of land into the farm category from the "grazing land not in farms" category. The cropland category remained relatively constant after 1920, when

TABLE 23. Farms, Land, Land Use, and Average Farm Size in the
United States, 1910–1964

Year	Farms (1,000)	Land in farms	Farmland as % of total land	In crops	Cropland Idle or in cover crops	Total	Grazing land not in farms	Average farm size
		million acres	%	. . . .	million acres	. . . .		acres
1910	6,362	879	46.2	324	23	367	739	138
1920	6,448	956	50.2	374	28	402	661	148
1925	6,372	924	48.6	365	26	391	646	145
1930	6,289	987	51.8	379	34	413	578	156
1935	6,812	1,055	55.4	375	41	416	533	155
1940	6,097	1,061	55.7	363	36	399	504	174
1945	5,859	1,142	59.9	379	24	403	428	195
1950	5,382	1,159	60.9	387	22	409	400	215
1954	4,782	1,158	60.8	380	19	399	353	242
1959	3,704	1,120	58.9	358	33	391	317	302
1964	3,153	1,106	58.2	335	52	387	294	351

Source: U.S. Department of Agriculture, Agricultural Statistics.

402 million acres were counted; this figure increased to 416 million by 1935, owing largely to vast areas of the central Great Plains falling under the plow— only to be caught in the drought of the 1930's, which caused much of the same area to revert back to grassland. By 1964, the area had dropped to 387 million acres. Thus, cropland area had remained relatively stable since 1920, with a slight increase in the total land in farms primarily through shifts of grazing land from unassigned uses in the public domain to assignment uses for specific farms.

For all practical purposes, the total amount of agricultural land in the United States has not changed since the second decade of the 1900's. A combination of a decrease in the number of farms since 1916 and the transfer of unassigned public domain to specific farm units substantially increased average farm size. In the five decades between 1910 and 1964, average farm size more than doubled— from 138 to 351 acres.

While the national supply of land in acres is fixed for most practical purposes, an acre of land is not a homogeneous unit either through time or across the country. Cropland, rangeland, and improved pastures measured in acres do not provide the same flow of services. Further, the degree of capital investment in land such as clearing, draining, and irrigating varies from one region to another. Thus, if one is to detail the intensity of land utilization more fully, some type of unit other than an area measurement such as the acre is needed to distinguish among different land qualities. Arne Larsen [1966] developed such a measure in the "pasture-acre equivalent"; this weights cropland acreage, both irrigated and dry, irrigated pasture, and other land by the ratio of their prices to the price of dry-land pasture over time and for each state. While this procedure leaves many questions from an analytical point of view, it does provide some, if limited, basis for time and spatial comparisons.

Table 24 presents percentage changes in pasture-acre equivalents by regions and for the whole of the United States for selected periods between 1917 and 1962. The table shows that the amount of farm land for the United States as a whole changed little during the period even when measured in pasture-acre equivalents. A closer inspection shows, however, that some substantial inter-regional shifts in land use occurred. A significant decrease of almost 20 percent in the number of pasture-acre equivalents is observed in the Northeast region between 1917 and 1929. This decrease is explained primarily by technical developments that permitted exploitation of Western regions relative to the North-east, which was at a comparative disadvantage. Increases in the number of pasture-acre equivalents were substantial in the Mountain region, the Northern and Southern Plains, and the Pacific area. The increases in the Northern Plains are accounted for to a large extent by the plowing of vast areas of the virgin plains for grain production. Since much of this land was in the semiarid portion of the Northern Plains, cultivation was subsequently abandoned during the 1930's due to lack of moisture, the land reverting back to grass. The shift to

TABLE 24. Percentage Changes in Pasture-Acre Equivalents by Regions and for the United States for Selected Periods, 1917-1962

(percent)

Region	1917-29	1930-33	1934-41	1942-47	1948-54	1955-62
United States	+1.2	+2.0	+2.7	+1.7	+0.7	−4.0
Northeast	−19.2	+2.7	−5.3	−5.6	−8.9	−19.5
Corn Belt	−4.9	+0.6	+0.8	−1.7	−1.7	−2.8
Lake States	−1.7	+4.3	+4.2	−3.3	−2.7	−7.0
Appalachian	−7.8	+1.9	−0.6	−3.8	−7.3	−16.4
Southeast	−7.5	+3.3	+7.6	+2.3	−2.3	−23.5
Delta States	+1.7	+4.5	+4.3	+1.4	+1.3	−17.3
Southern Plains	+14.9	+4.9	0.0	+2.8	+3.6	−0.8
Northern Plains	+10.9	+1.4	+2.8	+2.3	+3.6	+2.1
Mountain	+30.9	0.0	+20.4	+12.7	+6.8	+4.9
Pacific	+12.4	0.0	+5.6	+11.6	+10.8	+4.2

Source: Data from Van Gigch [1968, p. 282].

more intensive use of land in the Southern Plains was due largely to increased production of cotton stimulated by high prices resulting from boll weevil infestations in competing regions. The greatest expansion in cotton took place in the mid-1920's when over 45 million acres were planted. Between 1919 and 1926, Texas emerged as the state accounting for about one-third of the total cotton acreage as a result of additional cotton plantings of 5 to 6 million acres [Barger and Landsberg, 1942, pp. 76-77].

The increase in agricultural use intensity in the Pacific region was in response (1) to the general development of the region, which increased the demand for agricultural products locally, and (2) a national increase in demand for products of the region resulting from the changing patterns of consumption brought about by growing national income and population. Both the Southern Plains and the Pacific region also experienced expansion of irrigated land acreage.

The U.S. agricultural land base measured in pasture-acre equivalents increased by about 1 percent during the 1917-29 period. During the much shorter interval, 1930-33, a 2 percent increase was estimated; this was relatively uniform throughout the country except for the Mountain and Pacific regions where no change occurred. The period 1917 to 1929 was characterized by an increase in the proportion of other factors of production relative to land. Productive factors other than land moved geographically with the observed regional changes in land use. In contrast to that period, changes in the input mix in the 1929-33 period primarily concerned the volume of land stock. In part, land stock increased as a result of the "back to the farm" movement associated with the general economic depression. In addition, several programs in the 1930's dealt with land improvement.

The farm land base continued to increase during the 1934-41 period. However, expansion was not uniform throughout the country and, in fact, three

regions—the Northeast, Appalachia, and the Southern Plains—decreased or remained constant. Adjustment of the land input in the Northeast was a continua-
tion of the interregional adjustment process also observed in the 1917–29 period
but interrupted in the 1930–33 period by the depression. Appalachia was
dependent primarily on tobacco and cotton, crops that became subject to
acreage control early in the period. The Southeast, also heavily dependent upon
cotton, did increase land use; the decline in land devoted to cotton was offset
with expansion in other crops. The large earlier land use increase in the Southern
Plains, due primarily to expansion of cotton acreage, was halted by acreage
controls imposed early in the New Deal era.

Between 1942 and 1947, land use intensity increased at a 1.7 percent rate,
slower than during either of the two immediately preceding periods. By 1942
much of the complementary capital which could be added to U.S. land to
increase pasture-acre equivalents had been added. Also much of the readjustment
which could be made in the use of land to increase pasture-acreage equivalents
had been made. However, some shifts in the regional land use pattern in the
1942–47 period helped in fulfilling war-production requirements. These shifts
were spurred on by changes in the structure of agricultural product prices. Land
use increased in the Southern states, where labor was relatively abundant and
where alternatives to cotton—such as peanuts, soybeans, and corn—were encouraged through price incentives and the removal of acreage restrictions. In the
Plains states, part of the increase in the land input was attributable to physical
expansion of the land base through recultivation of land that the drought forced
out of production during the 1930's. Further, improved planting materials and
fertilizer were already being added to utilize the land base more fully and from
World War II on, increases in farm production came, in substantial part, from
extending the land base with a substitute for additional land. The use of improved seeds and fertilizers is not reflected in pasture-acreage equivalents; from
World War II on, pasture equivalents became a poor proxy for the total input of
land and land substitute capital actually used. Between 1948 and 1954, the
increase in land use intensity, as measured by pasture-acreage equivalents, was
less at 0.7 percent than during any prior period. Measured in acres, farm land
input reached a peak somewhere between 1945 and 1954 and declined thereafter (Table 23, above). The increases in pasture-acre equivalents since then,
despite fewer acres of land, indicate that the use of land extenders and substitutes were being expanded sufficiently to offset the acreage decreases. A substantial amount of land intensification took place through land improvements
resulting from government-sponsored projects that encouraged irrigation, drainage, flood protection, and conservation practices under the agricultural conservation program, as well as federally sponsored flood control projects. Irrigated land
in farms increased by about 3.8 million acres between 1949 and 1954 [U.S.
Dept. of Commerce, Statistical Abstract, 1964, p. 53]. About half the increase

in irrigated land was located in the Southern region, one quarter in the Pacific region, and most of the rest in the Northern Plains and the Delta region. Land drainage projects were located primarily in the Southern region and particularly in the Delta [ibid., p. 52]. By 1951, the Corps of Engineers had reclaimed an estimated 8 million acres from flood damage. Of the 1.1 million acres included in pasture improvement programs between 1944 and 1953, nearly 80 percent was in the Southern region [ibid., p. 50]. The large increase in pasture-acre equivalents in the Mountain states was probably due to the tillage of previously opened range land.

Between 1955 and 1962, the land input measured in pasture-acre equivalents decreased by 4 percent. Though this was the only period when a net decrease in land intensification occurred, it definitely indicated a shift from the use of complements that extended pasture-acreage equivalents. Instead, extension of the land base was accomplished with land substitutes such as fertilizers, improved varieties, and plant protection, which are not measured in terms of pasture-acre equivalents. The latter decreased by almost one-quarter in the Southeast region and by more than 15 percent in the Northeast, Appalachian, and Delta regions. Increases were recorded in the Mountain, Northern Plains, and Pacific regions. This, however, was not a period in which the use of land plus land substitutes decreased. Land substitutes expanded steadily to more than offset the decreased use of land. While government policies with respect to land were partially responsible for the decrease in the land input, they also encouraged the use of capital both to replace the land withdrawn from production and to extend land use.

The Agricultural Act of 1956 established the soil bank program under which land was shifted from farming by placing it in either the acreage reserve or the conservation reserve. Between 1957 and 1962, about 25 million acres were diverted from agricultural production under the soil bank. Starting in 1959, eligibility for price supports for certain commodities was made contingent upon diversion of acreage to soil-conserving practices. Between 1957 and 1962 fertilizer usage increased from 21.6 to 27.4 million tons (over 25 percent), the increase amounting to almost a quarter ton per acre of land going into the soil bank. The agricultural conservation program has been one of the major causes of increases in pasture-acre equivalents. A review of shifts in land intensification indicates that the agricultural conservation program was more effective in the Western region than in the Southern, Central, and Lake regions, and it was particularly ineffective in the Northeast and Appalachian regions.

The pasture-acre equivalent measure of land use intensification applied to various regions of the United States over time measures only part of the changing influence of various economic and political factors. As noted above, the use of such land substitutes as fertilizers, pesticides, improved varieties, etc., has extended the effective land base of the United States in ways not measurable in terms of pasture-acre equivalents.

THE PRODUCTIVITY OF LAND AND
LAND-SAVING OR LAND-EXTENDING CAPITAL

The consequences of the changing composition and levels of economic and technological variables are evident in differential changes over time in the marginal physical products and marginal value products of land in various areas of the country. Table 25 presents average yearly rates of change in estimated marginal physical products of real estate in 1947-49 constant dollars and marginal value product of real estate in current dollars for nineteen types of farming areas for selected time periods between 1930 and 1962. These estimates were calculated by using a combined cross-sectional, time-series, Cobb-Douglas production function [Rossmiller, November 1965]. With few exceptions, the rate of change in MPP's for all areas in all time spans is positive. Of the exceptions, those occurring in the 1940-49 period are negative, following substantial increases in MPP's in the early part of the period due to generally favorable weather in 1942 and 1943 and decreases in 1949 due to unfavorable weather [Stallings, February 1960, pp. 180-86].

A lower rate of increase for MVP than for MPP indicates that the average change in product prices for the period was negative. This was true, with five exceptions, for the 1933-39 period; in three of the five exceptions, prices did not change; in two, prices increased.

The 1950-54 period was characterized by falling product prices that had started in late 1948. Even though MPP changes in most areas were positive, the effect of the price decline overwhelmed the impact of rising MPP's so that the MVP's trended downward except for the Southern Piedmont cotton and Washington and Oregon wheat fallow areas. At this point, we should call the reader's attention again to the shift after World War II to the use of land substitutes which, in effect, expanded the U.S. agricultural land base in a manner not well measured by the concept of pasture-acre equivalents. It is also true that these increases were not well measured by the real estate data used by Rossmiller in making the MPP and MVP estimates under discussion here. Even that is not the end of the difficulty, because the fertilizers, improved seeds, pesticides, etc., which *substitute* for land, appear as operating expenses in the Cobb-Douglas function Rossmiller used to estimate the MPP's and MVP's. Use of the Cobb-Douglas function assumes implicitly that real estate and operating expenses are imperfect substitutes and partial complements for each other rather than substitutes. Thus, serious questions exist concerning Rossmiller's use of the Cobb-Douglas function in this regard.

TABLE 25. Average Yearly Rates of Change in Real Estate in Marginal Physical
Products (MPP's in Constant 1947-1949 Dollars) and Marginal
Value Products (MVP's in Current Dollars per Acre), Selected Areas
and Periods, 1933-1962

(percent per acre)

Area	1933-39		1940-49		1950-54		1955-62	
	MPP	MVP	MPP	MVP	MPP	MVP	MPP	MVP
Central Northeast dairy	+0.73	+0.44	-0.02	+1.19	-0.12	-0.39	+0.84	+0.93
Eastern Wisconsin dairy	+ .98	+ .58	+ .08	+1.72	+ .21	- .34	+1.04	+1.13
Western Wisconsin dairy	+ .54	+ .35	+ .08	+1.23	+ .12	- .37	+ .40	+ .55
Minnesota dairy-hog	+ .52	+ .47	+ .27	+1.54	+ .16	- .19	+ .96	+1.03
Corn Belt hog-dairy	+ .87	+ .66	+ .26	+1.98	+ .05	- .05	+ .89	+1.11
Corn Belt hog-beef raising	+ .30	+ .30	+ .12	+ .98	+ .12	- .05	+ .58	+ .67
Corn Belt hog-beef fattening	+1.06	+ .84	+ .39	+3.14	+ .65	-1.03	+3.16	+3.24
Corn Belt cash grain	+ .85	+ .30	+ .25	+1.73	+ .15	- .35	+ .60	+ .26
Southern Piedmont cotton	+ .40	+ .08	- .02	+ .60	+ .41	+ .16	+ .28	+ .32
Texas Black Prairie cotton	+ .48	+ .10	+ .31	+1.20	+ .41	- .20	+ .21	+ .21
Northern Plains wheat-small grain-livestock	+ .14	+ .09	+ .01	+ .44	- .04	- .12	+ .11	+ .15
Northern Plains wheat-corn-livestock	+ .15	+ .15	+ .10	+ .55	+ .03	- .16	+ .04	+ .16
Northern Plains wheat-roughage-livestock	+ .07	+ .06	+ .03	+ .30	+ .05	- .09	0.00	+ .04
Southern Plains winter wheat	+ .10	+ .09	+ .02	+ .47	- .05	- .16	+ .23	+ .25
Southern Plains wheat-grain sorghum	+ .07	+ .06	+ .07	+ .43	- .10	- .25	+ .60	+ .56
Washington & Oregon wheat fallow	+ .18	+ .04	- .04	+ .40	+ .07	+ .06	+ .11	+ .11
Northern Plains cattle	+ .03	+ .03	0.00	+ .08	- .01	- .14	+ .02	+ .08
Intermountain cattle	+ .02	+ .07	+ .01	+ .22	+ .13	- .36	+ .15	+ .36
Northern Plains sheep	+ .01	+ .02	0.00	+ .08	- .01	- .17	+ .04	+ .03

Source: Rossmiller [1965].

These questions are particularly relevant for the period following World War II. More specifically, the positive rates of change in MPP's and MVP's of real estate for the 1955–62 period in Table 25 are probably questionable and over-estimated. Had an index of the combined use of land and land substitutes been used along with operating expense data precluding expenditures on fertilizers, improved seeds, pesticides, etc., it is likely that the higher input of "real estate equivalents" would have had lower MPP's and MVP's. At any rate, an acre of land and an acre-equivalent of, say, fertilizer would be expected to have about equal MVP's and about equal values. Interestingly enough, Quance's estimates of the ratios between land and fertilizer MPP's and between the prices of land and fertilizer show a remarkable degree of equality (see last columns of Table 11 in Chapter 7). Theoretically, the picture is illustrated in Figure 14.

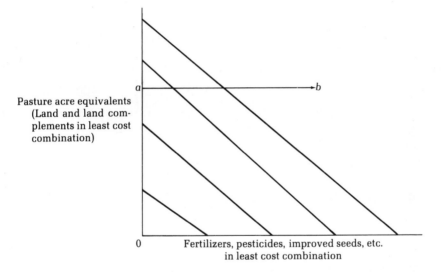

Figure 14. Land, land complements, and land substitutes in agricultural production.

In recent years, U.S. agricultural production can be viewed as expanding mainly along the line *ab* (Figure 14) unless some program, such as the Soil Bank, has forced it to a lower parallel line. In theory the following equality between the indicated ratios should hold along this line:

$$\frac{MPP_{PAE}}{MPP_{Fert}} = \frac{P_{PAE}}{P_{Fert}}.$$

This is empirically true according to Quance's Table 11. In the case of land, for the individual farmer, the differential between acquisition cost and salvage values is not very large, being in the neighborhood of 5 to 10 percent to cover broker-age fees, closing costs, etc. Thus, whether P_{PAE} in the above equation is an on-farm opportunity cost, salvage value, or acquisition cost is of little statistical significance, given the accuracy of the data, despite the importance of land prices to a farmer with, say, 640 acres of Eastern Central Illinois land valued at $900 an acre.

In connection with his analysis of capital use and earnings in Chapter 7, Quance also estimated the MVP of land with results similar to the Rossmiller estimates on which the data in Table 25 are based (see Table 26). The technique

TABLE 26. Marginal Value Products of Land in the Farm Sector and the USDA Index of Land Values, United States, 1917-1962

Year	Discounted MVP of the value of an acre of land[a]	USDA index of land value (1956-60 = 100)	Year	Discounted MVP of the value of an acre of land[a]	USDA index of land value (1956-60 = 100)
1917	$43.24		1941	$23.14	31
1918	45.87		1942	25.52	33
1919	48.43		1943	27.64	36
1920	56.84		1944	30.86	42
			1945	35.27	46
1921	51.95				
1922	53.68		1946	39.57	52
1923	45.70		1947	44.22	58
1924	46.25		1948	47.08	63
1925	43.60		1949	46.92	66
			1950	47.00	65
1926	40.54				
1927	39.85		1951	55.78	74
1928	38.76		1952	62.01	82
1929	37.61	43	1953	61.90	83
1930	35.45	42	1954	61.50	82
			1955	64.84	85
1931	31.35	38			
1932	26.40	32	1956	68.49	89
1933	23.16	26	1957	73.85	94
1934	22.69	28	1958	78.48	99
1935	22.81	28	1959	84.07	106
			1960	93.14	111
1936	23.54	30			
1937	23.71	31	1961	96.32	112
1938	23.24	31	1962	101.80	118
1939	22.93	30			
1940	22.37	30			

[a]Computed for Quance by Shyamalendu Sarkar of Michigan State University, using the estimating techniques employed by Quance [1967] and treating the current value of farm land in the United States as the input and the farm mortgage credit rate of interest as the cost of a dollar invested in land. Sarkar's MVP's have been multiplied by the price of an acre of land.

used by Quance to estimate MVP's can be called the factor-share, lagged-adjustment method. As a first step, the annual income accruing to a factor is estimated; this is the factor share. In the case of land, it includes interest on the
value of land and whatever other charges are deemed appropriate to cover depreciation, taxes, repairs, complementary inputs, and land substitutes. In
Quance's estimates, the interest charge was the main item included. It was estimated, in effect, by multiplying land acreage by current land prices by the
interest rate. In the next step, the factor share was divided by gross income to
estimate the proportion of income going to the factor concerned (land, in this
case). The estimated equilibrium value of this proportion is interpreted as the
elasticity of farm output with respect to the factor. In the case under consideration, it is the elasticity of gross income with respect to changes in the *value*
(price X quantity) of land used, and not of the quantity alone as in the case of
the Rossmiller estimates. By assuming the appropriateness of using a Cobb-
Douglas function at the aggregate level, the estimates of elasticity are then used,
along with input and output quantities to estimate MVP's.

Quance's results are suspect for the post–World War II years and for reasons
somewhat similar to those for suspecting Rossmiller's estimates. In the earlier
years, land and land complements were used in U.S. agriculture in a manner
which changed the quality of land in ways not well measured by the concepts of
ordinary acres, pasture-acre equivalents, or factor shares, while in recent years
land substitutes were used with land to extend the land base also in ways not
accurately measurable by real estate factor shares, ordinary acres, or pasture-acre
equivalents. The difficulties with the factor share lagged-adjustment approach
are that unless the lag in adjustment is large or there are large changes in use (in
this case, in the value) of the factor, marginal value product estimates are
forced to be close to marginal factor costs and, of course, equal to the average
factor costs. Thus, when and whether farmers overvalue or undervalue land by
pricing it at more or less than the present value of its stream of MVP's, the factor
share, lagged-adjustment approach to estimating MVP's produces estimates tending to equate MVP's with marginal factor costs based on the under- or over-
evaluation of land.

The conclusions to be drawn from the above evaluations of the Rossmiller
and Quance estimates are: (1) that little significance should be attached to the
close correspondence between these estimates, (2) that there are reasons to expect Rossmiller's MVP to be high for the post–World War II period, and (3) that
Quance's estimates should be expected to err with the errors of farmers in
evaluating land, errors that have been very large (both positively and negatively)
in the past.

Quance's estimated MVP's for land are compared in Table 26 with the USDA
index of land values. In general they move together—too well, in fact, in recent
years in view of increased interest rates.

Land is a specialized durable, not readily reproducible as such in either the farm or the nonfarm economy, though relatively easily (1) improved in quality with the application of complementary capital and (2) extended through the use of land-saving or substitute capital. As a specialized, nonreproducible durable, land (as distinguished from its substitutes and complements) has a low salvage value in the nonfarm economy and has for society a very high acquisition cost. Some of its reproducible complements such as drainage and irrigation facilities also have low salvage values but acquisition is closely related to the cost of producing the complements. Many of the substitutes for land are specialized, one-use, expendables (such as fertilizer, improved seeds, and pesticides), whose salvage values are low (but not very relevant as farmers seldom own large unutilized stocks) and whose acquisition costs are moderate and often falling (in real terms) because of technological advances and the overcommitment of resources by supplying firms to their production.

Another relevant characteristic of the markets for land and for its closely related complements and substitutes is imperfect knowledge. Though opportunity costs and the range over which the MVP of land can vary are closely bounded for any one farmer at any point in time by salvage values near to acquisition costs, agriculture as an industry has near-zero salvage values and near-infinite acquisition costs for land. Thus, when large numbers of farmers hold uniform but erroneous expectations with respect to the price and the technological and institutional forces governing land prices, very serious mistakes of overpricing and underpricing land do occur. The consequences are large-scale capital gains and losses. Reference to Table 1 in Chapter 2 indicates that, in current dollar terms, annual gains and losses of over $2 billion are commonplace and that, in the 1911–59 period, annual losses often exceeded $7 billion while annual gains often exceeded $11 billion. Since much of the value involved in the losses was often pledged, such losses often had to be repaid in current dollars.

In constant (1910–14) dollar terms, losses once exceeded $3 billion and gains once exceeded $4 billion in the 1940–59 period (Table 2 in Chapter 2). Thus, while there is a close correspondence between current ex post MVP's and land values, neither current ex post MVP's or current land values are good measures of long-term land values. Still further, the relatively small difference between salvage values and acquisition costs for land for any farmer at any point in time offers little protection against capital losses and does not prevent receipt of capital gains.

INCOME TO OWNERS OF REAL ESTATE

Payments for farm real estate services embody several components. These include, as the definition of farm real estate implies, payment for the services of farm buildings used in the normal operation of the farm unit. In addition, payments are made for improvements on land—such as clearing, fences, irrigation, drainage, leveling, and other man-made improvements. Finally, payments are made for the land itself, that is, for the original properties of land as found in nature.

The role of land in economic progress is a major concern to economists. It was generally believed that the factor share accruing to land would increase over time. This was implied by John Stuart Mill:

> The economical progress of a society constituted of landlords, capitalists, and laborers tends to the progressive enrichment of the landlord class while the cost of the laborers' subsistence tends on the whole to increase and profits to fall. Agricultural improvements are a counter acting force to the two last affects, but the first, though the case is conceivable in which it would be temporarily checked, is ultimately in a high degree promoted by those improvements and the increase of population tends to transfer all the benefits derived from agricultural improvements to the landlords alone [Mill, 1849, pp. 731–732].

In other words, the increased supply of agricultural products brought about by technological progress is matched by an increasing demand due to population increase. Technological progress would therefore not lead to less expensive food prices, and thus benefits from that progress would be transferred to the landowners through higher land rents. Land rents are then an increasing part of the value added in the economy.

Time has, however, proven this analysis wrong. Agricultural production improvements have been large enough to more than balance the increased demands for food. In the developed parts of the world land-saving technology has made land relatively abundant. This has led to a decline in the proportion of national income accruing to land. From this observation Schultz [1953, p. 128] set forth the following proposition as historically valid with respect to the economic development characterizing Western countries:

(1) A declining proportion of the aggregate inputs of the community is required to produce (or to acquire) farm products.

(2) Of the inputs employed to produce farm products, the proportion represented by land is not an increasing one, despite the recombination of inputs in farming to use less human effort relative to other inputs including land.

The value of farm real estate reflects not only services of land itself but also services of land improvements and farm buildings. During the 1917–65 period, a continual net investment in farm buildings occurred except during the 1930's and early 1940's. The amount of farm land as measured in pasture-acre equivalents was rather stable in the period of 1917-29 and then increased slowly until 1953-54. Since 1954 the figure has decreased. Nevertheless, that some changes in farm real estate reflect both quantity and price changes in the stock of farm buildings and land improvements seems fairly clear. This variation in farm real estate values does not give a good indication of variation in land values.

Variation in the total value of farm real estate is shown in Table 27. The variation is closely related to the variation in agricultural product prices and, consequently, net farm income. Thus, there was a large decrease in the value of farm real estate from the early 1920's to the mid-1930's. During World War II the value of farm real estate was far below the level warranted by net income in agriculture. This indicated that farmers did not expect the favorable prices of the war years to continue. Since the end of the war, prices of real estate have increased rapidly, even during periods with rather unfavorable net incomes in agriculture. Land rent for the economy also increased rapidly, and increases in farm real estate values were generally larger than increases in the GNP. Since there were net investments in buildings and land improvements during this period, it follows that land rent currently constitutes a smaller part of the GNP than it did twenty years ago [Boyne, 1964, Chap. 4]. Thus, the U.S. economy is earning an ever-decreasing proportion of its income from agricultural land rent, as Schultz postulated.

TABLE 27. Farm Real Estate Value and Gross National Product in the United States for Selected Periods, 1916-1970

	Value of farm real estate		Gross national product (1957-59 = 100)
Period	Billion current dollars	1957-59 = 100	
1916-20	5.17	44	
1921-25	53.6	46	
1926-30	48.0	41	
1931-35	35.4	30	
1936-40	34.5	30	
1941-45	43.1	37	40
1946-50	71.0	61	55
1951-55	94.3	81	79
1956-60	116.7	100	100
1961-65	144.3	123	107
1966-70	176.4	169	123

Source: USDA, Agricultural Statistics, Annual; and U.S. Department of Labor, Bureau of Labor Statistics, Survey of Current Business.

But we must look more closely to determine just how this change has occurred. A decline in the proportion of national income produced by agriculture continued throughout the time period of this study. This is expected, as economic growth causes a movement of factors from primary to secondary and to tertiary sectors. As agricultural production expanded in the agricultural sector, labor moved to other occupations.

The second of Schultz's propositions [1953], which argues that the proportion of agricultural inputs represented by land should not increase over time, is consistent, or at least not inconsistent, with the empirical results of the later years.

Two measures of the real estate share of gross agricultural income are shown in Table 28. The computed share in Column 1 of the table was obtained by attaching an opportunity cost interest rate to the value of farm real estate. Thus, in this case the return to labor is the residual of gross income left over when operating expenses, working capital, and real estate are paid. If, instead, the returns to labor are computed, the residual is the return to farm real estate as shown in Column 2 of Table 28. The computed land share in Column 3 differs from the computed real estate share in that returns to improvements are subtracted out. All three measures suggest that earlier tendencies of declining land and/or real estate share are at least temporarily reversed. During the 1920's and the beginning of the 1930's, the computed share was much larger than the residual share; however, during the 1940's, the residual share was more than twice the computed share. Since it is doubtful that labor input should be so seriously undervalued, the situation in the 1940's indicates the uncertainty with which most farmers regarded the future.

TABLE 28. Real Estate Share of Gross Income in U. S. Agriculture, Selected Periods, 1911–1965

Year	Real estate share		Computed land share
	Computed	Residual	
1911–15	32.6%	–	24.9%
1916–20	24.7	–	18.2
1921–25	32.7	23.7%	23.5
1926–30	25.8	16.5	16.7
1931–35	30.4	16.0	19.2
1936–40	18.2	23.7	10.5
1941–45	11.0	28.7	6.4
1946–50	12.1	28.2	7.2
1951–55	15.2	19.9	9.2
1956–60	18.8	16.4	12.3
1961–65	21.4	16.7	14.7

Source: Lerohl and MacEachern [1967].

In addition to the low expectations of the 1940's, another reason for the increasing land factor share since that time has been the increasing change of technological progress to land-saving and labor-saving inputs. Thus the residual computations leave with land all profits from such highly productive modern land-saving inputs as fertilizers, improved seeds, pesticides, insecticides, etc. The increased use of these inputs has been so great as to render the data for "computed land share" in Table 28 virtually meaningless. In addition, some capitalization of benefits from government programs contributed to increasing land-factor shares of gross agricultural income.

In summary, the computed share of real estate and of land and its substitutes in agricultural income in the U.S. increased during the two decades 1940–60, mainly because of (1) an exceptionally low share during the 1940's, (2) larger land-saving technological changes, and (3) benefits from subsidies. The land, per se, share of *total* income has probably decreased both in agriculture and in the total in the U.S. economy.

COMPONENTS OF THE FARM
REAL ESTATE MARKET

Farm real estate market values in the United States have followed an upward trend ever since the mid-1930's. Even though net farm income per farm declined from its 1949 high and fluctuated between 1949 and 1955 at relatively lower levels before beginning its present rising trend in 1956, farm real estate prices rose steadily through the entire period with only two minor setbacks occurring in 1950 and 1954 [USDA, Agricultural Finance Review, 1964]. Moreover, numerous studies reveal net farm incomes insufficient to pay opportunity cost returns to residual claimants—labor, real estate, and other capital.

One of the first questions asked, in attempting to understand changes in the total current dollar values of farm real estate, is what change in quantity has occurred. Boyne analyzed changes in major reproducible capital investments tied to land such as irrigation facilities, buildings, and reclamation and drainage investment, as well as changes in quantity of land in farms. He concluded that the stock of farm land between 1940 and 1960 increased only 1 percent and the cost in dollar value of farm buildings increased about 2 percent [Boyne, 1964].

A second question concerns the relationship between changes in farm real estate prices and the general price level. The trends correlate quite closely between 1930 and 1964 with the farm real estate price index increasing at a somewhat more rapid rate than the consumer price index. Boyne found that real capital gains accruing to farm operators due to farm real estate investment between 1940 and 1960 amounted to $26.5 billion in 1960 [Boyne, 1964].

A third question concerns trends in the nonfarmer participation in the farm real estate market. One type of purchase in this category is for nonfarm use. As discussed earlier, the influence of these nonfarm demands for land on land values is quite small. The other type of transaction in this category involves the nonfarmer entering the farm real estate market as an investor. The net of farm buyers over nonfarmer sellers as indicated earlier reached a peak of 21.3 percent of the total farm real estate market in 1956 (the year of the Soil Bank program) and then declined rapidly to 3.4 percent in 1966 [USDA, Farm Real Estate, 1967].

The expansion farmer buyer is an increasingly dominant force in the farm real estate market. In 1948, 35.5 percent of the market transfers were for expansion purposes. By 1966 this figure increased to 53.8 percent [USDA, Farm Real Estate, June 1967].

The expansion buyer category includes both those who are receiving parity returns on resources used in agricultural production and those who are not. But both types of expansion buyers create upward pressures on real estate values through their activities in the real estate market. According to a report to the U.S. Congress [USDA, Document No. 44, 1967], the parity returns position of all farms improved between 1959 and 1966. However, returns from farming in 1966 averaged between 4 and 21 percent below parity returns depending upon the components of the measurement used. Parity returns are defined as returns to resources used in agriculture equal to returns to comparable resources used in nonagricultural production. This is in close accord with the theoretical analysis in Chapter 3.

When farms are classified by value of sales and the returns from farming by class compared to parity returns, the report shows that farms with sales over $20,000 had returns well over parity returns under all methods of calculation used. Farms with sales less than $20,000 received returns below parity and those with under $5,000 sales received less than 50 percent of parity. Farms with sales of over $20,000 accounted for 16.2 percent of total farms in 1966 and for 68 percent of the total value of products sold. Since expansion buyers in this class are receiving returns on their resources used in agriculture above returns for comparable resources outside of agriculture, they can well afford to bid up the price of farm real estate for farm expansion purposes. In the aggregate, resources on these farms are not trapped in the sense that total returns are lower than returns to comparable factors in the nonfarm economy and pressures for expansion in the number and sizes of these units exist.

But for expansion buyers in the sales classes below $20,000 a somewhat different situation prevails. With some situations as described in previous chapters, labor and capital are economically fixed on these farms and the process becomes one of minimizing losses on labor and capital by opportunity costing. One way to minimize such losses is to organize farms as efficiently as possible, given the fixed resources. To minimize losses in recent years has often required large operating units [Quenemoen, 1966]. Such expansions sometimes involve investments in large new labor-saving equipment. If mistakes are made in such investments, still further loss-minimizing expansions are required. In many instances, farms with parity returns one year become loss-minimizing farms in subsequent years due to such errors. Since many commercial farmers have found themselves in this position in recent years—too little land to efficiently use available fixed resources including those embodying new technology—they continue to bid actively for the relatively small proportion of farm land that is available for sale each year [Scofield, 1964].

Since much of the new technology is now of a land-saving type, land MVP's decrease or do not advance as rapidly as they would in the absence of the newer land-saving technologies. Nevertheless, it is rational for loss-minimizing expansion buyers in this category to be willing to pay high prices for land, even though their overinvestment in capital may not be receiving acquisition costs.

The expected effect of government programs on the value of farm real estate, where economic fixity of labor and capital exist and, given rapid technological advance resulting in excess capacity with regard to these inputs on individual farms, is quite different from the case of farms that are in initial equilibrium in the classical economic sense with acquisition costs equal to salvage values. Programs that hold commodity prices above market-clearing levels cause the marginal value products of all inputs to increase and more of all inputs to be used. The amount of increased use of each is determined by the relative elasticities of their supply curves and the elasticities of substitution.

But where labor and/or capital overcapacity already exists with acquisition costs in excess of salvage values, opportunity costs of those inputs employed will be below acquisition costs and above salvage value. In this case, returns from the government programs are allocated to the fixed inputs (perhaps including but not necessarily solely land) and capitalized into a higher price for such fixed resources. Thus, the impact of government programs was to add more pressure to an already strong land market and to keep labor and durable capital in agriculture somewhat longer at opportunity costs that are higher (but still below acquisition costs).

SUMMARY

While acres of agricultural land remained relatively constant between 1917 and 1962, pasture-acre equivalents increased until the 1954–1962 period when a decrease of 4 percent was recorded. Between 1930 and 1962 the marginal physical product of farm real estate generally increased throughout the country with minor setbacks in a few areas in the 1950–54 period.

Farm real estate prices exhibited an upward trend throughout the period even during times when net farm income was decreasing, thus indicating that factors other than the immediate return to farm real estate influenced its price.

These factors included in later years an increasing portion of the total value of inputs in the agricultural sector represented by the total of land, nonland real estate, and land substitutes, even though the inputs in agriculture represented a declining portion of the inputs used in the total economy. The increased share of agricultural income accruing to real estate and land substitutes is due to

(1) land-saving technology that extended the total use of land, its substitutes, and its complements, and (2) economic fixity and underemployment of labor and capital in the agricultural sector. As a result expansion buyers attempted to minimize losses on mistakes of overinvestment in capital items and in overcommitment of operator labor, acquiring real estate above its capitalized marginal value product to utilize fixed capital and labor more fully. Further, the benefits derived from government agricultural programs were capitalized into real estate even though other fixed resources were not covering acquisition costs.

A Summary View, Evaluative Conclusions, and Recommendations

The purpose of this study was to examine both in theory and empirically how the U.S. agricultural economy allocates resources. Part I posed the problem, with Chapters 3 and 4 providing the theoretical and evaluative structure for the empirical analysis of resource use in Part II. Chapter 5 provided measures of farmers' product price expectations and Chapter 6 summarized the overall pattern of production, disappearance, income, and resource use in the U.S. farm sector. And Chapters 7 to 9 considered utilization and earnings of the traditional factors of capital, labor, and land, from 1917 to the late 1960's.

Part III summarizes and draws evaluative conclusions. Chapter 10 sums up the historical developments in agriculture—described in more detail in earlier chapters—and includes some information developed in the project but not dealt with earlier. Chapter 11 presents a normative analysis of the good and bad aspects of resource adjustments in agriculture, and summarizes what the authors believe are right and wrong policy actions in light of the basis for evaluation presented in Chapter 4 of Part I. Because the conclusions reached are based on a fairly long sweep of history, 1917 to the late 1960's, their validity would not be seriously affected by last-minute updating to include more detailed estimates for the last half of the 1960's.

CHAPTER 10

Historical and Economic Summary of U.S. Agriculture

FRANCIS VAN GIGCH

The period of history of U.S. agricultural resource use considered here starts with World War I and ends during the 1960's. The objective of this chapter is to bring sharply into focus, and to treat briefly, by historical periods, the more detailed information contained in the foregoing more specialized chapters. Our study proceeds in the particular context of the policies, programs, and other circumstances, such as wars and phases of the business cycle, that characterized selected epochs of the post-WWI period.

1917–1929: FROM WORLD WAR I
TO THE CRASH

The exceptional demand for farm products generated by World War I made acceleration in the growth of farm output desirable. Farm programs such as price guarantees, crash publicity programs, distribution of seeds, and draft deferments were geared in that direction. The exceptional demand, however, resulted more in high prices and appreciation of farm asset values than in large output.

As noted in earlier chapters, several factors were responsible for the failure of agricultural production to expand immediately under the stimulus of higher wartime prices: (1) adoption of labor-saving and output-expanding innovations had not yet taken place, and agriculture was still mostly dependent upon nature, land, relatively unskilled labor, and farm-produced capital; (2) the war itself competed with farming for the use of some factors, notably manpower; and (3) massive additions to land stock were no longer possible through extension of the frontier.

High product prices resulted in high net income for agriculture, high rewards to factors of production, and high price expectations promoting substantial appreciation in the value of farm assets. Between 1917 and 1919, the value of farm assets increased faster than the rise in the general price level—at a rate of more than $8 billion annually, of which 80 percent was for land.

The high wartime income created a promising outlook for farming that invited new resource commitments. During the late teens, the stock of capital in agriculture increased, land input increased, and, in the immediate postwar period, a net influx of labor into farming occurred. To expand farm capacity, large numbers of farmers made the mistake of going into debt at inflated prices.

The Armistice brought the collapse of both war and foreign demand and a drastic reduction in farm prices. Between 1919 and 1922 prices received by farmers decreased by more than 40 percent. The dramatic fall in prices indicated that the prevailing land values were based on unwarranted long-run price expectations. Actual value productivities of farm resources turned out to be far below expected value productivities. Residual returns to farm labor fell relative to returns for its urban counterparts, while earnings for many farm durables did not cover acquisition costs. Consequently, the high value of land and other farm assets created by faulty expectations could not be supported and their values fell, wiping out the capital gains received during the war years. Farmers suffered capital losses for most categories of farm assets. Appreciation and later depreciation of farm assets appear to have offset each other between 1917 and 1929. It should be emphasized, however, that the losses imposed upon farm asset holders after 1919 had few offsetting counterpart gains within the farm sector. Many farmers were caught with devaluated assets, high debts incurred in financing the purchases of farm assets at boom prices, and low revenues—out of which not only debts had to be serviced but also factors of production rewarded. During the 1920's, bankruptcy and other forms of financial distress reached record levels.

The post-WWI decrease in demand for U.S. farm output suggests that a decrease in the rate of growth of farm output would have been desirable. Nevertheless, agricultural output tended to grow faster after 1920 than during the war years. Many resources committed to farm production during and just after the war became economically fixed in agriculture, including soldiers returning to the farms from whence they came. This fixing of inputs was followed by further loss-minimizing, output-expanding investments and by commitments of resources which expanded production when, superficially, contraction was expected.

Land, mostly because of its special immobility, has a very low opportunity cost outside of agriculture—i.e., its "out-of-sector" salvage value approaches zero. Thus, there was practically no contraction in the use of land between 1920 and 1929 while land values fell catastrophically.

Despite adverse price relationships, net additions were made to the stock of farm durables and a conspicuous expansion took place in the use of many expendable forms of capital from 1925 to 1929. The hypothesis that producers were using more inputs to minimize losses on economically fixed farm resources is consistent with events. Such adjustments from an initial position of overproduction often result in further increases in production. Part of this expansion may have been promoted by technological innovations, yet, as a cause of "overproduction" (where overproduction is defined as failure to achieve earnings commensurate with acquisition costs simultaneously for all factors of production) technological change was not the leading culprit. Rather, it must be considered only one among the other unpredictable and exogenous forces that produce errors in resource allocation.

Study of U.S. agriculture between 1917 and 1929 revealed a propensity to overproduce, even in the absence of price supports. During this period the symptoms of overexpansion were decreasing farm incomes, low rewards to factors of production, and capital losses. The war appears not to have been the sole expansive force. Had it been, farmers would have taken their capital losses after the decrease in farm prices of the early 1920's, resources would have been progressively taken out of agriculture, output would have fallen, and returns would have moved in the direction of acquisition cost. Our study, however, does not show an overall decrease in the use of agricultural resources during the immediate postwar period; instead, it shows a net increase in the use of land, durables, and expendable forms of capital after 1925. Resources invested as a consequence of the war became economically fixed at rates of return that would not cover acquisition costs; hence, heavy capital losses were experienced. To minimize these losses, farmers brought still more resources into production despite the fact that farm product prices could not cover acquisition costs for all factors.

Farm policies from the Tariff Acts to the Federal Farm Board's activities did little to alleviate the pressing ills of agriculture—rather, these policies demonstrated a lingering faith in the ability of the free market, bolstered somewhat by farmer cooperatives and improved credit institutions, to regulate farm markets. Restrictive tariffs, short-term price stabilization policies, and the inaccuracy of farmers' own long-run product price expectations all contributed to the unrealized severity of agriculture's chronic adjustment problem.

1930-1933: FROM 1929 TO THE BOTTOM

If America's farmers had failed to benefit from the industrial prosperity of the 1920's, they were nevertheless full partners in the progressive impoverization of the early 1930's. They continued to develop excess capacity during 1930-33 despite worsening terms of trade and falling farm price expectations. In the absence of effective government intervention, agricultural prices fell freely, as a result of both deflation and excessive agricultural production relative to effective demand. As during the previous period, farmers bore the brunt of the losses. It is estimated that between 1930 and 1933, real average annual net income originating in agriculture was only $7.2 billion—nearly 35 percent below the 1920-29 average, while the average total change in asset position in real terms was a *larger* negative $9.1 billion. As a result, the sum of the conventional income and nonconventional (capital gains and losses) income achieved during the interval was negative.

Despite the postwar farm recession aggravated by the general depression, the level of production achieved during 1930-33 was higher than for any four previous consecutive years, despite rather mediocre weather conditions and one of the worst economic environments on record. The expansion of agricultural output recorded between 1920 and 1933 was brought about by an increase in the use of most agricultural inputs. The study of agriculture during this period reveals: (1) little net change in population and thus in available farm labor, (2) an increase in land use measured in pasture-acre equivalents, (3) decreases in some categories of durables more or less offset by increases in others, and (4) increases in the use of farm-produced expendables.

An absolute increase in farm population took place between 1930 and 1933 to more or less cancel the corresponding decreases of 1917-29. High industrial unemployment reduced effective "out-of-sector" salvage values for farm labor to near zero. Farming, which produces more laborers than required for replacement, developed a growing unemployable labor force. Residually computed returns to labor were often negative, indicating low marginal value productivities for farm labor during the depression.

The rate of growth in land use was faster during the 1930-33 interval than during the preceding period. The value productivity of land generally decreased during the depression. Expected earnings from land were not achieved, and land values fell drastically. The increased physical use of land in the light of falling expected returns was an attempt to minimize losses. Increased use of land was prompted by the need to raise the marginal productivity of labor remaining in agriculture because of very low off-farm salvage values, or returning to agriculture at very low acquisition costs (for the farm sector).

Farmers used an increasing amount of farm-produced durables and expendables during the depression, while there are indications that they let some nonfarm-produced, durable capital goods depreciate without replacement. During the depression, the estimated marginal value productivity of much farm-produced capital did not cover acquisition costs. The forces determining such costs for these assets are not independent of those determining their value productivity. Hence, acquisition cost and value productivity tended to fall together, somewhat encouraging the use of farm-produced durable capital inputs despite the depression.

It would be far-fetched to argue that the expansion in resources use from 1930 to 1933 was due to the lagged stimulus of World War I, which by then was about fifteen years removed. The agricultural experience of 1930–33 can reasonably be interpreted as a confirmation of the conclusions arrived at in the study of the preceding period. As during the 1920's, agriculture showed a propensity to overcommit resources. The brutal fall in prices caused a severe decrease in returns to factors of production and led to a massive devaluation of assets. Theories assuming no divergence between acquisition and salvage costs would have predicted a reduction in the use of farm resources. Yet deterioration in the terms of exchange for agriculture failed to achieve a reduction in the use of farm resources. Instead, the use of labor, land, and many forms of farm capital expanded. The years 1930–33 were ones of very imperfect knowledge and uncertainty. This uncertainty set the stage for entrepreneurial errors, leading to the overcommitment of resources as a result of producers' attempts to raise the productivity of farm resources that had become fixed in agriculture as a result of errors committed prior to or during the depression.

Public farm policy was not a dominant feature of the depression years, but it had at least two effects: (1) commodity price support policies were unable to sustain prices as had been expected; and (2) continuing restrictive trade policies contributed to the reduction in farm exports when domestic demand for food and fiber also declined.

While the farm program of the early 1930's had little success, some students of the field suggest that it was a necessary experiment to ensure public acceptance of the New Deal. But public policies of the period, such as the Smoot-Hawley Tariff of 1931 and the feeble efforts of the Federal Farm Board, were notably unsuccessful. They increased the adjustments required of agriculture and acted through product price expectations to provide farmers with inaccurate price signals. Nevertheless, many believed that greater public involvement was the key. The result of unsuccessful public programs was more public programs.

1934–1941: THE NEW DEAL

When President Roosevelt was inaugurated in March 1933, the depressed state of the economy called for direct and drastic action. In part, through the emergency measures taken during his first hundred days in office, the beginning of 1934 saw the general economic situation in a slightly improved state: general unemployment was subsiding and output showed a slight increase.

Although domestic demand for farm products improved, the foreign demand did not increase substantially during this period. At the beginning of the period the capacity of the agricultural plant remained in excess of needs, but a reduction in the rate of farm output expansion was never really achieved. If allowance is made for exceptionally unfavorable weather, farm output probably did not decrease during the mid-1930's, despite adverse economic conditions. As soon as weather conditions normalized after 1936, farm output resumed growth.

After 1933 both the farm population and the farm labor force decreased rapidly. Some authors have argued, however, that the heavy labor outflow was made up mainly of underemployed and unemployed people accumulated in agriculture from 1930 to 1933. Although farm wage rates increased, they fell relative to nonfarm wage rates, indicating that out-migration was not proceeding fast enough to bring returns in agriculture to levels which farmers would have attained had they left as young men. The rates of withdrawal in older age brackets were very low, suggesting that off-farm labor salvage values were so low as to leave a substantial amount of farm labor fixed in agriculture at low marginal value productivities.

The use of land increased from 1934 to 1941. Both current and expected value productivities of land increased due to increased use of capital (other than land substitutes) and to higher actual and expected prices. The higher value productivity of land was also due to a related series of additional factors—among them conservation payments to subsidize investments and practices which increased productivity, acreage controls, and direct government payments which were capitalized into asset values. As a result, land appreciated considerably during the period with a good deal of improvement of land values resting upon government programs.

There was substantial investment in most types of durables and expendables between 1934 and 1941. Except for draftstock and farm buildings, all categories of capital inputs showed increases, including both farm and nonfarm durables and expendables. Estimates indicate, however, that specialized durables often failed to earn enough to cover acquisition costs.

After no accumulation from 1933 to 1936, government stocks increased every year between 1937 and 1941. The lack of stock accumulation in the early years of the period, despite price support and generally ineffective production controls, is attributed to the drought. By 1941 the Commodity Credit Corporation held 10 million bales of cotton, 419 million bushels of wheat, and 403 million bushels of corn. These carry-overs became the most notable, though not the sole, symptom of overcommitment of resources.

Both in nominal and real terms, net income originating in agriculture averaged higher during 1934–41 than during the preceding period. On the average, farming made capital gains although capital losses appeared at the end of the period. These losses indicated that carry-overs were not the only symptom of overcapacity and that public expenditures were not sufficient to completely transfer the cost of overcommitted resources from farmers to the government and the taxpayers.

The study of U.S. agriculture between 1934 and 1941 reveals a propensity to overproduce and overvalue farm resources under price supports and production controls. Overproduction during the period was not solely the result of price support stimulation with ineffective production controls. As soon as weather conditions normalized, the farm sector failed to achieve returns, at support prices, which were sufficient simultaneously to cover the acquisition costs farmers incurred for all assets. Either farmers produced or purchased too many, or paid too much for, farm assets, or did both. Capital losses to the sector as a whole, losses on some categories of nonhuman capital, and relative decreases in the rewards of farm labor, despite large government payments to farmers, tend to support that contention.

The New Deal policy objectives to improve farm incomes involved direct payments to producers in the form of parity and other payments for compliance with acreage allotments and for carrying out conservation practices. Supply reduction was sought through acreage limitations on basic commodities, through conservation programs, and by channeling output away from the market by diverting it into storage. The production controls were ineffective, and the parity payments essentially established minimum prices that falsely inflated farmers' product price expectations and were capitalized into land values.

A further disequilibrating influence was that land diverted from the basic commodities was shifted into producing other crops. Thus, supplies of the next-best alternative crops increased, causing their prices to decrease and encouraging consumers to shift consumption from the basic to the alternative commodities. As a result, less of the basic commodities were demanded and excess production intensified.

Other New Deal policies included the Federal Emergency Relief Administration (FERA) which began to provide supervised rehabilitation loans and small grants in 1934. Supervised credit encouraged entry into, and discouraged withdrawal from, farming at a time when the reverse encouragement was perhaps needed.

1942-1946: WORLD WAR II

With the beginning of World War II in September 1939, when Germany invaded Poland, and the fall of France in early 1940, world agricultural production was seriously disrupted. In March 1941, the United States launched the Lend-Lease Program to aid the Allies.

Unanticipated wartime demands allowed fuller use of resources recently over-committed to agricultural production. Thus, the typical signs of overcommitment noted for earlier periods were generally absent between 1942 and 1946. This period is nevertheless a revealing one for the study of agriculture's propensity to overcommit resources. The reaction to lifting the restrictions of the 1930's—acreage and others—and to limited price incentives during the war shows very clearly that excess capacity was present in agriculture. As U.S. agriculture had developed such capacity both with and without price supports prior to World War II, it may be argued that this capacity resulted from circumstances other than the price supports of the 1930's.

Early in the period, the lend-lease arrangements made a substantial addition to foreign demand for U.S. farm products. Additionally, domestic demand for farm products increased because of the armed forces, growing nonfarm incomes, and the limited range of consumer choice. Hence, an acceleration in the growth rate of agricultural output was desirable. The acceleration was subject to the restriction that it should be achieved with moderate increases in the farm price level.

The compromise between output expansion and increases in farm prices was achieved through the Stabilization Act of 1942, which guaranteed 90 percent of parity after the cessation of hostilities for basic commodities and for any commodity in which production was encouraged as a contribution to the war effort. The Act exchanged high actual prices for future price supports.

Agriculture responded well to the incentives generated by the war, despite such adverse factors as: (1) loss of manpower, (2) relative scarcity of nonfarm-produced capital, particularly of the labor-saving type, and (3) the need for many farmers to shift into unknown lines of production. The index of average farm output during 1942–44, the three full years of war for the United States, averaged 28 percent above the 1935–39 level. Part of this increase can be attributed to generous weather, but, if the index of output is deflated by an appropriate weather index, growth was still remarkably high for such a short interval, nearly 16 percent. A slight increase in land input and a relatively small increase in farm durables other than land and good weather were not sufficient to explain the phenomenal increase in farm output during the war. An important contribution to output expansion was the excess capacity that had built up during the 1930's and had remained partially hidden by unfavorable weather and production restrictions. The termination of the restrictions and the arrival of normal weather unleashed the accumulated capacity.

Labor left agriculture during World War II. The decrease in farm population was nearly six times greater than the estimated reduction in the labor force during the same interval. The difference was probably due, to some extent, to many rural women and children joining the labor force in response to patriotic appeals as men left for war. The exit was also due to an increase in the "out-of-sector" salvage value for overcommitted and underemployed labor accumulated in agriculture. This explanation is substantiated by cohort analysis, which shows for the period exceptionally high rates of withdrawal from "older" age brackets where salvage values are typically low during times of high unemployment such as those just prior to the war. Simultaneously, cohort analysis also shows relatively high rates of entry for the "younger" age groups. Jones attributes the high rate of entry into farming from the young age brackets to draft deferments, which increased the commitment of young farmers to agriculture and thus contributed to achieving the necessary output expansion at relatively low output prices. Labor use was more intensive than if deferments had not existed.

Land use increased by 1.7 percent between 1942 and 1947. The earnings of land (and, thus, land values) increased substantially during the period. The stock of other farm durables and the use of expendables also increased. All categories of durables increased except draftstock. In general, earnings of farm durables covered their acquisition costs; earnings of specialized farm durables, however, sometimes failed to do this.

Farm incomes increased sharply during World War II. With few exceptions, returns during the war were sufficient to simultaneously cover acquisition costs of all factors engaged in agriculture. Adjustments gave the appearance of proceeding in the right direction—for example, farm labor earnings gained, relative to nonfarm labor earnings.

The turn-around in farm policy orientation from restricting production to encouraging it was rather gradual. Supplies of commodities accumulated during price support and largely ineffective controls of the 1930's turned into a blessing. By the beginning of 1943, however, the slack was largely removed and further increases in production came only with higher product prices. Despite rising product prices, expected prices tended to lag. Expectations were tempered by the downturn in farm prices during 1938–39 following recovery from depression lows, persistent debate over price ceilings, and lingering memories of the price tumble following World War I. But production incentives in the form of guaranteed prices to extend two years beyond the war's end, incentive payments, and price ceilings contributed to rising product price expectations. And although the substantial "lag effect" was to keep expected prices below realized prices until 1952, the gate was open for a continued flow of resources into agriculture at the end of World War II.

Farming was relatively prosperous in the 1942–46 period and, contrary to the previous period, improving farming's economic lot was not a purposive transfer of wealth from society at large. Wars hide the normal overexpansion symptoms.

1947–1954: FROM WAR TO PEACE
TO WAR TO PEACE

Price supports which were exceeded by actual prices during World War II became effective after the cessation of hostilities and were stretched into the peace by successive acts of Congress. Weak production controls were ineffective in preventing the development of excess productive capacity which was profitable at post-war price-support levels. However, resource commitments were so substantial that prices failed to cover acquisition costs even at supported levels. The general tendency, observed since 1917, of agriculture to overcommit resources relative to existing prices continued. The Marshall Plan relieved the pressure of overproduction during the first years after World War II. However, stocks began to accumulate in 1948 and 1949 when agriculture in Europe and Japan began producing heavily. The outbreak of the Korean War provided a new source of demand that, again, obscured the signs of overproduction.

With post-war recovery of agricultural production abroad, there was a need to slow down the rate of growth in domestic agricultural production. However, despite acreage allotments, output grew 12 percent between 1948 and 1954, slightly faster than the U.S. population. Agricultural exports were at extraordinarily high levels between 1948 and 1951. As noted above, high exports resulted from the Marshall Plan and, after European countries began to stand on their own feet, from Korean War pressures. Carry-overs developed between 1948 and 1950 but in general were mostly depleted between 1950 and 1952. After 1952, carry-overs again rebuilt rapidly. At the end of 1954, the United States had stocked 934 million bushels of wheat, 920 million bushels of corn, and 11 million bales of cotton.

The period 1947–54 witnessed rapid farm population out-migration relative to previous periods. Even so, government programs such as the G. I. Bill retarded the out-mobility of farm labor. Although labor earnings appeared to increase absolutely between 1948 and 1954, they lost ground relative to urban labor earnings, and this indicates that farm labor was still overcommitted to agriculture.

There was a small but positive increase in land use, between 1948 and 1954. The trend in land value appreciation showed signs of slowing after a sharp upsurge during the Korean War. This was associated with a reduction in conservation expenditures, one means through which the government supported land values.

Farm-produced durables increased in use during the period by about 2 percent, despite a decrease in farm buildings—the largest item in the group. Livestock (except horses and mules) and machinery inventories increased throughout the period. Quance has estimated that earnings of many farm-produced durables failed to cover acquisition costs (see Chapter 7). Milk cows at the end of the period and various types of specialized farm durables were sources of capital losses. The use of expendable capital was substantially expanded. Nonfarm-produced expendables such as fertilizers and gasoline increased in use between 20 and 50 percent. Farm incomes, in total, did not simultaneously cover acquisition costs of both farm- and nonfarm-produced durables and expendables.

During the 1948–54 period farm incomes were lower in both nominal and real terms than in the preceding period, but particularly in real terms. The average real farm income over the 1948–58 period (conventional and nonconventional plus government payments) was 35 percent lower than during the 1942–47 period.

Practically all signs of excess capacity were present for agriculture between 1948 and 1954: farm incomes showed consistent deterioration, and earnings were not sufficient to cover acquisition costs of all farm inputs simultaneously. Despite price supports, stocks accumulated, exports were subsidized at taxpayers expense, and consumers paid high prices for some commodities. The Korean War masked the more severe symptoms of the disease. Government programs shifted part of the burden of overproduction away from the farmers with price supports, which encouraged further expansions in production. However, indications are that output increased beyond the stimulus of the price supports. Production controls geared solely to limiting the land input were ineffective in containing excess capacity, since fertilizer is a relatively good substitute for land.

Many farmers who were encouraged to remain in agriculture through draft deferments and others who were enticed back into farming with subsidies from the G. I. Bill and certain credit programs became economically fixed in agriculture. Laborers who joined agriculture after World War II also acquired wealth in the form of farm training which enhanced their productivity in farming while making them a "specialized" farm input. Falling returns with uncontrolled excess production encouraged, in turn, further loss-minimizing investments complementary to resources that had become economically fixed. These loss-minimizing, output-expanding investments tended to increase production to further depress farm prices, thereby making public expenditures less effective in sustaining farm incomes. Asset fixity, output expansion in the presence of falling prices, and capital losses indicate that agriculture during 1948–54 behaved in reasonably close accord with the theory presented in Chapter 3.

1955–1970: THROUGH UNEASY PEACE TO THE INTERNATIONAL FOOD GAP AND PARTIAL WAR

Whereas the 1947–54 period ended with less optimism in the farm sector than it began, much confusion has accompanied the period since 1955. The technological revolution continues to reduce the average cost of producing farm products, but expanding output and potential surpluses place downward pressure on both supported and free-market prices. There is much hunger in the world, but effective demand for food and fiber does not provide an outlet for potential supplies. Domestically, the balance of political power shifted to the urban sector with an insistent demand for low-cost food and fiber, while huge stocks of durable assets were committed to farm production with long-run expectations of supported prices. Our urban-oriented generation, which sends manned explorations to the moon, transplants human hearts, and faces staggering social and environmental problems, views farming as a means of producing the necessities of life—not an end in itself. And the military conflict in Southeast Asia, while not significantly increasing world demand or prices for farm products as World Wars I and II did when the food-producing and distributing capacity of the world was impaired, contributes to inflated input acquisition costs and marketing charges and uncertainty as to future food and fiber needs.

Flexible price supports and, on occasion, relatively strict production controls have been in operation from 1955 to the present (early 1970's). These measures were not sufficient to contain excess capacity in U.S. agriculture, which amounted to about 6 percent of potential farm output during the 1960's. Aggressive disposal programs were inaugurated and continue today. Other symptoms of excess capacity, e.g., falling farm incomes and the inability to cover acquisition costs of all production factors even with support prices, indicate that the overexpansion was not the sole result of price supports.

After the Korean War, U.S. agriculture relied heavily upon the domestic market, a competitive world market, and disposal programs abroad. Although a reduction in the expansion of agricultural output was in order, the growth rate accelerated. Between 1955 and 1970 agricultural production grew at a faster rate than population. This acceleration in growth took place despite worsening actual terms of trade, worsening price expectations, diminishing incomes, and capital losses—part of which were borne by taxpayers and another part by the actual investors who made overcommitment errors.

The phenomenal increase in carry-overs immediately following the Korean War was brought to a halt during the second half of the 1950's through (1) aggressive, subsidized, foreign disposal programs launched during the period and (2) in some cases by increasingly severe production controls. The index of agricultural exports doubled relative to the average for the period 1948–53. Less than half of the value of U.S. agricultural exports, however, moved through strictly commercial channels.

Off-farm prosperity encouraged farm out-migration between 1955 and 1970. During this period the farm population was reduced by more than one-fourth. This sharp decrease in labor use was not sufficient, however, to close the gap between farm and nonfarm labor earnings; instead, labor earnings on farms decreased relative to those of their urban counterparts. Moreover, information on residual earnings of farm labor both for the sector and for typical commercial farms indicates a decrease in farm earnings relative to the preceding period.

Land use decreased by 4 percent between 1955 and 1970. Though there are some indications that the value productivity of land fell throughout the period, land-use policies appear to be responsible for the decreased use. The Agricultural Act of 1956 established the Soil Bank under which land was shifted away from farming by placing it either under the acreage or conservation reserves. Both diversion programs subsidized the exit of land from agricultural production.

Between 1957 and 1962 about 25 million acres were diverted from farming by the Soil Bank. Though high price supports increased the marginal value productivity of land, the expanded use of fertilizers as a land substitute decreased it. Government payments for conservation were a factor in the increase in land values between 1955 and 1970.

The total stock of farm durables (in constant dollars) decreased after 1959. Livestock and building inventories increased while the machinery inventory decreased. The decrease was not sufficient to maintain earnings high enough to cover acquisition costs for many asset categories. The use of most farm-produced expendables increased, but their earnings often fell short of acquisition costs.

Net farm income originating in agriculture was smaller on the average than in the previous period both in current and constant dollars. This loss was partially made up by larger government payments which increased threefold relative to the yearly average of 1948–53 and by capital gains. About 85 percent of these capital gains originated in real estate. Evidence exists that changes in the value of real estate are associated with government payments. The income position of farming in the late 1950's and 1960's would have been considerably worse had the government not supported the nonconventional portion of total farm income.

Flexible but higher than equilibrium price supports were in effect after 1954 for several commodities. Production controls were mostly in the form of restrictions on the use of land. Examination of individual programs to restrict land use indicates that high price supports created high price expectations and encouraged additional investment in land substitutes and other durables, thereby increasing yields. Many farm durables specialized in the production of the supported commodities were a source of capital losses as producers overinvested relative to both market-clearing equilibrium prices and price supports. And successive reductions in price supports did not per se result automatically in output contractions because many resources committed to agriculture were specialized resources with low off-farm opportunity cost. Under these conditions farmers often found it to their advantage to bring more resources into production to raise the productivity of fixed factors, further expanding output. High support prices reduced disappearance. As a result of increased supply, diminished disappearance, and price supports, either carry-overs increased or disposal programs were required, both at considerable expense.

The livestock economy, though free of direct government intervention, was affected by the support program in the grain economy. Higher feed prices discouraged heavy feeding and restricted output of livestock products. Restricted output resulted in higher actual livestock prices and these led to higher expected prices, which in turn encouraged investment in the livestock economy. The primary forces encouraging output expansion were later reinforced by successive decreases in feed price supports which encouraged heavier feeding and thus still larger output. As a result, expected prices were not fulfilled. The reaction to frustrated price expectations varied according to the enterprise concerned: (1) in hog production, only small capital losses ensued because of the shortness of the productive cycle; (2) the beef economy appears to have been spared, at least during the period, from major capital losses because of the high income demand elasticities for beef; and (3) in dairying serious capital losses apparently occurred, because as milk prices fell the discounted present value of milk cows fell to their value as cutter and canner beef.

HISTORICAL GENERALIZATIONS

U.S. agriculture operated between 1917 and 1970 under a variety of circumstances, and yet adjustments were not attained in resource use which would equate acquisition costs with factor earnings. Overcommitment of farm resources was observed in the presence and absence of price supports, in the presence and in the absence of production controls, and during different phases of the business cycle. Only during World War II did the most obvious signs of excess capacity fail to appear, although there are some indications that excess capacity was latent even during the war years.

The fact that excess capacity developed during different phases of the cycle, regardless of the presence or absence of price support programs and production controls, is consistent with the theoretical analysis presented in Chapter 3, which implies such a propensity to overcommit resources. This propensity is not explained satisfactorily by the neo-classical theory of production economics based on assumptions (1) of perfect knowledge and (2) of acquisition costs equal to salvage values. Such theory fails to explain the expanded use of agricultural resources that was recorded despite falling prices between 1920 and 1933. Neither does it explain the commitment of resources beyond the stimuli of price supports which was indicated after 1933 by (1) the existence of unused capacity at the outbreak of World War II, (2) acquisition costs in excess of factor earnings, and (3) capital losses even at existing price supports.

On the other hand, the behavior of agriculture during the period under study is in reasonably close accord with modified neoclassical theory based on the simultaneous assumptions of (1) imperfect knowledge and (2) acquisition costs greater than, or equal to, salvage values. This theory implies that unforeseen errors of management resulted in asset fixity, which in turn may cause less than expected returns and capital losses. The theory also explains how, in many initial situations of overcommitment, producers may be wise to indulge in additional output-increasing investments and expenditures to minimize losses. Both micro and macro data indicate that such has indeed been the case on U.S. farms from 1917 to 1970.

CHAPTER 11

Evaluative Conclusions and Recommendations

GLENN L. JOHNSON

Empirical evidence, marshaled in the chapters of this book according to a theoretical framework outlined in Chapter 3, logically leads to an overall evaluation of U.S. agricultural policy, and to some brief recommendations for future restructuring of that policy.

EVALUATIVE CONCLUSIONS

Based on the factor and historical studies summarized in Chapter 10, we offer some evaluative conclusions with respect to: favorable and unfavorable aspects of U.S. agricultural policies and programs; problems in the uncontrolled sectors of agriculture; and explanations (from the theoretical apparatus of Chapter 3) of allocative difficulties experienced in both the controlled and uncontrolled subsectors of the farm economy.

Favorable Aspects of U.S. Agricultural Policies and Programs

The favorable aspects of U.S. agricultural policies, 1917 to date, should be summarized in some detail to see what should be left alone and to glean hints on how to proceed in improving our policies and programs. In general, we must appraise as highly successful our policies of distributing land ownership widely; of giving farm people much freedom and opportunity for education and improvement; of supporting agricultural research and extension publicly; of supporting with public funds the development of transportation, credit, and communication facilities; and of developing institutions for maintaining law and order, including property rights. Many of the better aspects of our overall agrarian policy originated in the colonial period. Our abundant, relatively inexpensive food supplies and our enlightened progressive farm population all testify to the general wisdom of our policies and programs.

Price supports have had limited success in maintaining prices for commercial farmers nearer levels that cover acquisition costs. Within the price support and production control programs, it is worthwhile noting that the effective production controls that accompanied burley tobacco price support programs eliminated some inefficient investments (particularly within individual farms) and tended to prevent excessive investment in early technologies to the exclusion of later technological advances. However, political considerations prevented the elimination of obsolete inefficient firms as contrasted to parts of firms and have dispersed production from efficient to less efficient areas.

From time to time, the removal of price supports of some commodities and the lowering of support prices for others have eliminated part of the stimulus to (1) overinvest in productive capacity and (2) retain obsolete productive plants. The Soil Bank demonstrated that some reduction in production is possible by programs designed to remove a *necessary* factor of production. Where land substitutes were available and their use was permitted, however, land removal was not effective in controlling production.

The removal of price uncertainty by price supports for burley tobacco, dry edible beans, and potatoes increased the quantity farmers were willing to produce at a given real price. Government stocks of farm commodities built up under the price supports accompanied by ineffective production and investment controls played important roles in international and domestic relief.

Unfavorable Aspects of U.S. Agricultural Policies and Programs

Despite the above list of favorable items, all is not right with respect to our policies and programs. In terms of the criteria developed in Chapter 4 and the facts presented and interpreted throughout this book, farm prices and incomes are not at "right" levels. Resources are being applied to encourage farm products which are less needed than schools, hospitals, armament, churches, industrial capacity, etc.; our farm programs are interfering with our international objectives with respect to underdeveloped areas and the containment of authoritarian governments; some aspects of our programs compete with other aspects; and lastly, our price support programs have retarded technological advances produced by other agricultural programs. More specifically, price supports have increased farmers' price expectations which, in turn, stimulated overinvestment in productive capacity not containable with available production controls. The results were a combination of extra costs to taxpayers for supporting prices and/or low earnings on different farm investments. In general, these earnings were too low to cover (1) original acquisition costs in the case of durable, nonhuman resources, including land, and (2) lifetime labor earnings in alternative employments if people whose lives were committed to farm production had left farming in their youth.

For both "free" and "controlled" farm products, prices are and have often been inappropriate or "wrong" in the sense that they do, or did not, result in returns covering acquisition costs on inputs and equate production with consumption. The evidence for this includes low returns to capital and labor in agriculture (hence, capital losses) and/or accumulating governmental stocks when prices are supported. Either farmers have received substantial capital losses, or taxpayers have been subject to substantial burdens. Farmers stand to bear even greater capital losses if price supports are withdrawn. When an annual average of $2 billion of government subsidies finds its way into farm incomes, as much as $30 billion of the total present value of farm assets (currently well over $200 billion) may rest on the subsidies. Further, to the extent that price support programs transfer additional money from consumers to farmers, still more potential capital losses may exist. These potential losses would be on the values of (1) land used to produce corn and other feed grains and wheat and cotton, (2) breeding stock, and (3) farm machinery. In addition, potential additional losses exist with respect to the lifetime earnings of operators and family labor now overcommitted to farming.

While our price support programs brought forth overproduction, there is evidence that they are also partially responsible for the obsolete nature of many of our farms. Observations by technical scientists, sociologists, farm management experts, and general agriculturalists indicate that a high proportion of our dairy, beef, and cotton farms are using technologies appropriate for one or two generations ago. The corresponding figures for wheat, hog, and corn farms are lower, but still high. These observations square with theoretical analysis, which indicates (1) that price supports would extend the economic life of investments in old technologies in existence when the supports were inaugurated; (2) that price supports, unaccompanied by strict production controls, would stimulate overinvestments in technologies available at the inception of a price support program, thereby making it unprofitable to invest in the more advanced technologies becoming available at later dates in the programs; and (3) that high initial but declining price supports such as have characterized the post-WWII period would produce even more obsolete technology at later stages in the program.

Our price support programs have also reduced the effectiveness of several other federal programs by conflicting with the attainment of their objectives: for example, (1) price supports for corn, wheat, and cotton increased or maintained the value of land useful for producing these crops, thereby increasing the Soil Bank payments necessary to attract such land into the conservation reserve; (2) price support programs competed with, or offset, research and extension expenditures to develop and distribute new technologies. This second effect of the support programs has been especially serious by making retention of investments in obsolete technologies advantageous and stimulating overinvestments in earlier technologies, thereby preventing investment in later and superior technologies (as outlined above). Indeed, price support programs masked the need for new technologies (particularly labor as contrasted to land-saving and feed-saving technologies) and, by stimulating overinvestments in productive capacity, made it appear to superficial observers that the advance in technology brought by technological research is a major cause of "the" farm problem.

Price supports diminished the usefulness of public expenditures on agricultural economic research and extension by maintaining price expectations that promoted less optimal adjustments instead of the more optimal adjustments which would have been attained in the absence of price supports.

By maintaining domestic prices above world levels, exports were curtailed unless stimulated with subsidies and bargaining schemes. These schemes and subsidies disrupted relations with the developed countries of the western world, especially Canada in the case of wheat. They also prevented the United States from making its maximum contribution (for the value of resources expended) to the growth of undeveloped countries, and thus reduced our ability to fulfill our international commitments.

The export difficulty is only one phase of a broader difficulty. By raising prices but failing to control output, surplus governmental stocks were created as the support prices expanded production and contracted domestic and foreign disappearance. Unwillingness to engage in adequate production control to bring market prices up to support levels was matched by alacrity in devising programs to research, administer, and operate demand-expansion, domestic surplus disposal, and various forms of dumping programs in foreign markets. Many of these efforts have run up against low-income demand elasticities and rising real per capita incomes. Others encountered monetary problems abroad, including aspects of the U.S. gold flow problem. Still others interfered with the economic development of countries whose long-run support is needed by the United States. The difficulty here is not so much one of conflict among U.S. governmental programs as it is one of having unnecessarily ineffective price support and production control programs and a malfunctioning private agricultural economy create the need for demand-expansion programs where the possibilities of success are slight.

By promoting overproduction, our price support programs retained in, or diverted to, the production of unwanted farm products, resources that were badly needed, (1) in the public sector for urban renewal and poverty elimination, educational construction and education, medical facilities, road construction, production of armament and construction of military facilities, development of recreational and cultural facilities, and (2) in the private sector for construction of homes and for industrial capacity to satisfy the expanding multitudinous needs of both the private and public sector.

Problems in Periods and Subsectors
Free of Price Supports and Production Controls

Despite the numerous apparent defects in our price-support and production-control programs, empirical observations and the theory presented in Chapter 3 indicate that subsectors and periods free of production controls and price supports have bred problems—among them excess productive capacity, unsatisfactory returns to labor and investments, capital losses, failure to contract over-expanded production, and obsolete productive plants.

U.S. price-support and production-control programs were inaugurated following the farm recession after World War I and during the Great Depression. They followed an extended period that was much freer of price and production controls. In neither period, however, can the U.S. agricultural economy be characterized as free of overcommitted resources, by easy downward adjustment of production, free of capital losses, and as producing "right earnings" for labor and capital in agriculture in the sense that acquisition costs were covered.

Further, the post-WWII record for farm products not subject to price and/or production controls is far from encouraging to free price advocates. Beef and hog production, despite freedom from price supports and production controls, were not free of their traditional cycles of overexpansion, lower prices, contractions in production, high prices, re-expansion, etc., with consequent capital losses and low average resource earnings. Relaxation of price supports and production controls in the mid-1960's demonstrated again the tendency of a free uncontrolled U.S. agricultural economy to overinvest in agricultural production.

The post-WWII era revealed that imperfect knowledge on the part of farmers not subject to production controls and price supports caused them to make repeated errors in investment. Errors of underinvestment were readily correctable. On the other hand, some errors of *under*investment involved subsequent *over*investment to minimize losses. Still other overinvestment errors were not correctable at all, while some required further expansions in production to minimize losses imposed by the original errors. Among the causes of the errors were those revealed by the Schultzian modification of the neoclassical analysis: (1) low-income demand elasticities for carbohydrates, fat meat, and fats which caused farmers to overestimate prices for these products in an economy with rising per capita real incomes, and (2) rural-urban birth rate differentials, high economic growth, and labor-saving technological advance in farming which caused young farm people to overestimate the future earnings of their own labor in farming.

There were also complex impacts of technological advance not covered by the earlier Schultzian modification of the J. S. Mill neoclassical analysis of the agricultural sector. For one thing, land, feed, and capital, as well as labor-saving advances occurred, which were often initially very profitable. But the long-run profitability of investments in these technologies was easily overestimated when expectations were formed without due regard for the macro-economic impact of expansions in overall production in product prices. Such overestimation of earnings led to overexpansions and low earnings for capital as well as labor. By contrast, the Schultzian modification of the neoclassical analysis predicted low earnings for labor (to move surplus labor out of farming) and high earnings for capital (to move capital in) instead of low earnings for both labor and capital.

D. Gale Johnson's application of Frank Knight's risk and uncertainty analysis is also revealed to have considerable validity. Analyses of the burley tobacco, dry edible bean, and potato industries indicate that risk discounting leads to internal and external capital rationing which (1) restricts investments and resource use, and hence (2) reduces production. The result is production of less product than can be sold at prices that cover resource acquisition cost. Despite the validity of this argument, there is also evidence that the process of adjusting to risk and uncertainty goes beyond discounting to much more complex adjustments. We must examine the errors which farmers make and the processes they follow in correcting those errors.

Explanations of Allocative Difficulties with
Controlled and Uncontrolled Commodities and Subsectors

The explanations in this section are advanced to help us understand some of the difficulties encountered by the U.S. farm sector. The Schultzian and D. Gale Johnsonian modifications of the neoclassical secular analysis plus the use of more realistic assumptions within the neoclassical analysis of production (as presented in Chapter 3) provide a framework for understanding (1) why certain aspects of price-support policies and programs have not worked well, and (2) why a policy of entirely free, uncontrolled farm prices would not produce a farm economy free of overexpansions, low earnings for capital and labor, capital losses, and malallocated resources.

The explanation is not simple—if it were it would have been developed long ago. It involves almost every factor considered by postwar policy analysts yet does not ascribe a central position to any one of them. The crucial elements of the explanation involve:

1. The Schultzian secular analysis (obviously in accord with reality): that the economy is getting richer (in real terms on a per capita basis); that birth rates, death rates, and technological advance require movements of labor out of agriculture and capital into agriculture; and that income demand elasticities are low and declining for most farm products.

2. Recognition that: farm firms occupy considerable area and, hence, are located at considerable distances from each other, their suppliers, and their markets; costs are involved in moving factors of production physically from suppliers to farms, from farm to farm, and eventually in moving products to

market; institutional arrangements create costs of changing title and of moving durables from seller to buyer. These three problems imply differences between acquisition costs and salvage values for factors of production.

3. The added recognition that imperfectly foreseen changes occur which shift factor prices and the earning power of inputs by changing either product prices or their physical productivity.

Historical study indicates that some of the relevant changes are wars, price declines in response to increases in per capita real incomes, low-income demand elasticities, and expansions in production; changes in foreign demand; specialization; inflations; technological advance; improvements in the human agent; and advancing nonfarm wage rates and levels of living. Obviously such changes have affected agriculture since World War I.

Recognition is needed that farmers, in accord with the D. Gale Johnson analysis, often incorrectly anticipate the changes in factor prices and earnings noted above. Such incorrect anticipations lead to errors in organizing farms. Our analysis then indicates (in Chapter 3 and in the empirical work in Chapters 4 to 10) that these errors have at least the following nine impacts for commodities not subject to price supports: (1) overexpansions of production due to the particular problems encountered in correcting errors when acquisition prices exceed salvage values; (2) the fixing of durables in agricultural production; (3) low earnings for both labor and various durable forms of capital employed in agriculture; (4) capital losses on overinvestments in durables; (5) the overpricing of land with consequent capital losses thereon; (6) exit of some excess farm laborers generated by rural birth and death rate differentials without equating labor earnings in farming with earnings in the nonfarm economy; (7) technologically obsolete farm production plants; (8) the fixing of durables, including labor, at marginal rates of return below acquisition costs explains why the constant returns to scale observed for agriculture when all inputs are regarded as variable does not lead to larger than family-farm operations on farms where part of the resources are, in fact, fixed; and (9) sequences of resource fixities at earnings below acquisition costs result from repeated changes beyond the control and knowledge of individual farmers plus the wide differentials between acquisition costs and salvage values. These sequences may explain the continued failure of larger than family-sized farms to develop.

The theoretical analysis also indicates that price supports without strict production controls would serve to accentuate most of the conditions listed above. Further, it indicates that the automatic adjustments which farmers make under a free price system do not necessarily lead to maximization of general welfare even from a given initial distribution of resource ownership. The conclusion that free price equilibria maximize welfare is not logically sound. Thus, an alternative method of evaluating the operation of economies is required. A way of "muddling through" to partial conclusions was outlined in Chapter 4. That method is the one used to produce the evaluative conclusions reached herein.

With repeated errors of overproduction, the prices which equate use with production are not equilibrium prices of the type ordinarily considered in theory. While it is true that such prices "clear the market," it is not true that they clear the market at prices which cover acquisition costs for nonlabor inputs and nonfarm wage rates and/or levels of living for labor. Equilibrium prices, defined in the latter sense, would be higher than those which clear the market and would be "right" in terms of the definitions of Chapter 4.

In summary, our major conclusions are that (1) U.S. agricultural policies and programs have involved grave shortcomings despite the high productivity and generally excellent performance of the U.S. agricultural economy; (2) while a policy of entirely free prices might not have involved as many shortcomings as encountered by post World War II policies and programs, grave problems would still have existed; and (3) some combinations of more coordinated controls and freer prices would have been superior either to the policies and programs used or to a policy of entirely free prices.

RECOMMENDATIONS FOR IMPROVING U.S. AGRICULTURAL POLICIES

When one examines the history of U.S. agriculture and the implications of the theory presented in Chapter 3 in view of the changing characteristics of our agriculture, certain additional structural changes appear to be needed. These principally involve (1) improved knowledge on the part of farm entrepreneurs; (2) a reduction of differences between acquisition and salvage values for farm resources; and (3) an improved combination of private and public controls over the entry of men and resources into agricultural production.

We believe that the public service organizations for agriculture, namely the U.S. Department of Agriculture and the land grant colleges and universities, have not done as well as they could in reducing the imperfections in knowledge faced by individual farmers. Much better and more relevant research than has been done *can be done* on the implications of technological changes, changes in the training and education of people, income changes, income-demand elasticities, foreign demand, institutional changes, etc. Recently, for instance, little that is adequate has been done on the implications of the so-called "international food gap." Much more specific research is needed on the quantities of resources that can be committed to agriculture by individual farmers, by all producers of given products, and in the aggregate, without producing so much product that it cannot be sold except at prices that will not cover acquisition costs.

While researchers can do much better than they have done, they probably cannot produce enough knowledge to cure the long-term tendency of agriculture to overcommit resources to agricultural production. Furthermore, even if researchers could produce the knowledge, we may doubt whether even a greatly expanded and improved extension and information distribution system would really convey the improved knowledge to farmers and ensure that it is used by them. One reason for pessimism here involves the atomistic organization of agriculture. Knowledge of macro-consequences is of little real private value to a competitive entrepreneur unless he has an institutional structure which permits him to act in concert with other entrepreneurs.

If the above conclusions with respect to public reduction of imperfect knowledge are correct, then steps should be taken to more nearly equate acquisition costs and salvage values for agricultural inputs. However, these differences are due, in the final analysis, largely to the geographic dispersion of farms and transportation costs. Except for expensive subsidies, differences between acquisition and salvage prices are hard to eliminate. This combines with the above conclusions about the difficulty of solving the problem through research and extension to indicate that agriculture needs to seek structural changes involving the creation of public and semipublic institutional control mechanisms.

Better control mechanisms are needed to regulate the rate at which resources are committed to agricultural production. On the basis of the historical record, the government is not a completely adequate agency for doing this, because it tends to protect the value of resources that farmers and farm firms overcommit. Also, private nonfarm input suppliers are unlikely to perform this function well; they simply do not have incentives to control the overcommitment unless they become owners of the agricultural producing firms. Similar conclusions are reached with respect to control mechanisms which would originate with the processors and distributors. However, we must hasten to add that for private agricultural entrepreneurs to come under the control of supplying and/or distributing firms and agencies would not necessarily be wrong. Real political problems would be involved and the controllers would have a vested interest in overcommitment rather than in controlled commitment of resources in agricultural production.

Considerable attention should be given to the possibility of creating new control mechanisms owned and managed by agricultural producers. After researchers and extension workers have made their best efforts to produce new knowledge and to educate the public and the individual farmers, this same information could be used by organizations of producers in operating controls on (1) the entry of firms into agricultural production, (2) investments in new major pieces of capital equipment such as bulk tanks, power units, etc., and (3) the commitment of youths to agriculture.

When the U.S. Government granted similar powers of control to nonfarm firms by permitting them to incorporate, sufficient attention was not given to governmental arrangements for maintaining public responsibility on the part of these new institutions. Similarly, when labor was granted the right to organize and bargain collectively, as well as individually, sufficient attention was not given to the need for public regulation of the unions. In both cases, public control of the new institutions was developed and extended *subsequent* to the legal changes permitting them to be established. If we change our institutional arrangements to develop producer-run institutions to control investments in agricultural production, a change in the role of government must occur. The legal changes providing for the creation of control institutions should simultaneously provide for public regulation of the resultant agricultural monopsonies and monopolies. This area needs much research by agricultural economists, particularly those in the policy field.

Another aspect of the quest for a more appropriate combination of public and private controls over the commitment of resources to farm production still needs discussion. Even if expanded and more effective research and extension were provided and even if institutional arrangements to permit producers to develop control mechanisms were developed, organizations of producers are not likely to be successful in controlling commodities so widely dispersed and so diverse as, say, wheat or feed grains. Therefore, a need is likely to continue for government to operate price-support and production-control programs despite our rather unfortunate experiences with these institutions to date. Again, a need for more agricultural policy research is indicated.

As a final comment, there are reasons to believe that the solution of the problem of overcommitted resources might eliminate the U.S. family farm's economic *raison d'être*. Thus, if we adopt the structural changes suggested above and should they prove effective, separate attention needs to be given to determining whether or not we want to maintain family farms and if so, how [Glenn L. Johnson, 1969].

For a long while, people in this country worried about the replacement of the family-operated "pop and mom" grocery stores by chain stores. However, pop and mom were finally replaced (although not entirely) for the most part by supermarket workers and managers. Since we cannot see how the moral fiber and other aspects of American society were damaged by this transition, we cannot conclude, a priori, that American society would necessarily be damaged by a restructuring of our agricultural society to put agricultural production in the hands of input suppliers or processors, distributors, or corporate owners. Actually, such a restructuring might mean that agricultural labor would receive returns commensurate with those received by laborers in the rest of the economy and that investments in agricultural production would earn returns comparable to those in the rest of the economy. If this came about, such a restructuring, like the abandonment of the pop and mom grocery store, might be a good thing.

In the last chapter of this book, we must stress again that the study's purpose was to investigate the allocative efficiency of the U.S. agricultural economy. In this connection welfare problems have arisen, for the uses to which resources are put affect welfare; and, as is equally obvious, mistakes in the use of resources affect the welfare of both resource owners and consumers. However, such problems are only a few of the aspects of the overall welfare problems of the United States, urban as well as rural. Earnings for capital and labor in agriculture that cover acquisition costs do not guarantee adequate incomes to persons with insufficient property, skills, off-farm employment, and ability. Direct attention to increasing the skills, ability, and property in the possession of disadvantaged people (rural as well as nonrural) is required. Price manipulation and production control should not be expected to be an effective sole means of accomplishing such ends. Nor should we expect to do the job with demand-expansion schemes for food (except insofar as such schemes result in basic improvements in the personal capacities and increases in the owned resources with which the disadvantaged produce their incomes). In any event, demand-expansion schemes are not likely to solve the problem of overcommitted resources in farming—even if demand were doubled or trebled, both theory and experience indicate that we would soon have so much capital, labor, and money invested in land that earnings would not cover acquisition costs unless we greatly improve our combination of private and public controls over investment in agricultural production.

It is appropriate here to stress that the process of improving policies and programs is a continuous joint enterprise by (1) researchers who systematize and organize both normative and nonnormative knowledge and, sometimes, get through to solutions of policy and programmatic problems; (2) administrators whose normative and nonnormative experiences help reveal, define, and solve problems; and (3) lawmakers who need all the assistance they can get from researchers and administrators as they tackle the really intractable problems that cannot be left to the marketplace, academicians, researchers, civil servants, and administrators (both appointed and elected).

Mathematical Notes on the Neoclassical and Modified Neoclassical Theory of the Firm

GLENN L. JOHNSON

In these mathematical notes, the usual neoclassical analysis is presented as the first set of assumptions and covers equations (1) to (6). Modifications of neo-classical theory followed in this book are partially explicated under the second set of assumptions that includes equations (7) to (14). Finally, differences in the consequences of the two sets of assumptions are sketched.

At the individual firm level, we are interested in the different consequences of two alternative sets of assumptions [Edwards, 1958] for the inputs X_i $(i = 1, \ldots, n)$.

First set of assumptions

$$(1) \quad \infty \geq P_{AX_i} = P_{SX_i} \geq 0 \qquad\qquad (i = 1, \ldots, d)$$

$$\infty = P_{AX_i} > P_{SX_i} = 0 \qquad\qquad (i = d + 1, \ldots, n)$$

where P_{AX_i} = acquisition price of X_i and P_{SX_i} = salvage value of X_i. We assume a one to one correspondence between prices of stocks and service flows for the X_i.

For set of assumptions (1), let G stand for gain (or loss, if negative) for reorganizing a given firm.

$$(2) \quad G = \sum_{j=1}^{m} P_{Y_j} (Y_j - Y_j^0) - \sum_{i=1}^{n} P_{X_i} (X_i - X_i^0),$$

185

where Y_j = products $(j = 1, \ldots, m)$, and Y_j^0 stands for initial output of the product j while Y_j stands for the reorganized output of Y_j by the reorganized firm. Similarly, X_i^0 and X_i stand for the initial and reorganized input of X_i $(i = 1, \ldots, n)$.

The problem of the manager of a firm is envisioned to be that of reorganizing an initial organization to maximize G subject to

(2a) $b_i = \sum\limits_{j=1}^{m} X_{ij}$ $(i = d + 1, \ldots, n)$

(2b) $X_{ij} \geq 0,$ $(i = 1, \ldots, n)$

where X_{ij} is the amount of the ith input used in producing the jth product, and b_i is the amount of the fixed resource on hand.

(3) $G^* = \sum\limits_{j=1}^{m} P_{Y_j} (Y_j - Y_j^0) - \sum\limits_{i=1}^{d} P_{X_i} [\sum\limits_{j=1}^{m} (X_{ij}) - X_{ij}^0] ,$

where X_{ij} is the amount of the ith input used in producing the jth product, and independence among the j production functions, (3) can be maximized by methods developed by Kuhn and Tucker [1951]. When the Lagrangian function is formed as in

(4) $L \equiv G^* + \sum\limits_{i=d+1}^{n} \lambda_i (X_i^0 - \sum\limits_{j=1}^{m} X_{ij}) ,$

it can be maximized subject to (2a) and (2b) above "if and only if there is a set of λ_i (for $i = d + 1, \ldots, n$) such that (4) is maximized with respect to the X_{ij} and minimized with respect to the λ_i."

For each of the variable inputs $(i = 1, \ldots, d)$ used in producing a product j

(5) $P_{Y_j} \dfrac{\delta Y_j}{\delta X_{ij}} - P_{X_i} = 0$ $(i = 1, \ldots, d; j = 1, \ldots, m)$

for the most profitable reorganization of the firm. For each of the "fixed inputs $(i = d + 1, \ldots, n)$" used in producing a product j

(6) $P_{Y_j} \dfrac{\delta Y_j}{\delta X_{ij}} - \lambda_i = 0$ $(i = d + 1, \ldots, n; j = 1, \ldots, m)$

λ_i can be interpreted as the "on-farm" opportunity cost of X_i.

Off-farm opportunity costs for X_i are zero as $P_{SX_i} = 0$. Acquisition costs for X_i are assumed infinite. Hence, the X_i^0 for $i = d + 1, \ldots, n$ are fixed regardless of P_{Y_j} and of subsequent X_{ij} for $i = 1, \ldots, d$ and $j = 1, \ldots, m$.

Second set of assumptions

(7) $\infty \geq P_{AX_i} \geq P_{SX_i} \geq 0$ $(i = 1, \ldots, n)$

(8) $G = \sum_{j=1}^{m} P_{Y_j} (Y_j - Y_j^0) - \sum_{i=1}^{n} a_i (\sum_{j=1}^{m} X_{ij} - X_i^0).$

If $\sum_{j=1}^{m} X_{ij} > X_i^0$, then $a_i = P_{AX_i}$.

If $\sum_{j=1}^{m} X_{ij} < X_i^0$, then $a_i = P_{SX_i}$.

If $\sum_{j=1}^{m} X_{ij} = X_i^0$, then $P_{AX_i} > a_i > P_{SX_i}$.

Let W_i = amount of X_i purchased and V_i = amount of X_i sold. Hence,

$$\sum_{j=1}^{m} X_{ij} = X_i^0 - V_i + W_i,$$

subject to the restriction that $X_i^0 - V_i \geq 0$.
Equation (8) can be rewritten as

(9) $G^* = \sum_{j=1}^{m} P_{Y_j} (Y_j - Y_j^0) + \sum_{i=1}^{n} S_i V_i - \sum_{i=1}^{n} A_i W_i,$

where $S_i = a_i = P_{SX_i}$ and $A_i = a_i = P_{AX_i}$.
When placed in the Lagrangian form, (9) appears as

(10) $L \equiv G^* + \sum_{i=1}^{n} \lambda_i (X_i^0 - V_i + W_i - \sum_{j=1}^{m} X_{ij}) + \sum_{i=1}^{n} \mu_i (X_i^0 - V_i),$

which is maximized with respect to X_{ij}, V_i, and W_i and minimized with respect to λ_i and μ_i, following Kuhn and Tucker. For each product possibly using X_i, the solution involves, for all i and j

(11) $\qquad \dfrac{\delta L}{\delta X_{ij}} = Py_j \dfrac{\delta Y_j}{\delta X_{ij}} - \lambda_i \leq 0, \qquad \dfrac{\delta L}{\delta X_{ij}} X_{ij} = 0, \qquad X_{ij} \geq 0.$

Condition (11) indicates that the marginal value productivity of an input in producing a given product is less than or equal to opportunity cost if none of the input is used in producing that product.

The solution also involves

(12) $\qquad \dfrac{\delta L}{\delta W_i} = \lambda_i - A_i \leq 0, \qquad \dfrac{\delta L}{\delta W_i} W_i = 0, \qquad W_i \geq 0,$

which indicates that purchase of X_i involves an opportunity cost for X_i equal to its acquisition price at the optimum.

The solution also involves

(13) $\qquad \dfrac{\delta L}{\delta V_i} = S_i - \mu_i - \lambda_i \leq 0, \qquad \dfrac{\delta L}{\delta V_i} V_i = 0, \qquad V_i \geq 0,$

which indicates that sale of X_i^0 involves an opportunity cost for X_i equal to its salvage value when less than X_i^0 is sold. V_i is greater than or equal to zero when $S_i \geq \lambda_i$ and when all of X_i^0 is sold.

The solution also involves

(14) $\qquad \dfrac{\delta L}{\delta \mu_i} = X_i^0 - V_i \geq 0, \qquad \dfrac{\delta L}{\delta \mu_i} \mu_i = 0, \qquad \mu_i \geq 0,$

a condition made necessary by the fact that more of X_i cannot be sold than is on hand. The value, μ_i, is a measure of the gain obtained by selling X_i rather than using it; hence, $\mu_i > 0$ when $X_i^0 = V_i$; but $\mu_i = 0$ when $X_i^0 > V_i$.

Differences and Consequences of the Two Sets of Assumptions

The *first* set of assumptions states that acquisition and salvage values of inputs are either equal to each other or the acquisition value is infinite and the salvage value is zero. The *second* set permitted acquisition and salvage prices to be either equal or unequal.

I. Under the first set of assumptions:

A. Inputs with zero salvage and infinite acquisition prices are priced inter-nally at opportunity costs determined by product prices, initial quantities of these inputs on hand, the nature of the production function using them, and prices (including opportunity costs) of other inputs.

B. Some erroneous reorganizations of farms are reversible. These reorganiza-tions can result from changes in (1) product prices and (2) prices of other inputs. Erroneous reorganizations are irreversible which result from changes in initial quantities of inputs on hand with infinite acquisition costs or zero salvage values, as are those resulting from technological change or education as argued by Willard Cochrane.

C. B, above, implies reversible supply functions of individual firms for products and reversible demand functions of individual firms for inputs.

D. If $d = 2$ and $n = 3$, the iso-value product and iso-cost functions for the jth product would appear as in Figure A. LL is a line of least-cost combinations.

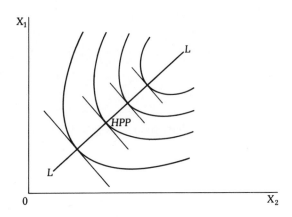

Figure A.

HPP is the high profit point. The cost functions would appear as in Figure B if P_{X_3} used in computing average total cost (ATC) is equal to its marginal value productivity.

E. If imperfect knowledge is assumed, failures to organize at the HPP can be corrected at no cost by selling any of the X_i which are in excess and buying any of the X_i in deficit, $i = 1, \ldots, d$. Hence, no capital losses need be incurred on X_i for $i = 1, \ldots, d$.

F. Capital losses and gains can occur on the X_i for $i = d + 1, \ldots, n$, however. The capital value of any durable in this set of X_i will be the present value of its expected λ_i's, and λ_i is a function of product prices, technology

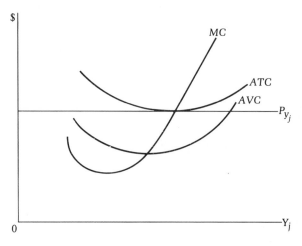

Figure B.

(nature of the production function), and P_{X_i} for $i = 1, \ldots, d$. Changes in these determining variables can create gains and losses for the fixed resources.

II. Under the second set of assumptions, i.e., $\infty \geq P_{AX_i} \geq P_{SX_i} \geq 0$ for $i = 1, \ldots, n$.

    A. Inputs with $P_{AX_i} > P_{SX_i}$

        (1) were priced internally at opportunity cost, λ_i when $P_{AX_i} > \lambda_i > P_{SX_i}$, and *are fixed*;

        (2) are priced at P_{AX_i} when $\lambda_i \geq P_{AX_i}$ and *are variable*,

        (3) are priced at P_{SX_i}, which might be termed an external opportunity cost when $\lambda_i \leq P_{SX_i}$, and *are variable*,

        (4) have λ_i's (opportunity costs) determined by product prices, initial quantities of the all X_i's on hand for which $P_{AX_i} > P_{SX_i}$, the nature of the production functions using them, and the prices (including opportunity costs) of other inputs.

    B. The optimizing reorganizations of farms which result from the changes listed in II.A.(4) *are not reversible*.

    C. B, above, implies irreversible supply functions of individual firms for products and irreversible demand functions of individual firms for inputs. Irreversibility is taken to mean responses to price decreases which are not the exact opposites of corresponding increases. Generally, the theoretical output responses to product price increases should be expected to exceed the contractions associated with product price declines. Similarly, expansions in use of inputs resulting from product price increases and input price decreases should be expected to be greater than the contractions resulting from comparable product price declines and input price increases.

D. If $n = 3$, $\infty \geq P_{AX_1} > P_{SX_1} > 0$, $\infty \geq P_{AX_2} > P_{SX_2} > 0$ and $\infty = P_{AX_3} > P_{SX_3} = 0$, then the iso-value product map for the jth product will appear as in Figure C.

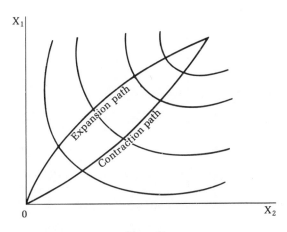

Figure C.

The line of least-cost combination when X_1 and X_2 are priced at acquisition costs need not be the same as when they are priced at salvage values. Though the first can still be dubbed an "expansion path," the second is better called a "contraction path."

At this point it becomes advantageous to introduce the concept of an iso-marginal value product line. Four such lines are of interest in the $X_1 X_2$ dimension of the production function under consideration, two for X_1 and two for X_2. For both X_1 and X_2, we are interested in all combinations of X_1 and X_2 for which $MVP_{X_i} = P_{AX_i}$ and for which $MVP_{X_i} = P_{SX_i}$. An $X_1 X_2$ map of such iso-marginal value products for $Y = aX_1^{b_1} X_2^{b_2} \mid X_3^{b_3}$ when $\Sigma_{i=1}^{3} b_i = 1$ and $1 > b_i > 0$ appears as in Figure D.

For the first set of assumptions, the iso-marginal value product lines for P_{SX_i} and P_{AX_i} would be identical. The same would be true for P_{SX_2} and P_{AX_2}. Thus areas 2, 4, 5, 6, and 8 do not exist under the first set of assumptions. Area 5 is a point in that case while areas 2, 4, 6, and 8 are lines. While it is interesting to explore the values of V_i, W_i, λ_i, and μ_i for areas 2, 4, 5, 6, and 8, time can be saved and valuable simplicity gained by ignoring the iso-product lines which do not border area 5 and erecting perpendiculars and extending horizontals as in Figure E. In addition, one iso-product line representing the *HPP* output for P_{AX_1},

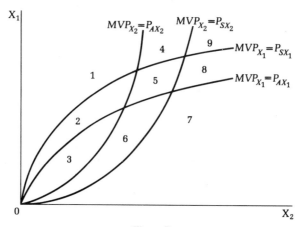

Figure D.

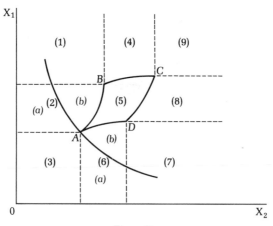

Figure E.

and P_{AX_2} has been added. This is, of course, a reproduction of Figure 1 in the main text. Let Y_{j_A} be the output of j at point A, Y_{j_B} at point B, etc.

For firms initially organized within area 1: $P_{SX_1} > \lambda_1$, $P_{AX_2} < \lambda_2$, $V_1 > 0$, $W_2 > 0$, and G is maximized at B, and $Y_{jB} > Y_{jA}$ even for $Y_j^0 < Y_{jA}$. The capitalized value of λ_1 after maximizing G is P_{SX_1} and greater than at (X_1^0, X_2^0) and the capitalized value of λ_2 after maximizing G equals the stock acquisition price of X_2. At both (X_1^0, X_2^0) and B the capitalized value of λ_1 is less than the stock acquisition price of X_1. If $B = A$, as it would under the first set of assumptions, $Y_{jB} = Y_{jA}$, and the capitalized value of λ_1 and λ_2 would equal P_{AX_1} and P_{AX_2} for stocks, respectively.

For firms initially organized within area 2: $P_{AX_1} > \lambda_1, P_{SX_1} = \lambda_1$ for X_1^0 along AB, $\lambda_2 > P_{AX_2}$, $V_1 = W_1 = 0$, $W_2 > 0$, G is maximized on AB at (X_2, X_1^0), and $Y_{j(X_1^0, X_2)} > Y_{jA}$ even for $Y_j^0 < Y_{jA}$. The capitalized value of λ_1 after maximizing G is P_{SX_1} and greater than at (X_1^0, X_2^0). The capitalized value of λ_2 after maximizing G equals the stock acquisition price of X_2. For $B = A$ under the first set of assumptions, see the last sentence for "within area 1."

For firms initially organized within area 3: P_{AX_1} can be made $< \lambda_1, P_{AX_2}$ can be made $< \lambda_2$, $V_1 = V_2 = 0$, $W_1 > 0$, $W_2 > 0$. G is maximized at A, and $Y_j = Y_{jA} > Y_j^0$. Capitalized values of λ_1 and λ_2 are equal to the stock acquisition prices for X_1 and X_2, respectively, at Y_{jA}. For $D = C = B = A$, nothing is changed.

For firms initially organized within area 4: $P_{SX_1} > \lambda_1, P_{SX_2} < \lambda_2 < P_{AX_2}$, $V_1 > 0$, except along BC where $V_1 = 0$; $V_2 = W_2 = 0$; G is maximized at $X_2 = X_2^0$ on BC, and $Y_{jA} < Y_{j(X_1, X_2^0)} < Y_j^0$. The capitalized value of future λ_2 after maximizing $G < $ at $(X_1^0, X_2^0) > P_{SX_2}$ and $< P_{AX_2}$ for stock X_2. The capitalized value of λ_1 after maximizing G equals $P_{SX_1} < P_{AX_1}$ for stock X_1. For $C = B = A$, see last sentence for "within area 1."

For firms initially organized within area 5: $P_{SX_1} < \lambda_1 < P_{AX_2}$, $P_{SX_2} < \lambda_2 < P_{AX_2}$, $V_1 = W_1 = 0$, $V_2 = W_2 = 0$, G is maximized at (X_1^0, X_2^0), and $Y_j = Y_j^0 > Y_{jA}$. The capitalized values of λ_1 and λ_2 at (X_1^0, X_2^0) are less than P_{AX_1} and P_{AX_2} for stocks, respectively. For $A = B = C = D$, see last sentence for "within area 1."

For firms initially organized within area 6: $P_{AX_1} < \lambda_1, P_{SX_2} < \lambda_2 < P_{AX_2}$ for X_2 along AD, $W_1 > 0$, $V_2 = W_2 = 0$, G is maximized at $X_2 = X_2^0$ on AD, and $Y_{jA} < Y_j > Y_j^0$ even when $Y_j^0 < Y_{jA}$. The capitalized value of λ_2 after maximizing $G > $ at $(X_1^0, X_2^0) > P_{SX_2} < P_{AX_2}$ for stock X_2. The capitalized value of λ_1 after maximizing G equals P_{AX_1} for stock at (X_1, X_2^0). For $C = A$ under the first set of assumptions, see last sentence for "within area 1."

For firms initially organized within area 7: $P_{AX_1} < \lambda_1, P_{SX_2} > \lambda_2$, $W_1 > 0$, $V_2 > 0$, G is maximized at D, and $Y_{jD} > Y_{jA}$ even for $Y_j^0 < Y_{jA}$. The capitalized value of λ_1 after maximizing G at D is equal to P_{AX_1}, while the capitalized value of $\lambda_2 = P_{SX_2} < P_{AX_2}$ for stocks. For $D = A$ under the first set of assumptions, see last sentence for "within area 1."

For firms initially organized within area 8: $P_{AX_1} > \lambda_1 > P_{SX_1}$ for X_1, and $P_{SX_2} > \lambda_{X_2}$ except along DC where $P_{SX_2} = \lambda_2, V_2 > 0, V_1 = W_1 = 0, G$ is maximized at (X_1^0, X_2) on DC, and $Y_j^0 > Y_{j(X_1^0, X_2)} > Y_{jA}$. $P_{AX_1} > $ capitalized value of λ_1 after maximizing G at $(X_1^0, X_2) > P_{SX_1}$ for stock and the capitalized value of $\lambda_2 = P_{SX_1}$ for stock. For $C = D = A$, see last sentence for "within area 1."

For firms initially organized within area 9: $P_{SX_1} > \lambda_1$, $P_{SX_2} > \lambda_1$, $V_1 > 0$, $V_2 > 0$, G is maximized at C and $Y_{jA} < Y_{jC} < Y_j^0$. After maximizing G at C, P_{SX_1} = capitalized value of λ_1 and P_{SX_2} = capitalized value of λ_1 for stocks. For $C = D = A = B$, see last sentence for "within area 1."

The cost functions that go with the first iso-product diagram (Figure C) of this section are segmented and irreversible. For example, output at successive points in time for the firm under consideration for $Py_{jt} < Py_{jt+1} > Py_{jt+2} > Py_{jt+3} < Py_{jt+4}$, where $t + i$ stands for successive production periods, could be as shown in Figure F, rather than as shown in Figure G under the first set of assumptions (see para. I.D).

    E. The consequences of imperfect knowledge are great.

        (1) Under perfect knowledge, the firm would organize at A in Figure E above. No overproduction, no capital losses, and no disappointed income expectations would follow and the differences between the two sets of assumptions would be slight.

        (2) Under imperfect knowledge, however, mistakes would be made and the firm would find itself in any of areas 1 to 9 in Figure E. A check of what can happen in each of the nine areas (see II.D above) supports the discussion of Figures 1 and 2 in Chapter 3. These theoretical events correspond closely with what has happened in agriculture. This in turn focuses interest on: improving knowledge; and preventing mistakes in farm organization, which would place farmers in areas 1, 2, 4, 5, 6, 7, 8, and 9. Mistakes in area 3 are easily and costlessly corrected.

    F. Capital losses incurred in areas 1, 2, and 4–9 are non-Pareto better. Evaluation of circumstances leading to such losses requires, therefore, analytical procedures going beyond modern welfare economics forcing efforts such as made in Chapter 5. Under the first set of assumptions, areas 2, 4, 5, 6, and 8 would not exist and no non-Pareto-better losses would occur in areas 1, 7, and 9 on X_1 and X_2 in the above example. Hence, modern welfare economics is sufficient under the first set of assumptions for evaluation. Under both sets, capital losses can occur on X_3. In theory, X_3 is ordinarily treated as land. As both land rent and land values are implicitly regarded as unearned in theory and, hence, as subject to destruction without raising evaluative questions, economists have worried little about non-Pareto-better adjustments in rents and land values, however illogical (and unjustified) that may be. Our book has attempted to remedy this difficulty by not distinguishing between *either* rental and other incomes *or* between capital losses and gains on land and other assets.

    G. Growth in demand becomes more important for the second than for the first set of assumptions.

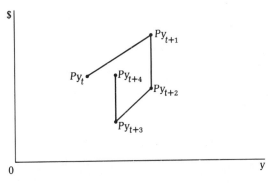

Figure F.

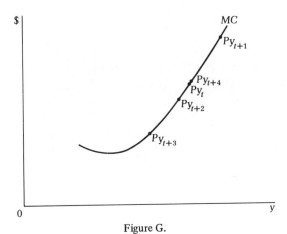

Figure G.

(1) Under the first set, unequal rates of growth in demand and supply have the consequences traced out by T. W. Schultz [1945].

(2) Under the second set: (a) If the growth in demand exceeds supply, many errors of organizing in areas 1, 2, and 4 through 9 (see Figure E) become errors of organizing in area 3 where correction is easy and costless. (Though growth in demand is rapid in the nonfarm industry, agriculture's low income demand elasticity means that producers experience only small growth relative to the number and magnitude of their errors in organizing farms.) (b) When growth in demand lags behind growth in output (partly as a consequence of errors of overproduction) errors of organizing in areas 1, 2, and 4 through 9 are correctable only slowly (less rapidly, perhaps, than new errors are made) and at great cost.

III. Under both sets of assumptions:

A. Serious problems exist about the optimum number of units of service to extract from a given durable in a given time period. For instance, in buying tractors, 500 hours of use per year might be the optimum rate of usage when a tractor is bought, while some other number becomes optimum in successive time periods after the tractor becomes fixed as a result of sequential errors made in organizing and reorganizing the business through time.

B. The aggregation problem going from firm supply and demand functions to industry supply and economy demand functions is obviously greater for the second than for the first set of assumptions. This problem has not been attacked for the second set and involves substantial difficulties for the first set. Some analysts have suggested that aggregate supply and responses would be similar under the two sets of assumptions. The following thoughts are offered:

(1) In reality, macro agricultural supply responses are more responsive to increases than to decreases in prices.

(2) Net prices received by sellers are not equal to gross prices paid by buyers after transaction and transportation costs are figured.

(3) Causes of imperfect knowledge are repetitive and never ending.

(4) Item (2) implies that acquisition and salvage prices never become equal in the long run. Item (3) implies that errors of production are repeatable in the long run.

Bibliography

Arrow, Kenneth J. 1951. *Individual Preferences and Social Choices*. New York: John Wiley and Sons.

Banks, Vera J., Calvin L. Beale, and Gladys K. Bowles. October 1963. "Farm Population Estimates for 1919–62." U.S. Department of Agriculture, ERS 130. Washington, D.C.

Barger, H., and H. H. Landsberg. 1942. *American Agriculture 1899–1939: A Study of Output, Employment, and Productivity*. New York: Bureau of Economic Research, Inc.

Barlowe, R. 1958. "Our Future Needs for Non-Farm Lands." In *Land–1958 Yearbook of Agriculture*. Washington, D.C.: U.S. Government Printing Office.

Benedict, Murray R., and Oscar C. Stine. 1956. *The Agricultural Commodity Programs, Two Decades of Experience*. New York: Twentieth Century Fund.

Bishop, C. D. 1961. "Economic Aspects of Changes in Farm Labor Force." In *Labor Mobility and Population in Agriculture*. Iowa State University Center for Agricultural Economic Adjustment, Ames.

Black, John D., and James T. Bonnen. 1965. "A Balanced United States Agriculture in 1965." National Planning Association, Special Report 42. Washington, D.C.

Boulding, Kenneth. 1948. *Economic Analysis*. New York: Harper and Row.

Boyne, David H. 1964. *Changes in the Real Wealth Position of Farm Operators, 1940–1960*. Michigan State University Agricultural Experiment Station, Technical Bulletin 294, East Lansing.

Carlson, Sune. 1939. *A Study in the Pure Theory of Production*. London: P. S. King.

Chennareddy, Venkareddy. 1963. "Present Values of Expected Future Income Streams and Their Relevance to Mobility of Farm Workers to the Nonfarm

Sector in the United States, 1917–62." Ph.D. thesis, Michigan State University, East Lansing.

_____, and Glenn L. Johnson. August 1968. "Projections of Age Distribution of Farm Operations in the U.S. Based Upon Estimates of the Present Value of Incomes." *Journal of Farm Economics*, vol. 50, pp. 606–20.

Chief of Investigations of the General Accounting Office. 1951. *General Accounting Office Report of Survey–Veterans Education and Training Programs.* 82 Cong., 1 sess., House Committee Part 160.

Clawson, Marion. 1963. "Aging Farmers and Agricultural Policy." *Journal of Farm Economics*, vol. 45.

_____. 1968. *Policy Directions for U.S. Agriculture: Long-Range Choices in Farming and Rural Living.* Baltimore: Johns Hopkins Press for Resources for the Future, Inc.

Cochrane, W. W. May 1947. "Farm Price Gyrations–Aggregative Hypothesis." *Journal of Farm Economics*, vol. 49, no. 2, pp. 383–408.

_____. 1958. *Farm Prices, Myth and Reality.* Minneapolis: University of Minnesota Press.

Congressional Quarterly Service. 1963. *U.S. Agricultural Policy in the Postwar Years, 1945–1963.* Washington, D.C.

Daly, Rex F. 1967. "Agriculture: Projected Demand, Output, and Resource Structure." In *Implications of Changes on Farm Management and Marketing Research.* CAED Report 29. Ames: Iowa State University Press.

Darcovich, William, and Earl O. Heady. 1956. "Application of Expectation Models to Livestock and Crop Prices and Products." Iowa State University Agricultural Experiment Station Research Bulletin 438, Ames.

Edwards, Clark. 1958. "Resource Fixity, Credit Availability and Agricultural Organization." Ph.D. thesis, Michigan State University, East Lansing.

_____. November 1959. "Resource Fixity and Farm Organization." *Journal of Farm Economics*, vol. 41, no. 4, pp. 747–59.

Fishlow, Albert, and Paul A. David. December 1961. "Optimal Resource Allocation in an Imperfect Market Setting." *The Journal of Political Economy*, vol. 69, no. 6, pp. 529–46.

Franklin, E. R. et al. July 1959. "Economic Progress and Problems of Columbia Basin Project Settlers." Washington State University Agricultural Experiment Station Bulletin 597, Pullman.

Goodsell, Wyllie D., and Isabel Jenkins. 1961. "Costs and Returns on Commercial Farms, Long-Term Study, 1930–57." U.S. Department of Agriculture Statistical Bulletin 297, Washington, D.C.

Gray, Roger W., Vernon L. Sorenson, and Willard W. Cochrane. June 1954. "An Economic Analysis of the Impact of Government Programs on the Potato Industry of the United States." Minnesota Agricultural Experiment Station Technical Bulletin 211, Minneapolis.

Griliches, Zvi. December 1960. "Measuring Inputs in Agriculture: A Critical Survey." *Journal of Farm Economics*, vol. 42.

Halter, A. N. 1956. "Measuring Utility of Wealth Among Farmers." Ph.D. thesis, Michigan State University, East Lansing.

Hathaway, Dale E. May 1955. "Effect of Price Support Program on the Dry Bean Industry in Michigan." Michigan State University Agricultural Experiment Station Technical Bulletin 250, East Lansing.

———. 1958. "Agriculture and the Business Cycle." *Policy for Commercial Agriculture.* Joint Economic Committee, 85 Cong., p. 5176.

———. 1963. *Government and Agriculture.* New York: Macmillan.

———, and Richard Duvick. 1967. "Parity Income—What Does It Show for Michigan Farms." From U.S. Department of Agriculture, 1967, *Parity Returns Position of Farmers.* Senate Document 44. Washington, D.C.

Heady, Earl O. 1952. *Economics of Agricultural Production and Resource Use.* Englewood Cliffs, N.J.: Prentice-Hall.

———, and Luther G. Tweeten. 1963. *Resource Demand and Structure of the Agricultural Industry.* Ames: Iowa State University Press.

Heidhues, Theodor. August 1966. "A Recursive Programming Model of Farm Growth in Northern Germany." *Journal of Farm Economics,* vol. 48, no. 3, pp. 668–84.

Hicks, John R. 1941. *Value and Capital.* London: Oxford University Press.

Johnson, D. Gale. 1947. *Forward Prices for Agriculture.* Chicago: University of Chicago Press.

Johnson, Glenn L. February 1952. "Burley Tobacco Control Programs." Kentucky Agricultural Experiment Station Bulletin 580, Lexington.

———. November 1957. "Sources of Expanded Agricultural Production." *Policy for Commercial Agriculture.* Joint Economic Committee, 85 Cong., 1 sess.

———. January 1960. "Book Review of Marc Nerlove's Dynamics of Supply." *Agricultural Economics Research,* vol. 12, pp. 25–28.

———. May 1960. "The State of Agricultural Supply Analysis." *Journal of Farm Economics,* vol. 42, pp. 435–52.

———. 1961. "An Evaluation of U.S. Agricultural Programs, 1956 to 1960." Mimeographed Report for the Committee on Economic Development. East Lansing, Michigan.

———. 1969. "The Modern Family Farm and Its Problems: With Particular Reference to the United States." Chapter 11 in Ugo Papi and Charles Nun, eds., *Economic Problems of Agriculture in Industrial Societies.* New York: Macmillan.

———, and Lowell Hardin. 1955. "The Economics of Forage Evaluation." Purdue Agricultural Experiment Station Bulletin 623, Lafayette, Indiana.

———, O. J. Scoville, George K. Dike, and Carl K. Eicher. 1969. *Strategies and Recommendations for Nigerian Rural Development, 1969–1985.* Consortium for the Study of Nigerian Rural Development. Michigan State University, East Lansing.

——— et al. 1958. "Supply Functions: Some Facts and Notions." *Agricultural Adjustment Problems in a Growing Economy.* Ames: Iowa State College Press.

——— et al. 1961. *A Study of Managerial Processes of Midwestern Farmers.* Ames: Iowa State University Press.

Johnson, Harry G. August 1960. "The Cost of Protection and the Scientific Tariff." *Journal of Political Economy,* vol. 68, no. 4, pp. 27–345.

Johnson, Sherman E. 1949. *Changes in American Farming*. Washington, D.C.: U.S. Government Printing Office.

Jones, Bob F. 1964. "Farm-Nonfarm Labor Flows with Emphasis on Recent Manpower and Credit Policies, 1917–62." Ph.D. thesis, Michigan State University, East Lansing.

Kaldor, D. R., and Earl O. Heady. 1954. "An Exploratory Study of Expectations, Uncertainty and Farm Plans in Southern Iowa Agriculture." Iowa State University Agricultural Experiment Station Research Bulletin 408, Ames.

Kanel, Dan. May 1961. "Age Components of Increases in Number of Farmers, North Central States, 1890–1954." *Journal of Farm Economics*, vol. 43.

Keynes, J. M. 1942. *The General Theory of Employment, Interest and Capital*. London: Macmillan.

Knight, Frank H. 1941. *Risk, Uncertainty and Profit*. Oxford: Oxford University Press.

Kost, William. 1967. "Investing in Farm and Non Farm Equities." M.S. thesis, Michigan State University, East Lansing.

Kuhn, H. W., and A. W. Tucker. 1951. "Non-linear Programming." In J. Neyman, ed., *Second Berkeley Symposium on Mathematical Statistics and Probability*. Berkeley and Los Angeles: University of California Press.

Larsen, Arne. 1966. "Changes in Land Values in the United States, 1925–62." Ph.D. thesis, Michigan State University, East Lansing.

Larson, Olaf, et al. 1947. *Ten Years of Rural Rehabilitation in the United States*. Bureau of Agricultural Economics. Washington, D.C.

Leftwich, Richard H. 1955. *The Price System and Resource Allocation*. New York: Rinehart.

Lerohl, Milburn L. 1965. "Expected Prices of U.S. Agricultural Commodities, 1917–62." Ph.D. thesis, Michigan State University, East Lansing.

――――, and G. A. MacEachern. 1967. "Factor Shares in Agriculture: The Canada U.S. Experience." *Canadian Journal of Agricultural Economics*, vol. 15, no. 1.

Lewis, A. W. 1949. *Overhead Costs–Some Essays in Economic Analysis*. London: George Allen and Unwin.

Lewis, C. I. 1955. *The Ground and Nature of the Right*. New York: Columbia University Press.

Lipsey, R. G., and Calvin Lancaster. 1955–56. "The General Theory of Second Best." *Review of Economic Studies*, vol. 24, pp. 11–32.

Manderscheid, Lester V. 1965. "Incorporating Durable Goods Into Consumption Theory." Paper read before the meeting of the Econometric Society. New York.

Marshall, Alfred. 1949. *Principles of Economics*. 8th ed., London: Macmillan.

Menzie, Elmer, and Lawrence W. Witt et al. 1962. "Policy for United States Agricultural Export Surplus Disposal." Technical Bulletin 150, University of Arizona, Tucson.

Mill, John Stuart. 1849. *Principles of Political Economy*. Book 4. London: Longmans, Green and Company.

Nerlove, Marc. 1958. *The Dynamics of Supply: Estimation of Farmers' Response to Price*. Baltimore: Johns Hopkins Press.

_____ . January 20–22, 1960. "Time Series Analysis of the Supply of Agricultural Products." Paper presented at Workshop on Estimating and Interpreting Farm Supply Functions. Chicago.

Parsons, Talcott. 1949. *The Structure of Social Action*. Glencoe, Ill.: Free Press.

Partenheimer, Earl J. 1959. "Some Expectation Models Used by Select Groups of Midwestern Farmers." PH.D. thesis, Michigan State University, East Lansing.

Petit, Michel. 1964. "Econometric Analysis of the Feed-Grain Livestock Economy." Ph.D. thesis, Michigan State University, East Lansing.

Quance, C. Leroy. 1967. "Farm Capital: Use, MVP's, and Capital Gains or Losses, United States, 1917–1964." Ph.D. thesis, Michigan State University, East Lansing.

Quance, Leroy, and Luther Tweeten. December 1967. "Elasticities of Production and Resource Earnings." *Journal of Farm Economics*, vol. 49.

_____ . February 2, 1971. "Simulating the Impact of Input Price Inflation on Farm Income." Paper presented at the annual meetings of the Southern Agricultural Economics Association. Jacksonville, Florida.

Quenemoen, Merle E. 1966. "A Study of Costs and Returns for Dry-Land Farms in the Triangle Area of Montana With Emphasis on Operator's Labor, Machinery, and Land." Ph.D. thesis, Michigan State University, East Lansing.

Rogers, Everett M. 1958. "Categorizing the Adopters of Agricultural Practices." *Rural Sociology*, vol. 23.

Rossmiller, G. E. November 1965. "Farm Real Estate Value Patterns in the United States, 1930–1962." Michigan State University Agricultural Economics Report 31. East Lansing.

Samuelson, Paul. 1948. *Economics*. New York: McGraw-Hill.

Schultz, T. W. 1945. *Agriculture in an Unstable Economy*. New York: McGraw-Hill.

_____ . May 1951. "A Framework for Land Economics—The Long View." *Journal of Farm Economics*, vol. 33, p. 204.

_____ . 1953. *The Economic Organization of Agriculture*. New York: McGraw-Hill.

Scofield, W. H. November 1964. "Dominant Forces and Emerging Trends in the Farm Real Estate Market." Paper presented at seminar on land prices, North Central Regional Land Economics Committee. Chicago.

Smith, Vernon L. February 1959. "The Theory of Investment and Production." *Quarterly Journal of Economics*, vol. 73.

Stallings, James. February 1960. "Weather Indexes." *Journal of Farm Economics*, vol. 42, p. 180.

Stigler, George. 1946. *The Theory of Price*. New York: Macmillan.

Tostlebe, Alvin S. 1954. "The Growth of Physical Capital in Agriculture, 1870–1950." Occasional Paper 44. National Bureau of Economic Research, Inc., New York.

_____ . 1957. *Capital in Agriculture: Its Foundation and Financing Since 1870*. National Bureau of Economic Research. Princeton, N.J.: Princeton University Press.

Tweeten, Luther G. 1968. Unpublished Manuscript, Oklahoma State University, Stillwater.

———, and C. Leroy Quance. May 1969. "Positivistic Measures of Aggregate Supply Elasticities: Some New Approaches." *American Journal of Agricultural Economics,* vol. 51, no. 2.

Tyner, Fred H., and Luther G. Tweeten. December 1965. "A Methodology for Estimating Production Parameters." *Journal of Farm Economics,* vol. 47, pp. 1462–67.

U.S. Bureau of Labor Statistics. 1961–63. *Employment and Earnings.* Washington, D.C.: U.S. Government Printing Office.

U.S. Congress, House Committee on Veterans' Affairs. 1952. *Hearings, Education and Training and Other Benefits for Veterans' Services On or After June 27, 1950.* 82 Cong., 2 sess.

U.S. Department of Agriculture, 1955. *Consumption of Food in the United States.* Ag. Handbook 62. Washington, D.C.

———. 1957. *Major Statistical Series of the USDA.* Ag. Handbook 118, vol. 1, Washington, D.C.

———. July 1958. "Livestock and Meat Statistics, 1957." SB 230, and later issues. Washington, D.C.

———. 1960. "Quantity Indexes of U.S. Agricultural Exports and Imports." FAS-M-76. Washington, D.C.

———. 1962. *Consumption of Food in the United States, 1909-52.* Ag. Handbook 62 Supplement for 1961. Washington, D.C.

———. 1963. "Farm Costs and Returns Series." SB 297. Washington, D.C.

———. August 1963. "Farm Real Estate Market Developments." Washington, D.C.

———. December 1964. *Agricultural Finance Review.* Washington, D.C.

———. 1967. Commodity Credit Corporation Charts. Washington, D.C.

———. 1967. "Farm Costs and Returns Series." AIB 230. Washington, D.C.

———. 1967. "Major Uses of Land in the United States: Summary for 1954." AIB 168. Washington, D.C.

———. 1967. "Parity Returns Position of Farmers." Document No. 44. Washington, D.C.: U.S. Government Printing Office.

———. 1970 and earlier issues. *Agricultural Statistics.* Washington, D.C.

———. 1970 and earlier issues. "The Balance Sheet of Agriculture." AIB 290. Washington, D.C.

———. June 1967. "Farm Real Estate Market Developments." Washington, D.C.

———. January 1968. "Quantities of Pesticides Used by Farmers in 1964." AER 131. Washington, D.C.

———. July 1970 and previous July issues. *Farm Income Situation.* FIS 199. Washington, D.C.

———. 1970 and earlier issues. "Changes in Farm Production and Efficiency, A Summary Report." SB 233. Washington, D.C.

———. 1963. "Farm Employment." SB 334. Washington, D.C.

U.S. Department of Commerce. Bureau of the Census. 1960. *Historical Statistics of the United States, Colonial Times to 1957.* Washington, D.C.: U.S. Government Printing Office.

_____. 1964. *Statistical Abstract of the United States, 1964.* Washington, D.C.

_____. 1964 and earlier issues. *U.S. Census of Agriculture.* Washington, D.C.

U.S. Department of Labor. Bureau of Labor Statistics. 1968 and earlier issues. *Survey of Current Business.* Washington, D.C.

U.S. Statutes at Large. vol. 58, Part I, and vol. 61, Part I.

Van Gigch, Francis. 1968. "Agricultural Policies, Programs and Resource Flows, U.S., 1917–1962." Ph.D. thesis, Michigan State University, East Lansing.

Vincent, Warren, ed. 1962. *Economics and Management in Agriculture.* New York: Prentice-Hall.

Waldo, Arley D. 1962. "The Off-Farm Employment of Farm Operators in the United States." Ph.D. thesis, Michigan State University, East Lansing.

White House Conference on Food, Nutrition, and Health (December 1969). 1970. Washington, D.C.

Young, Robert. 1965. "An Economic Study of the Eastern Beet Sugar Industry." Michigan State University Agricultural Experiment Station Bulletin 9, East Lansing.

Index

"Absolutes," in economic analysis, 47-48
Acquisition-cost and salvage-value differentials, 6-9, 21, 26-30, 32-38, 42, 48-50, 90, 172, 179-81
Acquisition costs, in agriculture: Compared with earnings, 168-69, 177, 183; effect of war on, 161, 170; of durables (capital), 91-92, 97, 100-12, 160, 164-65, 167, 171, 174-75; of labor, 11, 29, 32, 119, 129-30, 162; of land, 93, 145-46, 148, 154-55; and market prices, 39, 180; in theory of the firm, 84, 188-89, 191
Acreage controls, federal, 141-42, 164-65, 168, 170-71
Adjustment model, use of, 89-91
Agricultural Act (1956), 142, 170
Agriculture, U.S.: Basis for evaluation, 41-51; characteristics, 5-21, 48; evaluative conclusions and recommendations, 173-83; expected product prices, 55-66; historical and economic summary, 159-72; overproduction, 1-4 (see also Overproduction); production, disappearance, income, and resource use, 67-87; role of capital, 88-112; role of labor, 113-36; role of land, 137-55; theoretical considerations, 22-40
Agriculture Department, 24, 58, 62, 65, 75, 82, 89, 180
Allocation of resources. See Resource allocation

Appalachia, 141-42
Arrow, Kenneth J., 41

Bankruptcy, in farm sector, 160
Banks, Vera J., 75
Barger, H., 140
Beale, Calvin L., 75
Bean production, 23, 72, 141, 174, 178
Beef production, 65-66, 96, 98-100, 105, 172, 175, 177
Benedict, Murray R., 70, 74-75
Bishop, C. D., 129
Black, John D., 24
Bonnen, James T., 24
Boulding, Kenneth, 34n
Bowles, Gladys K., 75
Boyne, David H., 76, 150, 152
Brokerage fees, 6, 9, 146

Canada, 176
Capital, in agricultural sector, 4, 22-23, 81-82, 84-87, 155; acquisition costs of, 19, 91-92, 97, 100-12, 160, 164-65, 167, 171, 174-75; changing structure of, 97-112; durable (physical), 6-9, 26, 37, 88-91, 179; empirical techniques used in study of, 88-91; expendable (nondurable), 7-9, 104-05, 108-12, 168, 171; history of, 159-72; and technological incentives, 91-97, 105, 112. See also Capital gains; Capital losses; Labor-saving capital; Land-saving capital

Library of Congress Cataloging in Publication Data

Johnson, Glenn L
    The overproduction trap in U.S. agriculture.

    Bibliography: p.
    1. Agriculture—Economic aspects—United States—Addresses, essays, lectures. 2. Agriculture and state—United States—Addresses, essays, lectures.
I. Quance, C. Leroy, joint author. II. Resources for the Future. III. Title

HD1765 1972.J63   338.1'873   72–3613   72–186509
ISBN 0–8018–1387–5

THE JOHNS HOPKINS UNIVERSITY PRESS

This book was composed in Press Roman Medium by Jones Composition Company, Inc. It was printed on 60-lb. Sebago and bound in Holliston Roxite cloth by The Maple Press Company.